CONFER.
MOT, CROWN
HVP
32 WEEKS
BLOOD BED 1
GROWING OK.

Prepared for
Cornell University Home Study Program
Department of Agricultural Economics
New York State College of Agriculture and Life Sciences
A Statutory College of the State University

Managing and Training People

Fifth Edition

Edward M. Harwell

with selected chapters by
Robert Duvin and Laurence Taylor

Lebhar-Friedman Books
CHAIN STORE PUBLISHING CORP.
A Subsidiary of Lebhar-Friedman, Inc., New York

Fifth Edition

MANAGING AND TRAINING PEOPLE
formerly published as PERSONNEL MANAGEMENT AND TRAINING

Printed in the United States of America
Library of Congress Catalog Card Number: 74-25020
ISBN: 0-86730-308-5

Acknowledgments

This book is the result of the efforts of many people. First and foremost, credit must be given to my clients in the United States and Europe who, over the years, demonstrated a pioneering spirit in their willingness to test new management practices and training techniques. Without their cooperation and assistance, these ideas could not have been developed and this book could not have been written.

Appreciation is also due the 30 supermarket companies who cooperated by supplying the employee turnover information reported in Chapter 1 and in the Appendix, and to Robert Nolan of Cornell University who assisted by collecting the data.

Special recognition should be given to the following experts who contributed chapters to this book: Robert Duvin, labor relations attorney, Cleveland, Ohio (Chapters 17 and 18, "Laws Affecting Employment" and "Union Relations"); and Laurence Taylor, consultant and conference moderator, Hillsdale, Michigan (Chapters 11 and 12, "Motivation and Morale" and "Communicating"). The four chapters written by these outstanding experts have added immeasurably to the value of the book. Also, Arthur Wolfe, former director of industrial relations, Fisher Foods, Inc., Cleveland, Ohio provided information that was incorporated into other sections of the book (Chapters 4, 13, and 16, "Selecting Employees," "Evaluating Performance" and "Criteria for Promotions").

Particular thanks are also due to Marilyn Greenbaum Harwell, Tova Reich and Henry Rothman for their invaluable aid and suggestions in editing the manuscript.

EDWARD M. HARWELL

SARASOTA, FL

Training is everything.
The peach was once a bitter almond;
cauliflower is nothing but cabbage with
a college education.

Mark Twain
Pudd'nhead Wilson

Contents

Figures

Tables

Introduction

In recent years, supermarket executives have become increasingly concerned with two major problems: the need to develop and maintain store individuality and the urgency to make a reasonable profit.

It is well known that supermarkets have grown more and more alike each year. Despite the recent emergence of superstores, large combination stores and giant warehouse markets, there remains a great deal of sameness in the retail food industry in all major metropolitan markets. When the first innovator opens with a bang in a given marketing area, competition is quick to react with new or remodeled, larger stores offering the same types of mass merchandising, expanded varieties, specialty service departments and competitive pricing. Few operators are able to successfully penetrate a new market and maintain high volumes for any period of time. Even the most successful gradually lose their unique qualities as others open similar operations. With little difference in physical appearance, product quality, assortment, price, service operations or other conveniences, a company must achieve its own identity and individuality through its people. Accordingly, a handful of highly successful chains, including Ralphs and Von's in California, Publix in Florida, H. E. Butt in Texas, and Supermarkets General in the New York-New Jersey area, have created their distinctive images by "building" people.

Similarly, it has become increasingly difficult to make a respectable profit in the supermarket industry, one of the world's most competitive businesses. Many areas are over-stored, or are rapidly approaching that point. Profit margins have been squeezed to the danger point. In 1988, for example, average net earnings *before* taxes dropped to 1.2 percent of sales, one of the lowest profit margins in many years. During the previous four years, performance was relatively flat: 1984, 1.6 percent; 1985, 1.8 percent; 1986, 1.7 percent; and 1987, 1.6 percent.[1] After the dismal showing in 1988, there was a partial recovery to 1.5 percent in 1989; however, forecasts for 1990, a year of economic distress, are for another downturn.

Not surprisingly, total labor costs, including fringe benefits, rose steadily during this period. Expressed as a percentage of total company sales, total labor costs were: 1985, 10.9 percent; 1986, 11.0 percent; 1987, 11.1 percent; 1988, 11.0 percent; and 1989, 11.2 percent.[2]

To make matters worse, the increase in average order size has leveled off in recent years. The average sale per customer transaction increased from $16.33 in 1985 to $17.60 in 1989, or 7.8 percent, but food prices increased 19.9 percent during that same period.

Even more worrisome is the 8.9 percent decline in average weekly store sales, from $210,770 in 1988 to $193,500 in 1989.[3] This decrease is of serious concern to all supermarket operators.

Again, the problem of sameness looms. Today, price competition is fierce in all major cities and in most smaller towns. The cost of doing business is approximately the same for both the independent and the chain competitor down the street. Both pay the same prices for their merchandise. Innovations, such as unique merchandising methods or unusual operating techniques, at best, provide the innovator with the upper hand for only a very short time. Virtually every new product, technological development or promotional idea is very quickly available, in one form or another, to any interested supermarket. There are no real secrets in the supermarket business any longer.

Again, the solution rests with people. The store with capable, well-motivated employees usually runs circles around its competitors. In the race for profits, an efficient, cooperative, productive staff is the only edge a store has today in outpacing its competition.

---

[1] *The Food Marketing Industry Speaks* (Washington, D.C., The Food Marketing Institute, 1990).

[2] Ibid.

[3] Ibid.

But it is no secret that, at present, there is a shortage of competent supermarket personnel and the situation is becoming worse. The competition for high school, junior college and college graduates, and the certainty that supermarkets will continue to expand at least as rapidly as the population, all promise to aggravate the people shortage at all levels.

The people vacuum is most seriously felt in key store management positions. Enlightened supermarket executives realize that they cannot simply continue to promote people who have merely been successful stock clerks, meat cutters or produce trimmers. They have learned from experience that errors in selecting people for promotion are costly.

Yet the number of qualified applicants for executive training programs falls short of present and future needs. Every industry in the country is competing for key personnel. Moreover, very few suitable people are switching from other industries to supermarketing. Further compounding the problem is the supermarket industry's high rate of employee and manager turnover.

Supermarket executives are the first to admit that the industry's personnel and training practices are poor and that there is an urgent, even desperate, need for change. In some chains, the need for better tools and techniques in recruiting, selecting, training and developing personnel has been recognized. Some companies have started new training programs or are strengthening existing ones in an effort to teach managers how to manage. Personnel departments, whose primary function is to improve employee performance, are being given more support and autonomy, and more attention is being paid to forecasting future personnel needs.

However, despite attempts to create more enlightened personnel policies, most chains have not come to grips with the vital fact that today's part-time clerk will become tomorrow's manager because there simply is not enough trained personnel available from other sources. By necessity, the retail food industry will continue to obtain the large majority of its future managers from the ranks of people originally hired for part-time, lower-echelon positions. As it is, more than 90 percent of the typical company's key personnel started as part-time employees.

Nevertheless, a majority of chains still hire part-timers without the slightest consideration of the future roles such employees will play. For the most part, recruitment and training programs are still limited, still weakened by small budgets and the feeling that tomorrow will somehow take care of itself. As a rule, the part-timer is hired haphazardly and trained sporadically. If he or she survives the initial part-time stage, the next step is full-time employment.

Then promotions follow because there is no one else available, with a hope and a prayer that the employee will grow into the job, despite a lack of training in managerial skills.

While most of the industry laments the notorious turnover rate of part-timers, such turnover is, in fact, abetted by the poor employment practices and lack of effective policies that can identify and bring out the best in an individual. Competently conducted employment interviews and effective training are still rare. As a result, many potential managers, supervisors and executives move on to other industries and businesses.

Tremendous opportunities are available for those companies making intelligent attempts to solve the shortage problem among talented people. The company that develops personnel programs strong enough to establish a favorable image with potential employees and consumers has a significant competitive advantage over its rivals. The store manager who can successfully recruit, select and train people who are properly motivated, can dominate his or her area.

Moreover, a store manager's own growth depends on the staff he[4] builds. The store manager's future, as well as his company's success, will continue to depend on his own performance. His performance, in turn, will continue to depend on the image he and his employees create in the store.

Therefore, the personnel practices recommended in the pages that follow are aimed not only at supervisors and personnel department executives, but also at key store-level personnel, including managers, their assistants and department managers. Though many personnel practices are developed by personnel departments, the responsibility for carrying out these programs rests with *store-level* personnel.

This book's concern, then, is people—current and future supermarket employees. It is intended to help the manager recruit, select, train and develop people, and create an environment in which they are motivated, so that the needs of the store as well as of the individual employee are fulfilled.

---

[4] The use of the masculine gender is a traditional editorial style. Unless otherwise noted, it refers to male and female throughout this book.

Managing
and Training
People

1 | Employee Turnover

With costs rising and competition growing more fierce each year, how can a supermarket[1] increase its profits?

Most executives offer the same solution: increase employee productivity. In searching for methods to accomplish this goal, progressive companies are instituting programs to upgrade personnel management and training and to reduce employee turnover.

Enlightened executives realize that companies are paying dearly for excessive turnover even though such costs may not be as evident as the monthly checks they issue to pay taxes and rent. They are aware that high turnover and high wage costs are directly related: the loss in productivity which occurs while new replacements are learning to perform their jobs creates a major drain on store profits.

The measurable cost of employee turnover in the supermarket industry today is over 855 million dollars annually. Store managers and executives would do well to consider the substantial savings that

---

[1] This term refers to conventional supermarkets, combination stores, superstores and warehouse stores throughout this book.

would result if employee turnover were reduced by only a few persons each year.

The 1990 Turnover Study

Thirty chains representing 3,955 supermarkets (including superstores, combination stores, and warehouse stores) with 345,969 store employees participated in an in-depth turnover study conducted especially for the 1991 edition of this book. The chains that were investigated represented all areas of the United States and had a combined annual sales volume of more than thirty-five billion dollars. The study not only sought to determine current employee turnover ratios; it also examined reasons for employee turnover, its costs, and the extent to which turnover is excessive and preventable. Additionally, the study identified programs that were being planned or that had already been launched by many companies to reduce employee turnover. Finally, the 1990 study provided data to allow comparisons with similar surveys conducted in 1968 and 1983 for earlier editions of this book.

Many of the findings from the 1990 study are summarized in this chapter, and statistical data based on this study are presented in the Appendix. The full statistical data on the 1968 and 1983 studies can be found in earlier editions of this book.

The Problem

The study revealed that the average supermarket had an annual turnover rate of 23.8 per 100 full-time employees (compared to 10.5 in 1983), and 111.5 per 100 part-time employees (compared to 69.2 in 1983). The full-time employee turnover rate has more than doubled in the past seven years, while the part-timer rate has increased more than 60 percent, an alarming trend. Thus, the average nine million dollar supermarket with 87 employees—30 full-timers (35 percent of the staff) and 57 part-timers (65 percent of the staff)— had to hire 71 new employees every year to maintain its normal work force. More than 20 percent of its full-time employees (7) and more than 110 percent of its part-timers (64), were replaced each year. This means that managers, supervisors, and, personnel departments were faced with the problem of hiring approximately five new employees for each store every month, which is double the hire rate of 1983.

With a combined annual turnover rate of 81 percent of all full-
and part-timers, continuous gaps occur in a store's operating organization, which adversely affects profits. Moreover, according to one
Northeastern chain executive, a high turnover rate diminishes the
efficiency of other employees, too:

> Too much of our district managers' time is spent putting out people
> fires—finding and training replacements, talking an employee out of
> leaving, etc. Because of our relatively high turnover rate, our district
> managers have little time left to upgrade their managers' merchan-
> dising or operations skills. What makes it tougher today than ever
> before is that we're using more complex systems. Our front-end
> scheduling system, for example, makes a lot of sense once it's mas-
> tered. But it takes considerable time and energy to train people
> to use this and other complicated systems. Every time you lose an
> experienced employee, there's a major training job to perform in
> systems alone.

The average store's high rate of 71 employees being replaced each
year also creates a vacuum which must be filled by spending a good
deal of time hiring and training new people.

Turnover High During the First Year

Of the 71 employees who leave the average store in any twelve
month period, only ten have had more than a year's experience on
the job. The remaining 61 leave before they even accumulate a full
year's tenure. According to our study, of these 61, 21 left before
they finished a full month's employment; 19 more left with only one
to three month's experience; another nine left after they had been
employed three to six months; and 12 more left before their first
anniversary at the store. Thus, three of the seven full-timers and 57
of the 64 part-timers who were turned over in a twelve-month
period had been employed for less than one year.

However, most supermarket executives agree with the Midwestern vice-president for personnel who stressed that a certain amount
of turnover is both necessary and desirable: "Any dynamic organization requires new blood and new ideas for growth, even though that
growth may not be in the number of employees. Otherwise the
company itself becomes stagnant." Indeed, the nature of the supermarket business, including the hours it must operate, requires heavy
use of part-time employees. Higher turnover among part-timers is

to be expected because many are high school or college students whose planned tenure does not extend beyond their student days.

Excessive Turnover

Any resignation that is avoidable is considered excessive. An avoidable resignation is defined as a voluntary separation which occurs because of dissatisfaction with the job, wages, hours, working conditions or opportunities; plans to take a different job or to better oneself in some other way; or resignations without notice or for no given reason. An analysis of the 1990 turnover study revealed that 73 percent of full-timers, and 77 percent of part-timers were separated for these reasons. Such turnover is avoidable and is therefore considered excessive.

These rates are considered the minimum excessive rates for several reasons. First, they do not include any discharged employees. Several executives have noted that many such discharges can be avoided by hiring and properly training the right person at the outset. Second, many employees who resign do not give their real reasons for leaving, possibly because they are concerned about obtaining good recommendations when they apply for another job. Thus, it is possible that their resignations, too, swell the excessive turnover rates.

A large regional chain discovered the unreliability of the reasons given for employee resignations when it switched from manager-conducted termination interviews to exit interviews by letters sent from headquarters. Over a period of time, 24 percent of all those who had responded to the letters reported that they quit because they had not gotten along with their immediate supervisors. This reason, of course, had never shown up in manager-conducted termination interviews, making it difficult for the company to identify and then to deal with the problem. One executive in that chain commented: "We've reached the conclusion that approximately 90 percent of our current turnover rate is excessive and, to a great degree, preventable."

A fast growing East Coast regional chain, in an effort to take a deeper look at its excessive turnover figures, tried to separate the avoidable and unavoidable turnover rates. According to a company spokesperson:

> Some of our turnover is normal—Christmas hires of part-timers, for example. We consider this unavoidable turnover. These employees don't cost as much to hire, train and supervise as do our regulars.

The avoidable turnover includes part-timers who have the potential to become full-timers; employees with above average productivity; and hard-to-replace personnel, such as a good meat-cutter or a person who can work only specified night hours which others are unwilling to work. The turnover figures alone can be misleading if they do not take into account the particular individual who is leaving: turnover of ten poor employees isn't half as serious as turnover of four top performers. It is more difficult to replace someone with above average skills than someone who is just average. But just as important is the cost of training replacements until they become as competent as the terminated employees. Turnover rates must be coupled with turnover costs to get a true picture of the profit drain.

Turnover Costs

Until results of the 1983 turnover study were published, few supermarket operators even tried to estimate the cost of turnover. But today, more and more chains feel that these costs must be pinned down so that the extent of their turnover problem may be fully understood.

Employee turnover costs may be classified in four categories:

1. Employment costs
2. Learning costs
3. Supervision and trainer costs
4. Intangible costs

Employment Costs. The cost of recruiting, selecting and hiring replacements for employees who are separated varies widely among supermarket chains. These costs are directly affected by the company's turnover rate; the proportion of full- and part-time employees on the staff; the number of employees hired by store managers and supervisors in contrast with the number hired by a central personnel department; and the extent to which advertising, interviewing, employment forms and applications, record processing, reference checking, testing and other devices are used.

Because of the widespread differences in many of these procedures, average employment costs are difficult to pinpoint on an industry-wide basis. The one exception is in the area of unemployment compensation, which represents one of the major employment costs.

The latest available information on unemployment compensation, from the 1983 turnover study, showed that annual unemployment compensation averaged $111.14 for each terminated employee. To-day, the cost would be considerably higher, but the expense is bur-densome even at 1983 rates. With 71 employees turned over in each store in 1990, the annual cost for unemployment compensation would be $7,891 per store at 1983 rates, and considerably more when increases that occurred during the intervening seven years are factored in.

Moreover, when employment office hiring expenses, employ-ment agency fees, advertising, testing, record processing and other expenses are added to the unemployment compensation cost, the total annual employment cost is formidable.

Learning Costs.   Untrained employees, no matter what their jobs, cannot become skilled the moment they join a firm. They must first be trained, either formally, or informally on a watch-me-do-it basis. They are working at less than optimum proficiency until they perform at levels comparable with experienced employees.

Industrial psychologists have measured the loss of productivity during the learning period for manual tasks at approximately 30 percent of the average skilled or proficient employee's productivity. (See Figure 1.) One supermarket company found that its average skilled meat wrapper produced 220 packages per hour over an eight hour work day, hand wrapping meat with soft film. Meat wrapper trainees, on the other hand, averaged only 155 packages per hour during the eighty hour learning period, or about 70 percent of the packages wrapped per hour by skilled employees. In other words, 30 percent of the employees' working hours and wages during the full learning period may be considered learning costs. On the first day of training, a new meat cutter's productivity is very low and the learning cost will be almost 100 percent of his or her wages. Therefore, when employees are terminated before they have com-pleted training, learning costs increase.

The loss in efficiency during the learning period has long been recognized. However, only recently has learning cost been mea-sured as a cost of turnover. The relationship between learning cost and turnover is quite evident. When an experienced employee leaves, a replacement must be hired and put through training. The learning cost of this replacement is a cost of turnover, and the higher the turnover, the greater the learning costs. Thus, several companies are now using the 30 percent loss of efficiency during training as a base figure for computing turnover costs for all supermarket store-level jobs.

A typical cashier trainee needs 120 learning hours to reach the average performance level of the experienced cashier. Since the

FIGURE 1
Average Learning Curve for Manual Tasks

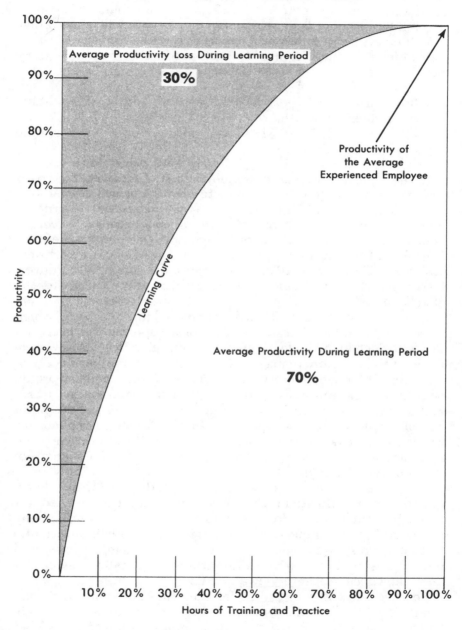

cashier trainee loses 30 percent of productivity during the 120 hour learning and practice period, each trainee is paid for 36 non-productive hours (30 percent × 120 hours = 36 hours). If the average full-time cashier trainee earns $8.50 per hour, and the average part-time cashier trainee $5.50 per hour, their learning costs can be determined by multiplying the non-productive hours by these hourly wage rates:

36 hours × $8.50 = $306.00 (Learning cost of one full-time cashier trainee.)

36 hours × $5.50 = $198.00 (Learning cost of one part-time cashier trainee.)

In the typical supermarket employing six full-time and ten part-time cashiers, the full-time cashier turnover rate was 24 per 100, and the part-time cashier turnover rate was 111 per 100. If turnover costs are computed in terms of learning costs, then the average annual turnover cost at the above wage rates (including benefits) is $441 for full-time cashiers (.24 × $306 × 6), and $2,198 for part-time cashiers (1.11 × 198 × 10). At these rates, the combined turnover-learning cost for full-and part-time cashiers in a typical store is $2,639 annually.

In the 1983 study, annual learning costs and turnover rates, which were computed for all positions in a typical supermarket, averaged $17,878. Such an average, though meaningful in itself, is obviously not as useful to a store manager as specific figures for his or her own operation. It is relatively easy for a manager to obtain a store's profile on turnover-learning costs by using his own figures on average learning time, average wage rates, average turnover rates and the number of employees in each position. In this fashion, the manager can learn the exact turnover-learning cost in the store. The same approach may be used to determine learning costs for a group of stores or for a company.

In the 1990 turnover study, each responding company determined its own estimated turnover costs using a recommended formula. It included costs for recruiting (search, interview, screen); hiring and initial employment (administration, induction/orientation, uniforms, equipment, training, travel, lodging, wages, and monitoring); and separation (administration, separation pay, severance allowance, exit interviews, and taxes).

The average cost was $1,021 for each full-time employee separated, and $557 for each part-timer. The typical store in the study had a turnover rate of seven full-time employees at a cost of $7,147 per year, and a part-time turnover rate of 57 employees at a cost of

$35,648 per year. Thus, the total annual turnover cost for the typical $9 million supermarket was $42,795. Since the net profit after taxes of the typical store in this study was approximately 1.0 percent of sales ($90,000), turnover costs were equivalent to more than 47 percent of net profit. This should convince any skeptic of the importance of controlling avoidable turnover.

Intangible Costs. There are several very important intangible costs related to employee turnover which cannot be computed in dollars and cents but which are undoubtedly responsible for further draining the profits in high employee turnover stores. One of these intangible costs is the reduced amount of attention store and department managers are devoting to other managerial responsibilities while training and supervising replacements. Another intangible cost is the depressing effect turnover has on employee morale. It is almost impossible to develop a high level of team spirit when team members are constantly coming and going. Poor morale always has a harmful effect on store profits.

One executive of a West Coast chain feels that the effect of turnover on morale is often underestimated. He said: "High turnover is contagious. That is why we periodically examine every store's turnover rate and try to get at the causes of rising turnover in individual units before we have a real problem on our hands."

Turnover can hurt store sales too. The inferior performance of green recruits will often cause additional stockouts and add service problems at the checkstand. Of course, a customer is not going to miss the brusque and inefficient clerk, or the discourteous manager. But a customer will surely be affected by the resignation of a manager who recognizes the shopper on sight and approves his or her checks immediately, or of a favorite cashier, or of a meat cutter who puts aside a rib roast for the customer until she does her usual Friday night shopping; these are the people who have brought the customer into the store. Moreover, if the store's turnover rate is too high, with employees constantly changing, the customer will not be able to build up a friendly rapport. Then the competitor down the street, with a more stable organization, can steal the thunder from the high employee turnover store.

Another intangible turnover cost, which is occasionally overlooked, is product spoilage during the training period, including miscuts by the apprentice meat trainee or by the new produce trimmer; wrong prices or cut packages by the new stockman; or errors by the new cashier. Moreover, many chains feel that there is a direct correlation between excessive turnover and high internal pilferage and/or above average cashier errors. Some companies have also discovered that there is a direct relationship between turnover and tardiness and/or absenteeism, both of which are early warning signals of a likely resignation.

Finding the Information

Because excessive turnover is costly, time-consuming and may be damaging to a store's sales and morale, it is important to find the chief causes of turnover. Computers have been used in recent years to help the industry to pin down the scope and causes of turnover. Without computerized data storage, it would be extremely difficult to determine exact turnover causes for large companies with thousands of employees. Today, over 90 percent of the supermarket chains that do an annual volume of 50 million dollars or more, either own or lease a computer. Many of these companies have programmed their computers to handle turnover data, while others are in the process of doing so.

Of course, human beings, not a computer, must determine the cause of each turnover incident. Some chains must still tighten and improve their methods of reporting turnover causes so that accurate information will be fed into the computer. Therefore, more and more chains are using exit interviews and/or exit questionnaires to compile turnover cause information. No longer satisfied with mere labels such as "quit" or "discharged"—labels that offer no insight into why the employee has resigned or was terminated—companies are beginning to investigate the real reasons for turnover.

Why They Leave

Employee separations fall into four categories:

1. *Resignations*: 72.6 percent—almost three of every four full-time employee separations—and 77.4 percent—more than three of every four part-time employee separations—are resignations.

2. *Discharges for cause*: 20.5 percent of separated full-time employees and 20.7 percent of separated part-time employees—more than one in every five—are discharged for such causes as violating company policy, unsatisfactory work, absenteeism, etc.

3. *Unavoidable separations*: 6.0 percent of full-time separations and 1.6 percent of part-time separations are due to such unavoidable reasons as retirement, illness or death.

4. *Operational discharges*: 0.9 percent of full-time separations and 0.4 percent of part-time separations are discharges for such operational reasons as store closings, layoffs or temporary hirings.

Resignations are by far the chief contributor to today's high turnover rate. The 1990 study showed that of 157,539 terminations reported by participating companies, 121,471—77.1 percent—were resignations.

Leaving for other employment is the single most frequent reason for resigning, accounting for more than one in four resignations. In most cases, the true cause of leaving for other employment is masked by the departing employee. It is highly unlikely that wages are the underlying cause; less than 1.0 percent indicate dissatisfaction with wages as their reason for leaving. This is not surprising because wages in the supermarket industry today are superior to those paid in other retail or service businesses. The real underlying reason is more likely to be unhappiness with the boss or co-workers, a low level of morale within the individual or in the store, poor training, or poor treatment of the employee.

Companies participating in the 1990 turnover study did not separate out data for department and store managers; however, data available from the 1983 study provides information that is useful and still timely. For example, many supermarket executives noted that the proportion of managers who leave is far more serious than the extent of resignations by full- and part-time employees. Competent managers are not only difficult to find, they also constitute a substantial investment. The cost of replacing and training a store manager was estimated at about $60,000 in 1983 and undoubtedly exceeds $100,000 today. As stores and their staffs have grown larger, and more sophisticated methods of management are in place, more skills are required of the manager. In fact, one company reported a significant negative correlation between store manager turnover and net profit; the lower the turnover rate, the higher the profit.

In 1983, as well as today, employees discharged for cause far outnumbered those separated for operational or unavoidable reasons. Among managers, the rate of discharges for cause was higher than for other employees. Almost one of four department managers and almost half the store managers who were separated were dismissed for cause. Of all store and department managers who were discharged for cause, the most frequent reason given was "unsatisfactory work." This fact seems to support the view of those who contend that many supermarket chains keep promoting people until they fail—a rather serious indictment. At best, the high rate of managerial discharges for cause indicated a need to determine ex-

FIGURE 2
Managerial Separations

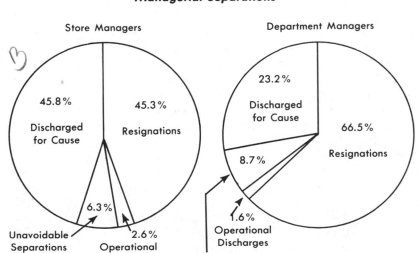

actly why so many managers failed to perform satisfactorily. Considering the financial investment that it has in its managerial staff, every supermarket company today would be wise to scrutinize its manager turnover rate and causes, to determine whether action to reduce avoidable turnover should be taken. Figure 2 summarizes the reasons for and rates of managerial separations in 1983.

Employee Turnover: 1983 vs. 1990

Following are some of the more interesting comparative observations from the 1983 and 1990 studies:

1. The average weekly sales per store increased from $158,350 in 1983 to $173,077 in 1990.
2. The number of employees per store increased from 63 to 87.
3. The ratio of part-timers increased from 57.2 to 65.2 percent.
4. the annual turnover rate for full-timers increased from 10.5 percent to 23.8 percent; and for part-timers from 69.2 percent to 111.5 percent.

5. Full-time separations during the first 30 days of employment increased from 5.6 percent to 19.3 percent; part-time separations increased from 26.2 percent to 29.0 percent.

6. Full-time separations after one year of employment decreased from 77.4 percent to 36.4 percent; part-time separations decreased from 34.2 percent to 12.0 percent.

Economic climate can be a major factor in turnover, as it was in 1983, when turnover rates were low, due in part to the recession in 1981 and 1982. However, ignoring the temporary nature of such external factors can lead to a potentially dangerous attitude of complacency. For example, one company in the 1983 study commented: "Our turnover is not excessive . . . we don't have a turnover problem." Yet, they had the highest full-time and store manager turnover rates among the six chains that participated in the study from their region. Another company had the highest turnover rate among all the participating companies in every employee and manager category. When asked what steps were being taken to reduce turnover, their vice-president responded, "Very little." The management of this large company obviously was not aware of the very heavy drain that turnover was having on their bottom line.

With today's turnover cost being equivalent to almost half the supermarket's net profit *after* taxes, employee turnover cannot be ignored. It demands constant attention and improvement.

Cutting Turnover

Once the seriousness of excessive employee turnover has been realized and the major factors that contribute to turnover have been revealed, it is necessary to devise ways to substantially reduce excessive turnover. Here is an effective five-step procedure for cutting turnover:

1. Maintain accurate turnover records, which help to pinpoint problem areas, for each department and for each store.

2. Conduct exit interviews to identify the real causes of turnover.

3. Inform all managers and key personnel of turnover rates and causes.

4. Develop and put into practice effective techniques to recruit, select, induct and train new employees.

5. Instruct managers and supervisors in the use of modern techniques for communicating, managing and getting work done through people.

Keeping Turnover Records

Any company that decides to really tackle its turnover problem must begin by setting up techniques for accumulating and reporting meaningful data on a regular basis. The simplest method of gathering turnover rate information is to examine the W-2 forms for separated employees, made up by every accounting department for all employees at the end of each calendar year. But annual turnover rates alone are of little value. For a company to act effectively to reduce turnover, data must be available at least quarterly, and must identify *where* and *why* turnover is occurring. In order to pinpoint and correct problems, quarterly turnover reports must be broken down by job classification, by department, by store, by district or division, and by the reasons for the terminations.

Most progressive chains have already placed all turnover data on computers. The advantages of using the computer for this purpose are that periodic reports can be produced faster, more accurately and at a lower cost than when such reports are manually produced. However, a computer can produce accurate information only when it is fed accurate information.

One of the real problems in gathering accurate turnover data is to determine the real, often hidden causes of employee terminations. When an employee claims he is leaving to take another job, or to better himself in some way, or because he is dissatisfied with his job, or for any of a number of other reasons, he may, in fact, be concealing the true reason for his departure. Careful probing is required to uncover accurate turnover causes.

Exit Interviews

The primary purpose of an exit interview is to obtain accurate information regarding deficiencies within the company so that corrective action may be taken to avoid excessive turnover in the future. Three types of exit interviews are commonly used: face-to-face interviews, telephone interviews, and mail questionnaires. Each has certain advantages and disadvantages, and each is best suited in specific circumstances.

The preferred approach is the face-to-face exit interview conducted by a skilled interviewer. When the employee gives notice that he is leaving, the face-to-face interview should be conducted a day or two before his departure. When he resigns or is discharged suddenly, it is conducted a few days after his departure, in many companies, when he returns to the store or main office for his final pay check.

The primary disadvantage of the face-to-face interview is its timing. Since the employee is often emotionally caught up in the circumstances leading to his resignation or dismissal, it is usually difficult, and sometimes impossible, to obtain accurate information from him. His emotional involvement makes it all the more important that a skilled person conduct the interview.

After commencing on an informal note, the interviewer should gradually lead to the main point: the real reason for the termination. As in any formal interview (see Chapter 4 for a discussion of interviewing techniques), the interviewer should spend most of his or her time listening instead of talking, and should not attempt to dissuade the resigning employee from leaving. (Where appropriate, this should be done before the exit interview.) Specific questions should be planned and notes taken on a form similar to the one shown in Table 1.

It is not always possible to conduct a professional face-to-face interview. Employees sometimes leave suddenly, giving no advance notice; some move to a different city or leave stores remote from headquarters and cannot return for their final pay checks. When face-to-face interviews are not possible, either a telephone interview or a mail questionnaire should be used about two to four weeks following termination. The advantage of these two types of interviews is that sufficient time has elapsed for the employee to have a chance to modify whatever strong emotions he or she might have had at the time of departure. On the other hand, it is often more difficult to elicit the real cause of termination during telephone interviews or through mail questionnaires.

When telephone interviews are used, the employee should be called at his home where he is free to talk, rather than at his new place of work. Interviewing techniques should resemble those of the face-to-face interview; the interviewer should gradually lead up to the most pertinent question: the reason for the termination.

The basic form of the mail questionnaire is generally the same as that of the face-to-face and telephone interviews. In this case, however, a self-addressed, stamped return envelope should be enclosed with the questionnaire, as well as a brief covering letter explaining the purpose of the questionnaire. Former employees should be encouraged to be honest and frank in their answers. They should, furthermore, be advised that they need not sign their name or otherwise identify themselves when completing the questionnaire. Properly handled, the mail questionnaire should bring a response from 60 to 80 percent of terminated employees.

Regardless of the approach used, the questions asked of the former employee should provide vital information about the reasons for leaving, as well as his or her views on the effectiveness of such personnel department responsibilities as employee induction and training, communication, opportunities for advancement, working conditions, fringe benefits and others. Many companies also find it helpful to have the immediate superior of the terminated employee give an explanation of the departure. The reasons given by the employee and his or her superior often differ widely, thus underscoring the need to identify the real cause of separation.

When stores are remote from headquarters or when terminated employees cannot be interviewed in person by a specialist, store managers should be trained in exit interviewing techniques. However, in such cases, the mail interview should also be used because managers are sometimes personally and emotionally involved in the terminations of their own employees and cannot be objective, and because very few managers become really skilled in conducting in-depth interviews.

Termination reasons should be classified in periodic turnover reports, and courses of action should be developed and implemented to eliminate excessive turnover.

TABLE 1

Sample Exit Interview Form

Questions	Employee Comments
I. Company and Store Induction:	
A. When you first started work with us,	
1. Were you made to feel at home in your store?	Yes_____ No_____
2. Were you given a tour of the store?	Yes_____ No_____
3. Were you introduced to the store and department managers and to other employees?	Yes_____ No_____
4. Were you assigned a "buddy" to guide you through your first few days?	Yes_____ No_____
5. Did your manager give you an adequate explanation of what your job was and of exactly what was expected of you?	Yes_____ No_____
6. Were the company's salary and benefit plans thoroughly explained to you?	Yes_____ No_____

	Good	Fair	Poor
II. Training:			
A. How would you rate the training you received for:			
1. Your first job	_____	_____	_____

TABLE 1 (Cont.)

Questions	Employee Comments

2. Your present job (if different from above)   _____ _____ _____

B. In what respects do you believe the training we
provide can and should be improved? _____

III. Working Conditions:

    A. How would you rate each of the following:

        1. Your immediate superior   _____ _____ _____

        2. Your superior's boss   _____ _____ _____

        3. Help and suggestions from superiors   _____ _____ _____

        4. Cooperation from others in your department   _____ _____ _____

        5. Equipment provided   _____ _____ _____

        6. Interest shown by your superiors in your
welfare and progress   _____ _____ _____

        7. Your opportunity for advancement   _____ _____ _____

        8. The importance of your work to the success of
the company   _____ _____ _____

        9. The working conditions of your job   _____ _____ _____

      10. The wages you received   _____ _____ _____

      11. Our fringe benefits:

           a. Hospitalization plan   _____ _____ _____

           b. Profit sharing plan   _____ _____ _____

           c. Vacation plan   _____ _____ _____

           d. Sick leave plan   _____ _____ _____

IV. Job Requirements:

    A. Was the amount of work you were expected to do:
Excessive _____ About right _____ Too little _____

V. Attitude Toward Company:

    A. What did you like most about working for our company? _____

_____

    B. What did you like least? _____

_____

VI. Reasons for Leaving:

    A. What would you say are the most important reasons why you are leaving the
company? _____

_____

VII. Other
Comments: _____

_____

_____

Keeping Personnel Informed

Many of the 25 supermarket companies that responded to our 1983 turnover study, understandably troubled by the results, have instituted programs to reduce turnover. Among other improvements, some developed a better communication system to keep operating managers up to date on information gathered by personnel representatives during store visits or during counseling or exit interviews with employees. Several also expanded the list of reasons for terminations and devised procedures to derive more meaningful turnover information in order to study the impact of special events on turnover, and to analyze particular causes of turnover so that programs for improvement might be initiated. Several chains who were conducting studies on turnover mailed questionnaires to people who had left during the prior twelve month period to determine whether there were any specific company shortcomings that caused employees to leave. Others sent confidential questionnaires to employees thirty to sixty days after resignation or termination. One chain investigated transfers more closely before they were made in order to study their possible effects on turnover.

Developing Effective Techniques to Cut Turnover

An examination of the turnover records of 21 participating chains disclosed such statistics as the following:

1. In chains where the personnel department hired all full-timers, the full-time turnover rate per 100 was 4.6, compared with a turnover of 10.8 per 100 full-timers in chains where the manager and/ or supervisor did all of the hiring.

2. In chains where the personnel department hired all part-timers, the part-time turnover rate per 100 was 40.9, compared with a turnover of 71.6 per 100 where part-timers were hired at store level.

3. Only one of the participating companies reported that they administered psychological tests to new full- or part-time employees. The turnover ratio in this company was 24 percent less than the average for full-timers and 42 percent less than the average for part-timers.

4. Chains conducting exit interviews for part-timers had an annual turnover ratio of 46.9 per 100 part-timers. In chains that did not interview departing part-timers, the turnover ratio was 77.0

percent. Exit interviews had no significant impact on full-time turn-over ratios.

5. Companies with written standard policy and procedure manuals for more than half their store departments had an average turnover rate of 10 percent for full-time employees. Where manuals were not used extensively, the rate was 15 percent for full-timers. The use or absence of such manuals appeared to have no effect on part-time turnover.

6. Nineteen chains that conducted performance evaluations for full-timers at least once a year had a full-time turnover rate of 10.3 percent. The two chains that did not conduct such evaluations had a turnover rate of 28.3 percent.

7. Nine of the 25 chains in the study, with 13 percent of the employees surveyed, were not unionized. All were local or smaller regional chains. The non-union companies had turnover ratios of 12.8 per 100 full-timers and 57.2 per 100 part-timers; in unionized companies, the ratios were 9.8 and 71.3, respectively. It is difficult to know, with any degree of certainty, why unionized companies have lower full-time turnover rates than non-union companies, but higher part-time turnover rates. One explanation may be that unions do a more effective job in representing the full timer.

Significant as these statistics may appear to be, it is unwise to jump to the conclusion that the implied relationship between employee turnover and various personnel practices is sufficient reason for instituting major shifts in present personnel policies and procedures. There is no guarantee that adopting any given personnel practice will, in itself, reduce turnover. Still, these figures represent a significant portion of the industry and the findings do point up some practices that chains seeking to cut excessive turnover would do well to examine.

What Needs to Be Done

Twenty-three of the 25 participating chains responded to questions relating to how excessive turnover can be reduced, and what actions they have taken to achieve that goal.

The vast majority of these chains saw an urgent need to: maintain and communicate turnover data and trends; improve their recruiting and selection techniques; use more professional, more thorough interviewing techniques; upgrade the indoctrination of new employees into the company and the store; inform new employees of what is expected of them *before* they start on the job; conduct annual or semi-annual performance evaluations of *all* store employees; train department and store managers in the skills of communication and getting work done through people; and finally, a point made by several companies, improve the quality of life in the workplace. As expressed by one participant, there is a need to "provide an environment that encourages employees to develop their abilities, use their full potential, and share ideas that further the success of the business, so they gain a sense of pride in their accomplishments, and confidence in their capabilities."

What Some Have Done

Several companies provided detailed descriptions of the actions they have taken to reduce turnover and the results of those activities. Following are some examples:

Chain A: (1) Instituted a program whereby all interviewing is conducted by the employee relations department. This provides consistency throughout the company with regard to hiring standards for new employees.

(2) Developed an in-depth orientation process that is conducted by the store manager. Included is a store employee handbook and induction checklist.

(3) Instituted a mobile training unit (classroom on wheels) that makes contact with new employees before the ninetieth day on the job. The mobile training unit provides orientation that supplements the program conducted by the store manager.

Results: Prior to the inception of this program, in-store turnover was in excess of 77 percent. Turnover rates dropped to 52.4 percent two years later; to 39.7 percent five years later; and to 32.0 percent after seven years.

Chain B: When turnover was measured at an unbelievable 88.7 percent, a company-wide management training program was implemented to upgrade store and department manager skills in (1) proper hiring and interviewing procedures, (2) proper orientation of new employees, and (3) thorough training of new employees. Also, a greater emphasis was placed on building store and department managers' human relations skills. Turnover data is communicated monthly to the store managers.

Results: In one year, turnover was reduced to 63 percent and in subsequent years leveled off in the 47 percent range.

Chain C: Developed and implemented a new, thorough orientation program, plus written training reports, which are followed up with a six-month performance evaluation for each new employee.

Results: The annual part-time turnover rate has been reduced to 29 percent, which is less than half the industry average.

Chain D: Started a program to administer employee attitude surveys and conduct performance appraisal reviews for all full- and part-time employees on a regular basis. Communication has been improved by having each district manager designate specific days in each store when any employee can schedule an appointment for a private discussion.

Results: Turnover rates are currently averaging 8.4 percent for full-timers and 58.7 percent for part-timers, which is significantly better than the rates for other companies in this chain's geographic area.

Chain E: Heavy emphasis was placed on new employee indoctrination and training.

Results: Turnover rates are currently averaging 7.2 percent for full-timers and 45.5 percent for part-timers. This company enjoys one of the lowest turnover rates of all the participating companies in the survey.

Reports of innovations by other chains also indicated success at drastically reducing the loss of manager trainees, full-time employees and management personnel.

Hiring, Induction and Training. In order to reduce turnover through improved hiring procedures, other chains have eliminated all store hiring, making employment a function of the central personnel office.

Induction and orientation methods have also been re-examined. Company orientation booklets are being distributed to all new employees in 23 of the 25 participating chains. Many companies have established a "buddy system" in all stores. Three chains send a personnel representative to make a follow-up visit during the employee's second or third week on the job. Even more significant, 21 of the 22 chains reporting on the time devoted to indoctrination indicated they are spending a minimum of one hour with all full- and part-timers; nine chains devote between two and eight hours to indoctrinating new employees. This is in stark contrast to earlier practices, when more than 75 percent of the participating chains spent an hour or less on introducing the new hire to the company and the store.

To reduce turnover, training methods have also been improved by several companies. Among the training innovations that are being introduced are self-development courses, Learner Controlled Instruction (LCI, described in Chapter 9), and a series of workshops for store and department managers, which are designed to improve training, supervision and leadership skills and to upgrade skills in human relations.

Each of the steps taken or planned by these companies can substantially cut turnover if the programs are designed to overcome the specific problems of the individual company. Every supermarket firm must pinpoint the causes of turnover within its own company, determine where and why turnover is excessive, and develop steps that will correct the problem. Chains that have handled this task competently have invariably reported exceptional results. According to one personnel executive, "We've put a lot of money into our turnover reduction program in the past two years. But by our reckoning, we've saved three dollars for every dollar we've invested."

Managers and Turnover

The efforts of headquarters executives to reduce excessive turnover at store level will be to no avail unless supervisors, and store and department managers are invited to participate in developing and carrying out such programs. Managers represent the company and its policies to line personnel. Unless these managers are made to understand how harmful and wasteful excessive turnover is, company programs will have little chance of succeeding.

In one Midwestern company, the manager whose store had the lowest employee turnover ratio in its district (a quarterly combined full- and part-time employee turnover rate of 7 per 100) exchanged stores with the manager who ran the district's highest turnover store (a quarterly combined average turnover of 25 employees per 100). Within a year, the manager who had been shifted to the high turnover store had reduced its quarterly turnover rate from 25 to 9 per 100. The other manager increased the rate of turnover in the low turnover store from 7 to 25 per 100, thus transforming the district's lowest employee turnover store to its highest. This experiment proved to the company the key role that the store manager plays in creating an atmosphere that leads to either high or low employee turnover.

It is becoming increasingly evident that store managers, rather than complaints about salaries or long hours, trigger much of today's costly turnover. More and more companies are finding that their store managers make too many hiring mistakes and are not properly prepared to interview, test, select and train employees. Today, many chains hire no full-time employees. The practice of promoting part-timers to fill full-timer vacancies is part of their "promotion from within" policy. Knowledgeable personnel executives estimate that more than 90 percent of the supermarket store employees hired today are part-timers. With almost 48 percent of all part-time turnover occurring during the first ninety days on the job, it is also obvious that a manager's orientation skills must be upgraded. Proper induction methods will help to reduce the number of separations of new recruits and to protect the training dollars which have been invested in them.

Too many companies accept turnover as one of the necessary evils of supermarketing. But turnover is more than a temporary irritation or inconvenience. It represents a substantial loss of money, money that many progressive supermarket companies are now saving through the implementation of improved personnel training and practices.

2 | Forecasting Personnel Requirements

Because of the high turnover rate common throughout the super-market industry, today's food companies are constantly faced with the problem of finding adequate personnel to fill their ranks. Unlike baseball clubs, they have no minor league farm clubs to guarantee an upward flow of talent protected by the reserve clause. They are compelled to build from within their ranks of employees only to see, too often, their most talented people move on to other chains and industries. While trying to hold current operating payroll in line, they must also invest in future manpower. Their personnel problems are all the more severe because the need for personnel grows steadily as the chains expand, not only with additional stores, but with larger stores as well.

To meet their labor requirements, many companies are raising such questions as the following:

What steps can be taken to avoid the necessity of luring key personnel from other chains?

To what degree can supermarket chains afford to prepare for future needs by overstocking on trainees beyond their immediate operating requirements?

Can and should training periods be shortened and made more concentrated so that "graduates" would come through at a faster rate?

The Need to Know

First, it is necessary to be aware of the personnel vacancies that are likely to occur during the next few years. Predicting future quota requirements enables chain operators to plan an orderly program for fulfilling such requirements. A company must begin planning for future store management personnel long before new stores are on the boards. It must determine in advance the number of months required to develop men and women into effective store managers. It must be able to predict the number of new store and department managers it would need in the next two years or even in the next five years. (Five years, remember, are only sixty short months away.) It must also identify the people who would be capable of filling such key positions.

The supermarket company that does not plan for the future is in trouble. It is necessary to establish an effective forecasting system or the company's growth may be stunted.

A Typical Problem

The director of store operations for a thirty-store Midwestern chain recently called a meeting of his field supervisors. "Here we go again," he said. "More problems on key personnel. Johnson, our store manager at Number 8, has been hired to run our competitor's store down the street. And that's not all; Jenkins, the assistant manager at 23, is going to work at a hi-tech assembly plant. He leaves us a week from Saturday. As you can see, we've got to make some pretty quick moves.

"We never seem to be able to keep up," he continued. "We get about set in our managers, and boom—we lose a couple of key people. I don't have to tell you we have nobody ready to fill these openings. The changes we made last month really cleaned us out. We'll just have to find the best people we've got and struggle along with them while they learn their new duties on the job.

"Let's start with your stores, Rick. What assistant managers have you got who might make us a manager at store Number 8?"

Two hours and 45 minutes later, they had selected an assistant manager to promote to store manager, as well as two stock clerks to promote to assistant managers. The supervisors all agreed that, "even with luck," it would be several months before any of these three employees would be capable of functioning properly in the new job. Moreover, there was always the possibility that one or more of these people would not grow into the new job because of inadequate training or inexperience and would eventually swell the company's already high turnover rate.

Forecasting Key Personnel Requirements

The problem illustrated by the above example can be alleviated, though not altogether routed out, by setting up workable personnel forecasting programs. Advance planning can effectively deal with both foreseen and unforeseen personnel needs. Nevertheless, even companies with such programs must occasionally call meetings to deal with unexpected terminations. However, such emergencies occur far less frequently and are far less serious because the company is equipped with a reserve force of employees who have already been trained and who are prepared to fill the new vacancies.

Thus, a good forecasting program is somewhat similar to a strong bull-pen in baseball. The relief man is out in the bull-pen warming up the minute there is a sign of a developing emergency.

A Forecasting Program

Here is a forecasting program which has helped several companies to anticipate and provide for their future personnel requirements.

1. *Determine turnover*: By examining personnel records over the last three to five years, the chains determine their actual turnover in every key job in the company. They set up charts which, in the case of each employee, indicate the reason for the termination of employment. (See Table 1.)

2. *Summarize findings*: The companies summarize these termination records to show the average number of terminations per year, excluding retirements. (See Table 2.)

3. *Project needs*: The known key personnel openings that will develop as a result of new stores, planned employee promotions and planned retirements are then listed by the company for each quarter over the next eighteen to 24 month period. Average terminations are also included, based on the data provided in Table 2. (See Table 3.)

TABLE 1

Analysis of Terminations of Key Store Personnel, 1987-1990

Position	Store Number	Reason for Separation	Year of Separation
Store Managers			
Henry Alcott	4	Retired	1987
David Madison	21	Deceased	1988
Herbert Faber	18	Poor Performance	1989
Helen Jones	5	Ill Health	1989
Frank Walsh	7	Other Employment	1990
Arthur Meadow	29	Other Employment	1990
Assistant Managers			
Jacob Brown	17	Poor Performance	1987
Jack Weinberg	19	Other Employment	1987
Richard Melson	3	Poor Performance	1988
Robert Dannick	21	Pilferage	1988
Harold Freeman	14	Retired	1988
Nancy Vincent	23	Other Employment	1989
Esther Hancock	18	Auto Injury	1990
Ernest Tucker	17	Deceased	1990
Andrew Harper	27	Poor Performance	1990
Meat Managers			
Adolph Weinberg	29	Other Employment	1987
Jerry Atkins	13	Alcoholic	1987
H. L. McDonald	7	Retired	1987
Joseph Bassett	9	Poor Performance	1988
Edward Hanson	17	Violated Company Policy	1988
Bruce Atteletti	11	Poor Performance	1988
Samuel Braesburg	11	Other Employment	1989
Ruth Flint	26	Other Employment	1989
Robert Hankins	1	Insubordination	1990
Gerome Woodward	16	Deceased	1990
A. L. McIvey	7	Entered College	1990
Jack Gordon	9	Pilferage	1990
Produce Managers			
Sam Siegel	1	Retired	1987
A. B. Martini	28	Insubordination	1987
James Ferrente	4	Poor Performance	1987
Robert Kalik	5	Deceased	1987
Manuel Christopher	5	Other Employment	1988
Freda Nutto	17	Other Employment	1988
Edwin Hall	21	Poor Performance	1988

TABLE 1 (Cont.)

Analysis of Terminations of Key Store Personnel, 1987-1990

Position	Store Number	Reason for Separation	Year of Separation
Doris White	18	Auto Injury	1988
David Jones	5	Pilferage	1988
Andrew Medina	9	Other Employment	1989
Fred Blake	23	Retired	1989
Orsini Ceyroski	26	Poor Performance	1989
Oliver Dandee	13	Other Employment	1989
Jerome Saletti	8	Other Employment	1990
Robert Franklin	2	Violated Company Policy	1990
Harriet White	11	Ill Health	1990
David Valenti	26	Poor Performance	1990
Henry Harvey	21	Ill Health	1990
Checkout Managers			
Ann Mogenson	16	Moved	1987
Susan Marko	4	Pregnancy	1987
Harvey Visco	27	Other Employment	1987
Isabelle Heath	15	Pregnancy	1988
Janet Cash	15	Poor Performance	1988
Louise Stiefer	9	Other Employment	1988
Roger De Lilo	11	Cash Shortage	1988
Georgia Brook	19	Pregnancy	1989
Harry Gryling	23	Moved	1989
Beth Bartle	29	Pregnancy	1989
Samuel Hartley	3	Other Employment	1989
Joyce Cimbry	16	Other Employment	1990
Martha Laker	7	Moved	1990
Ellen Tern	6	Pregnancy	1990

This forecasting program provides the basic data for the company's future key personnel needs. On the basis of this information, general target dates can be established for the completion of the training of personnel selected to fill projected openings. The program is not fool-proof, of course, because the exact dates of such terminations as resignations, discharges or deaths cannot be anticipated.

Forecasts of key personnel needs for the coming twelve months should be more accurate than long-term forecasts. They should form the basis for short-range planning. Every forecasting plan, however, should be reviewed once a month and revised to include new data that have become available.

TABLE 2
Summary of Key Store Personnel Requirements
Based on Terminations, 1987-1990

Position	Year of Separation	Total Terminations	Number of Retirements	Terminations Exclusive of Retirements
Store Managers	1987	1	1	0
	1988	1	0	1
	1989	2	0	2
	1990	2	0	2
	Total	6	1	5
	Yearly Average	1.50	.25	1.25
Assistant Managers	1987	2	0	2
	1988	3	1	2
	1989	1	0	1
	1990	3	0	3
	Total	9	1	8
	Yearly Average	2.25	.25	2.00
Meat Managers	1987	3	1	2
	1988	3	0	3
	1989	2	0	2
	1990	4	0	4
	Total	12	1	11
	Yearly Average	3.00	.25	2.75
Produce Managers	1987	4	1	3
	1988	5	0	5
	1989	4	1	3
	1990	5	0	5
	Total	18	2	16
	Yearly Average	4.50	.50	4.00
Checkout Managers	1987	3	0	3
	1988	4	0	4
	1989	4	0	4
	1990	3	0	3
	Total	14	0	14
	Yearly Average	3.50	.00	3.50

TABLE 3

Anticipated Openings in Key Store Personnel Positions, by Quarter for 1991-1992

	Anticipated Openings During							
	Quarters of 1991				Quarters of 1992			
Position ·	1	2	3	4	1	2	3	4
Store Managers								
New Stores	1	0	1	0	0	2	1	0
Planned Promotions	0	1	0	0	0	0	0	0
Planned Retirements	0	1	0	1	1	0	0	0
Average Past Terminations (1.25 per year)*	1	0	0	0	1	0	0	0
Total Openings	2	2	1	1	2	2	1	0
Assistant Managers								
New Stores	1	0	1	0	0	2	1	0
Planned Promotions (to store manager)	2	2	1	1	2	2	1	0
Planned Retirements	0	0	0	0	0	0	0	0
Average Past Terminations (2.00 per year)*	1	1	0	0	1	1	0	0
Total Openings	4	3	2	1	3	5	2	0
Meat Managers								
New Stores	1	0	1	0	0	2	1	0
Planned Promotions (to meat specialist)	0	0	0	1	0	0	0	0
Planned Retirements	1	0	0	0	0	0	0	1
Average Past Terminations (2.75 per year)*	1	1	1	0	1	1	1	0
Total Openings	3	1	2	1	1	3	2	1

TABLE 3 (Cont.)

Anticipated Openings in Key Store Personnel Positions, by Quarter for 1991-1992

| | Anticipated Openings During | | | | | | | |
| | Quarters of 1991 | | | | Quarters of 1992 | | | |
Position	1	2	3	4	1	2	3	4
Produce Managers								
New Stores	1	0	1	0	0	2	1	0
Planned Promotions								
(to produce specialist)	0	0	0	0	0	0	0	0
Planned Retirements	0	0	0	1	0	0	0	0
Average Past Terminations								
(4.00 per year)*	1	1	1	1	1	1	1	1
Total Openings	2	1	2	2	1	3	2	1
Checkout Managers								
New Stores	1	0	1	0	0	2	1	0
Planned Promotions	0	0	0	0	0	0	0	0
Planned Retirements	0	0	0	0	0	0	0	0
Average Past Terminations								
(3.50 per year)*	1	1	1	1	1	1	1	0
Total Openings	2	1	2	1	1	3	2	0

* Openings due to termination are anticipated to occur at equal intervals during the first quarters of each year.

Note: Any planned store closing would usually be listed as a negative entry and included in this Table. In this illustration, however, the only planned closing was in connection with a relocation of the store, and no changes were planned in key personnel. Therefore, it was omitted from the Table.

Any company with an escalated expansion program must, however, plan much further ahead. Such a company may be expected to have a fairly good idea of its needs over a five year period. Long-range planning means that top management must work closely with store operations and personnel department executives and communicate its growth projections. Cooperative planning between the personnel department and store operations provides the opportunity to prepare an effective recruitment and development program.

A good forecasting program must contain an account of the key personnel needs for all stores. However, the personnel forecasting program should be expanded to cover other key positions in the company, including administrative and service operations, field supervisory positions and key line jobs.[1]

A Personnel Inventory

After the key personnel needs have been established, an inventory should be made which describes existing personnel resources within the company. Such an inventory has a triple purpose: It identifies (1) the people who can be moved along to higher positions; (2) those who are performing satisfactorily in their present positions but who are not considered candidates for promotion; and (3) those who are not meeting company standards, and who must either be retrained or replaced. For example, some department managers, assistant managers, co-managers or store managers, or even supervisors, may not be performing satisfactorily even after repeated efforts have been made to correct their shortcomings. Whenever this occurs, the forecast of key personnel requirements should include planned replacements for such employees.

The company's inventory of key personnel, then, should identify the following: (1) managers rated excellent or very good who, with additional training, are considered definite or probable candidates for promotion; (2) managers whose performances in their present positions are considered satisfactory; (3) managers whose performances are considered fair, and who can hold down their present positions after retraining in specified areas; and (4) managers who are not performing satisfactorily and who must be replaced. (See Table 4.) The inventory of key personnel, and a similar one covering all full-time promotable store employees, should be updated every three months, with interim reports to show progress in correcting problem situations.

How does a company go about conducting an inventory of its key personnel? Techniques used to evaluate present performance vary from company to company. Some companies use performance evaluation techniques by which supervisors evaluate subordinates (as was the case with the company described in Table 4). A few companies rely on the use of psychological tests or evaluations by outside psychological consultants. Others place primary emphasis on in-depth interviews. Still others use measured performance on the job as their primary criterion. Many companies use a combination of

---

[1] *Line jobs*: the term *line employee*, as used in the text, refers to employees below the level of department manager; the term *line manager* refers to store employees at or above the level of department manager.

TABLE 4
Key Personnel Inventory Report

Date: October 6, 1990

Performance

Position	Excellent (definitely promotable with training)	Very Good (probably promotable with training)	Good (satisfactory in present position)	Fair (needs training in present position)	Poor (unsatisfactory; must be replaced)
Store Managers					
1. Smith, R.W.				X	
2. Kaplan		X			
3. Cook	X				
4. Ratterman			X		
5. Dolph					X
6. Trapp				X	
7. Griffin				X	
8. Brown			X		
9. Headley			X		
10. Wyziewski					X
11. Scott	X				
12. Brandt			X		
Totals	2	1	4	3	2
Assistant Managers					
1. West	X				
2. Smith, A.K.				X	
3. Hatton				X	
4. Lovitt	X				
5. Greenbaum					X
6. Crane		X			
7. Jasper			X		
8. Robinson		X			
9. Wakeman			X		
10. Ward				X	
11. Thompson		X			
12. Goldberg	X				
Totals	3	3	2	3	1
Meat Managers					
1. Duval		X			
2. Rainey			X		
3. Wetzel	X				
4. Baum					X
5. Henderson			X		

these techniques, some of which are described in some detail in subsequent chapters. The point here is that an effective personnel inventory is integral to successful forecasting of personnel requirements. Whatever system is used, it must be applied to line employees as well, because it is from that level that department managers eventually come.

Although a personnel inventory system identifies retraining and replacement needs, its primary purpose is to indicate the potential candidates for those key positions for which future needs have been established. Then it must specify exactly what additional training is necessary to qualify each candidate for the higher position. One company found it helpful to prepare a store manager prospect form. The purpose of this form was to (1) maintain an inventory of prospects for the position of store manager; (2) keep management posted on the additional training required to qualify the prospect for that position; and (3) pinpoint the current status of store management requirements. (See Table 5.) The company revises and updates this form on the first of each month.

Forecasting Line Personnel Requirements

The first step in any program for recruiting or selecting line employees, whether they be part-time baggers hired by the store manager or full-time meat cutters hired by the personnel department, is to forecast these personnel requirements. In one company, for example, the personnel department employs and trains all full-time cashiers, while part-timers are hired by individual store managers and trained at store level. This personnel department maintains up-to-date weekly projections of new cashier needs by considering the following: (1) planned separations or retirements; (2) average unplanned separations based on turnover records; and (3) new store requirements. (See Table 6.) The figures showing the planned separations are entered in the form in pencil and updated as information is received from stores. Store managers contribute to the success of the program by advising the personnel department as soon as they learn of a full-time cashier who is planning to leave.

This personnel department, in consultation with store operations, also has the responsibility to recruit and train apprentice meat cutters and full-time trimmers in the produce department. It forecasts personnel needs and trains new employees for these departments just as it forecasts the need for and trains full-time cashiers. Before adopting this method of forecasting labor requirements, this person-

TABLE 5
Store Manager Prospect Form
Weeks Required to Complete Training in Each Department   Date: October 6, 1990

Name	Position Prior to Training	Grocery	Meat	Produce	Checkout	Office	Assistant Store Manager	Anticipated Readiness Date
Henry Johnson	Assistant Manager 14	Complete	Complete	Complete	Complete	Complete	Complete	10/6/90
Sam Pakstan	Assistant Manager 37	Complete	Complete	Complete	Complete	Complete	3 weeks	10/27/90
Joe Bendella	Assistant Manager 51	Complete	Complete	Complete	Complete	Complete	5 weeks	11/10/90
B. L. Thornton	Produce Trainee 19	Complete	Complete	6 weeks	Complete	Complete	5 weeks	12/22/90
Norris Adger	Meat Trainee 5	Complete	7 weeks	Complete	Complete	2 weeks	5 weeks	1/12/91
Jerry Thomas	Assistant Manager 31	Complete	16 weeks	Complete	Complete	Complete	Complete	1/26/91
Harry Davis	Meat Manager 17	12 weeks	Complete	Complete	5 weeks	2 weeks	5 weeks	3/23/91
Sue Rudanski	Produce Manager 33	12 weeks	8 weeks	Complete	5 weeks	2 weeks	5 weeks	5/18/91

Anticipated Store Manager Requirements

Reason for Need	Month in Which Need Is Anticipated											
	Oct. 90	Nov. 90	Dec. 90	Jan. 91	Feb. 91	Mar. 91	Apr. 91	May 91	June 91	July 91	Aug. 91	Sept. 91
New Store 74	X											
New Store 75					X							
New Store 76								X				
Ludlow to Supervisor				X								
M. D. Smith Retire						X						
Terminations (2 per year)	X			X								
Anticipated Manager Needs by Month	2	0	0	2	1	1	0	1	0	0	0	0

TABLE 6

Forecast of Future Full-Time Cashier Requirements

	Week Ending			
Reasons for Anticipated Vacancies	*4/6/91*	*4/13/91*	*4/20/91*	*4/27/91*
Planned Separations or Retirements*	4	3	2	3
Average Unplanned Separations	2	2	2	2
New Store Requirements	0	0	7	0
Number of Cashiers to Be Trained During Preceding Week	6	5	11	5

*Total represents the personnel requirements of all four districts of this company.

nel department had continually been behind schedule, unable to meet demands as they arose.

"Forecasting" for Emergencies

One of the day-to-day problems of supermarket operations is the emergency that arises whenever a regular employee calls in sick at the last minute. In many companies, dealing with such emergencies consumes a major portion of the supervisor's time. One company has reduced this problem by maintaining a pool of trained cashiers, who want only part-time, intermittent work. They are called when they are needed. These reserves will work in any of the company stores in the metropolitan area and are paid a mileage allowance plus an hourly rate which is slightly higher than what is paid to part-time cashiers. Such a pool of cashiers, controlled and assigned by the personnel department, is a valuable asset to the chain and to its individual supervisors.

In another company, each store manager maintains a list of trained housewives or students who can be called to fill-in during an emergency. In any case, preparing in advance to meet such emergencies is an important responsibility of every store manager.

Summary

Forecasting needs for key personnel and line employees forms the basis of recruitment programs in any company. Needs must be established before they can be met. Along with effective recruiting, selecting and training programs, a sound system of forecasting personnel requirements enables the company to achieve the major goal of having the right person with the right skills in the right place at the right time.

3	# Recruiting Employees

The primary purpose of any recruitment program is to find the most competent applicant to fill each opening. No company can expect successful corporate growth unless it has an effective work force. Thus, a company's success or failure is often determined at the recruitment stage.

A good recruitment program requires thorough planning and efficient organization. Each phase of recruitment must be designed to take into account the particular goals of the employer. In general, recruitment procedures may be divided into four phases, as follows:

1. Policy development
2. Procedure development
3. Development of sources and recruiting techniques
4. Evaluation of the recruitment program

Policy Development

Before recruitment can begin, clear-cut policies must be established by headquarters regarding such basic questions as these:

To what extent should promotions come from within the company's organization?

What physical limitations does the company want to establish? For instance, at what age is a man or woman no longer capable of lifting heavy cases?

What is the company's policy regarding the hiring of the handicapped?

To what extent should part-timers be used? Which functions should be limited to full-timers only?

These are only some of the questions that must be answered before an effective recruitment program can be implemented. By solving such problems a company may avoid a helter-skelter program, with each store going off in a different direction.

Full-Time or Part-Time?

A major policy decision which most chains must face concerns full- and part-time employees: To what extent should part-timers be used? What percentage of the work force should full-timers represent? An examination of the problems involved in establishing just this policy emphasizes the need for careful planning before a recruitment program can be effectively instituted.

The extent to which a company hires full-timers or part-timers actually determines its hiring practices. Moreover, the full-time/part-time ratio influences the personnel department's work load with regard to the filling of vacancies, as well as to the amount of training to be provided and the best possible sources of recruitment to be used.

A proper decision regarding the balance of full- and part-timers must result from a complete examination of the factors that affect the choice. For example, the coverage problems of stores open seven days a week are different from those of stores that operate downtown on a 9 AM to 6 PM schedule and a few late nights. But on the whole, today's typical store, operating 72 or more hours a week, would find it difficult, if not impossible, to staff with full-timers only and still maintain a respectable payroll percentage.

Going wage rates in a community also play a major role in the decision. In some parts of the country, the differential between full-time and part-time rates is considerable, while in other areas there is very little spread. Another consideration is employee benefits. Full-timers usually are entitled to more generous vacation policies and, among other things, often participate in pension and insurance plans and sick pay benefits. These are only some of the factors which must be weighed in terms of dollars and cents.

But there are also other considerations, including the chain's experience with turnover rates of full- and part-timers. A company with a low full-time turnover rate and an extremely high part-time turnover may want to lean more heavily toward full-timers because of the savings in dollars when the cost of employee turnover is considered.

What, then, is the best policy to follow? A comparison of the 1968 and 1983 surveys shows some interesting contrasts with regard to full-time/part-time ratios. For example, in chains based in the East, the percent of store employees who were part-timers *increased* from 52.6 in 1968 to 69.7 in 1983. In chains based in the Midwest, the percent of part-timers *decreased* from 56.2 to 50.6 during the same period. In Western-based chains, the percent of part-timers *increased significantly*, from 32.3 in 1968 to 56.3 in 1983. For all U.S. chains, the average percent of part-timers increased from 48.4 in 1968 to 57.2 in 1983 to 65.2 in 1990.

Lack of Agreement. Although part-timers outnumbered full-timers in all three regions of the U.S. in 1983—East, Midwest and West—there was little consistency among the chains, even within the same operating area, on the use of part-timers vs. full-timers:[1]

Headquarters Location	Part-Timer Profile		Weighted Average of All Chains*
	Chain with Lowest Percent	Chain with Highest Percent	
East	56.7%	77.5%	69.7%
Midwest	25.1	70.3	50.6
West	53.0	71.7	56.3

*Weighted by the total number of employees in each region in companies participating in the 1983 study.

These figures clearly show that different chains have different views on how best to balance out part-time/full-time store staffs.

Following are some of the arguments made for maximizing the number of part-time store employees:

"Without part-timers, you simply can't run a supermarket with sales of $8 to $10 million a year and hope to maintain a decent wage percentage."

"The most important advantage of part-timers is flexibility. When someone calls in sick—and this happens often—a part-timer not

[1] Comparable data not available in 1990 study.

scheduled for that day is always on tap. Besides, part-timers cost less. On the average, they get 85 cents an hour less than regulars, and the company doesn't have to foot as large a bill for vacations and other benefits."

"This business is never constant—not from day-to-day or even from hour-to-hour. We just have to bring in people to cover peak hours when we need them. This very often means we simply must operate on work shifts as short as four hours a day for a large number of employees."

"Part-timers do create a lot of problems. They don't produce as much as full-timers, and they're not as dependable either. And every once in a while some green kid pulls a real boner and we start wondering if we shouldn't put on some more full-timers. It's about here that we remember the bottom-of-the-line figures and decide that we can live with the problems. Last year we made a net profit of 2.7 percent after taxes, which is a heck of a lot higher than the national average. And like they say, you can't argue with success."

"Three of every four store employees in our company are full-timers; that's our policy. But I think we should have more part-timers. Our stores are open from 8 AM to 10 PM six days a week, and from 10 AM to 6 PM on Sundays. The need for people in our service departments—cashiers, baggers, store office help, deli-bakery, service meats, produce weighers—varies directly with our customer traffic, which fluctuates a lot during the 92 hours that we're open each week. If we had more part-timers in those positions, we could give our customers better service, and at a lower cost, too."

But others feel just as strongly about full-timers. Following are some of their comments:

"Full-timers are far more productive, far more dependable and more trustworthy than part-timers. Because their jobs are their livelihoods, they are more interested in both the store and the company. This means the customers get treated with the respect they deserve."

"Full-time cashiers are far more accurate than part-timers by a wide margin. We have studies showing that part-timers make twice as many errors and have higher net loss ratios than full-time cashiers."

"A high percentage of full-timers not only means more experienced people are on the job; it also means a larger number of people from which to select candidates for promotion."

Optimum Balance. Good points are made in all of these arguments. Who is right? Neither side is entirely right because an extreme policy in either direction presents problems. The spokesperson for the company with 75 percent full-timers made a good point about providing better customer service with more part-timers in service functions during peak periods. However, it is all too easy to agree with the cliché, "you can't argue with success," made by the person from the high profit store of another chain. Few things prevent outstanding performance more than compliance with that faulty rationalization.

The real questions here are: How much greater would the profits be if an optimum balance were established between full- and part-time employees? And, even more significant, what is that optimum balance? | Though opinions vary, most successful companies view optimum balance in terms of the maximum number of full-time employees who can be kept productively employed for forty hours each week, and the minimum number of part-timers required to provide coverage during peak hours. |

The use of part-timers provides the manager with the most important advantage of scheduling flexibility. Full-time employees must work forty hours each week, in some companies on five consecutive eight-hour days. On the other hand, a manager can vary the number of hours worked by a part-timer from week to week. Because the work load in every supermarket fluctuates from week to week, each department in the store should have at least one part-timer (and service departments in large volume stores as many as required) so that labor-hour schedules can be adjusted to the anticipated labor-hour requirements. Only in this fashion can labor costs be kept at a minimum.

A supermarket that employs good scheduling techniques will usually establish a ratio of at least one part-time employee to each full-timer, with the majority of part-timers involved in the front-end operation. As store hours lengthen and/or the number of service departments increase, the percentage of part-timers should also increase. Of course, another determining factor in this ratio is the availability of qualified full-time employees. In many cases, it may be preferable to hire two good part-time employees rather than settling for one marginal full-timer.

Developing Procedures

Headquarters must also establish procedures as well as policies in order to insure a fully coordinated recruitment program. Unfortunately, however, few supermarket companies develop adequate procedures. Therefore, they often do not get either the quality or the quantity of personnel they require.

Even in metropolitan areas, where trained specialists are available for central recruiting, store managers and supervisors often bypass the personnel department when hiring non-management, store-level employees. Or, at best, the personnel department receives only verbal requisitions from the managers or supervisors and, then, only when a vacancy in the store's staff has already developed. Teamwork, the basis for successful recruitment, is very often disregarded. Any company that fills its personnel needs in such a hand-to-mouth manner, with last minute, day-to-day hiring practices, cannot possibly operate at peak effectiveness. Personnel needs must be anticipated well in advance. Moreover, new employee requisitions are integral to the successful forecasting of personnel needs.

More often than not, a store manager knows in advance when an opening is likely to occur. As soon as that information is available, he or she should prepare a written request to the personnel department for a replacement, specifying the anticipated termination date. Such cooperation between store operators and the personnel department must exist if the personnel department is to perform its recruitment function effectively and take steps to insure that staffing requirements are filled on schedule. Only then can optimum results be obtained.

On the other hand, where stores are scattered or located in remote areas, a central personnel department cannot perform the function of recruiting line employees. In such cases, the only alternative is for the company to train the store manager to perform this function effectively. But, contrary to common belief, this is more easily said than done.

Factors Affecting Recruitment

A number of factors affect a personnel department's or store manager's ability to recruit the best possible people. The most obvious determining factor is a tight labor market. When there are few prospective employees available in a community, it is often difficult to find applicants who meet company standards.

For example, if week-long advertisements for a sorely needed checkout clerk draw only two applicants, both of whom can barely add, the manager and personnel department are faced with a dilemma: Should they hire obviously incompetent help or should they operate with a serious gap in the store's organization? On the other hand, if the same advertisements draw twenty experienced applicants, there is little doubt that the only problem will be to select the best employee among the many who are qualified.

A company's reputation in a community influences the number of persons who will apply for a job. For example, two major chains operate in the same large metropolitan area. One has considerable difficulty with its recruitment program, while the other does not. Both pay the same wage rates and have very similar fringe benefits. Still, one day recently, both chains placed advertisements (almost identical in size and copy) in the local paper for apprentice meat cutters. One chain drew 23 applicants and the other only four. It is not coincidental that the first chain has a much lower employee turnover rate and obviously higher morale among its key personnel.

Though no formal research was conducted on this situation, casual discussions with employees and consumers of the respective companies revealed that the chain which received a better response to its advertisements was widely regarded as friendlier than the other. Its stores were considered to be "nice" places in which to work and shop. In addition, the "friendly" company grants its personnel department more responsibility in recruitment and training, and encourages it to establish rapport with store managers. This, in itself, may be a reputation-building factor.

No recruitment program can be properly established unless it conforms to current labor laws. For example, the Federal Minimum Wage Laws affect almost every supermarket in operation. (This subject is discussed more fully in Chapter 17.) It is difficult to imagine any store manager in mid-1991 not knowing that the federal minimum wage was $4.25, the rate to which it had been raised on April 1, 1991. Yet there probably were managers who did not know that, effective that same date, they could pay a "training wage" of $3.61 per hour (85 percent of the federal minimum), for the first 90 days of employment to people under age 20. If, however, a state's minimum wage is equal to or higher than the federal minimum, and the state does not provide for a lower training wage, then the state's minimum wage overrides the lower federal wage.

Federal, state and local agencies have legal restraints which must be followed, and the company personnel officer should see to it that each store manager is familiar with the latest labor statutes. This also means that programs and policies must be re-examined and updated as pertinent laws are revised and union contracts are renegotiated.

Development of Sources and Recruiting Techniques

Employees may be recruited from eight major sources. Some are commonly used to recruit full-timers, while others are used as

TABLE 1
Full-Time and Part-Time Employee Recruitment Sources

	Source for	
Recruitment Sources	Full-Time Employees	Part-Time Employees
1. Present Part-Time Employees	✓	
2. Referrals by Present Employees	✓	✓
3. Educational Institutions	✓	✓
4. Advertisements	✓	✓
5. Employment Agencies, Public and Private	✓	✓
6. Competition	✓	
7. Labor Unions	✓	
8. Unsolicited	✓	✓

sources of both full-timers and part-timers. Table 1 lists these eight sources and the type (or types) of employee most often recruited from each.

Present Part-Time Employees. Unquestionably, the most fruitful source of full-time employees is present part-timers. In most supermarket chains in the United States, 80 percent or more of the present full-time personnel were once part-time employees. In some companies, this figure is as high as 90 percent.

But the supermarket industry generally does a poor job of keeping capable part-timers. Most of the young men and women who work as part-timers are hired by store managers and given little or no training. Instead, they learn by trial and error. Too often, store managers as well as department managers show little interest in them. Small wonder that the industry is burdened with such tremendous turnover of part-timers. Most supermarket companies lose many talented youngsters who leave because they are ignored or poorly treated while they are part-timers.

Referrals by Present Employees. Recommendations by present employees probably constitute the second best source of full- and part-time employees. Dale Yoder, a prominent personnel authority, has observed that this source of personnel can have far-reaching value because "employees react favorably to the opportunity to help select their colleagues and fellow workers, and the practice encourages a high level of loyalty and morale."[2]

Many supermarket chains have repeatedly demonstrated the importance of this manpower source. The danger of cliques of close friends or family members may be avoided by assigning such new employees to different stores. These precautions should be taken in order to reduce the possibility of nepotism, or promotion as a result of "relative ability."

Educational Institutions. Educational institutions represent a third significant source of both full- and part-time line employees. As a rule, students are conscientious and competent. Those who start their supermarket careers as part-timers and, upon graduation, join the staff as full-timers, have two immediate advantages: on-the-job experience and education.

Still, many supermarkets have poor working relationships with educational institutions that can, and should, provide the largest share of part-time employees. The lack of interested, capable, hard-working part-time students is continually deplored throughout the industry. But investigations have shown that many supermarket companies make no real effort to establish productive relationships with local high school counselors, teachers and principals. In addition, most chains miss real opportunities by failing to establish a good rapport with local college administrators.

High school, junior college, and college and university officials and counselors will almost invariably welcome responsible business people who are searching for capable part-time employees. School counselors can provide the information which would enable supermarkets to obtain reliable young men and women who need work and possess leadership qualities. In many cases, schools will administer appropriate math or dexterity tests to students interested in part-time work.

Indeed, school officials have been known to go far beyond the call of duty in arranging to make talented students available to supermarkets. One small chain in New Jersey found that on Friday mornings it was unable to secure sufficient part-time help at the front-end operation to handle the surge of customers that came through. An official of the company visited the local high school and presented this problem to the principal who, in turn, discussed it with several of his counselors. A few weeks later the school had arranged to change the schedules of nine of its young men and

---

[2] Dale Yoder, *Personnel Management and Industrial Relations* (New Jersey: Prentice-Hall, Inc., 1962), p. 312.

women so that these students could work on Friday mornings, thus solving the supermarket's problem and helping students who needed the income. There are many other instances in which student schedules have been adjusted to accommodate local supermarket needs.

Specialized Schools: A number of American colleges or universities are offering degrees in food marketing. In addition, many high schools and vocational schools offer special programs and services. For example, in Ohio several schools which award high school credit for work performed in supermarkets have undertaken to train cashiers in electronic register operations before these cashiers are assigned to local supermarkets.

Distributive Education: A major source of potential managers and other executives is students attending Distributive Education courses at high schools, junior colleges, and adult vocational schools. Today, thousands of high schools throughout the United States offer DE programs. The number of students participating in such courses is estimated at more than one million.

Essentially, these programs involve a practical arrangement between the school, distributive businesses in the community, parents and students. DE is based on a combination of classroom instruction in marketing and distribution, and experience on the job.

Spreading the Word: A chain in Detroit established a policy of setting aside one day in each three month period on which local school officials, counselors and teachers visit its headquarters. The educators tour the offices and warehouse, after which they assemble for dinner. Following dinner, a discussion is conducted on the supermarket business and the opportunities it offers to talented young men and women. The tour, dinner and talk last about two hours. By rotating the invitations among local schools, this company has found it possible to meet with a group from each school about every three years.

Other chains around the country have established career days. Typically, once each year some of the more talented part-time employees are invited to spend the day touring the office and warehouse and examining supermarket service operations. Lunch is provided, following which the president discusses the company's plans and the opportunities available to young people in the supermarket business.

A supermarket chain in New Jersey uses the career day to bring to its offices students selected by the local high school. Each student spends the day with an officer of the company or a department head. At the end of the day, the students and key company personnel join for dinner, where a talk is usually delivered by the president of the company.

These methods used by supermarkets to communicate with local school officials and with students are relatively inexpensive, yet they are far-reaching in their effect. By employing such techniques, supermarkets can attract the most capable young men and women to their companies and establish important forums for improved customer and public relations.

Education and the Full-Timer: Because high school and college students hired as part-timers are often mistreated and accorded little respect by store and top management, many leave at the first opportunity. There is little doubt that few among the part-time employees who resign in order to return to school ever return to the industry. Many of the talented young people who are lost would have been willing to consider a future in the supermarket industry when they finished school had they been treated as potential managers or executives instead of as menial laborers.

Universities, junior colleges and high schools represent the most desirable sources of future managers and executives. Most supermarket companies, however, do a poor job of attracting these potential leaders. Even the companies that place college graduates in management training programs grant them little authority once they become full-fledged managers. Typically, these managers are not given the opportunity to become familiar with the overall operation of the company. They are not exposed to other aspects of the business, such as advertising, personnel and financial functions. In addition, many companies have no standard policy for promoting young managers based on objective periodic reviews of their performances. These employees are merely pressured to perform as store or department managers and are given no chance to see how their performances help the company.

Indeed, some top executives in the supermarket field consider their industry unworthy of college graduates. The president of a large chain commented during a panel discussion composed of supermarket leaders that the business does not offer sufficient challenge to sustain the interest of the average college graduate. Other members of the panel objected. They noted that if the store manager's job is not challenging in a company it is because the executives of that company have not made it so. Enlightened companies, they continued, see to it that a store manager is treated as the chief executive officer of an eight, ten or twelve million dollar business.

Few supermarket leaders would insist upon a college degree as a prerequisite for the job of store manager. But it is obviously a serious mistake to neglect the talent available among college graduates.

Use of Media.   Newspaper advertisements are an obvious source of manpower, but their effectiveness varies according to the location and the "want-ad pull" of the paper. As a rule, newspaper advertising is more effective in cities than in suburbs. It is usually better to advertise in papers that prospective employees are likely to read. At first it is advisable to place test ads in all major papers in order to determine which draw the most responses.

In some areas, advertisements in foreign language and ethnic-group papers work well. Such advertisements also tend to improve relations with the ethnic community. Usually, advertisements of this sort are relatively inexpensive. Radio advertising is also occasionally useful, though some executives caution that such advertisements can be a costly waste if the right station is not chosen.

Employment Agencies.   Federal, state and private employment agencies are often used as recruitment sources, particularly of line employees. State employment agencies vary in quality. It is important to evaluate the usefulness of each agency. Most federal and state employment agencies usually have some prospective employees available for interviews because unemployed workers must report to the agency to be eligible for unemployment benefits.

Reputable private agencies are used by many supermarket companies in their search for qualified personnel. Some of these agencies do an excellent job of providing counseling and placement services. Whereas a sizable proportion of persons listed in federal and state agencies are currently unemployed, persons listed with private agencies are more likely to be employed, looking for higher pay or for a more suitable job.

Specialized placement agencies can also be used as a source of personnel. For example, the Veterans Administration lists handicapped workers and will provide information relating to the nature and extent of a prospective employee's disability, as well as to his or her ability to handle the job in question. Local schools and universities also have records of handicapped students who might be available on a part-time basis. Most states maintain an industrial commission which keeps records on employees who have been handicapped as a result of industrial accidents. Handicapped non-veterans and non-students may also be located through private welfare agencies or through state agencies which list persons who suffer from a variety of disabilities.

The supermarket companies that employ handicapped people have learned from experience that absenteeism, turnover and accident rates for such employees are far lower than for others. One supermarket chain in Alabama uses handicapped workers in its central produce packaging operation. Some of these people are mentally retarded, others are physically handicapped, but the company's experience with them has been excellent. Indeed, handicapped workers have proven themselves in many industries. Generally, their productivity will match or exceed that of the average worker. Moreover, people who are certified to be mentally or physically handicapped for a particular job can be employed at a lower rate than other employees.

Competition.   Several supermarket companies regularly pirate personnel from their competition. Though at first glance this may be considered a viable solution for some personnel problems, in the long run such a practice damages company morale. It emphasizes promotions from outside the company rather than from within, and of course, damages relations with competitors. Pirating also brings into an organization personnel who are trained in different techniques by competitors; retraining is sometimes more costly and time-consuming than training a beginner.

Unions.   For those companies that are organized, unions are occasionally good sources for full-time employees. An alert union is often aware of and on good terms with labor sources unknown to management. Many run placement services for unemployed members. However, this is a delicate area which must be considered by each company in accordance with its own labor relations situation.

Unsolicited Applicants.   Unsolicited applicants for full-time employment are not unusual, even in a tight labor market. Although such walk-in applicants are not generally the best source for full-time employees, they often provide a good source for part-timers. Whether or not they are offered employment, such persons should always be accorded the kind of reception that would leave them with a favorable impression of the company. Applicants of this sort may be expected to transmit their opinions to others and, what is more, they may be customers or potential customers.

Perhaps the most common unsolicited applications for part-time work come from local high school students. Store managers should maintain a file of such applicants to which they can refer in order to satisfy future needs. The personnel department should also maintain an up-to-date file of persons who apply for regular or part-time employment.

Follow-Up

No supermarket chain would ever advertise exclusively in only one of several local papers or spend its entire advertising budget on radio spots unless it had some excellent reasons, as well as a statistical basis, for following such a course. Similarly, it is necessary to determine which recruitment sources and techniques bring the most responses, and even more important, the best personnel. The sources that don't provide the best qualified employees should be eliminated.

If, for example, an agency repeatedly sends prospective employees for interviews and none is suitable, further dealings with that agency are a waste of time. Similarly, it is unwise to continue soliciting part-timers from two local high schools if only one has shown itself to be cooperative and a useful source of good employees.

One of the yardsticks that should be employed to measure the effectiveness of recruitment techniques is the turnover ratio. Each major source of both full-time and part-time employees should be periodically evaluated in order to determine which provides steadier personnel. For example, if the Veterans Administration proves to be one of the best sources for low-turnover, good caliber handicapped workers, it might be a good idea to contact other sources of handicapped employees as well.

Source evaluations should also take the particular job into account. The best source for one position is not necessarily best for another. Window signs, for example, can often attract enough people to fill part-time cashier jobs. But such signs would seldom attract meat department managers.

Once policies, procedures, sources and techniques have been determined, a well-defined selection system must be instituted. Otherwise all the energies expended upon recruitment will afford no profitable results in terms of competent employees.

4 | Selecting Employees

A carryout clerk had just resigned to enter college and John, the store manager, needed a quick replacement. He advertised by placing a sign in his store window, to which a young man named Charlie responded.

John led Charlie to the backroom where the interview was to be conducted. When they reached the backroom, John asked Charlie a few questions and, before he half realized it, found himself saying, "Okay Charlie. Come in tomorrow right after school and we'll try you out."

John always told everyone he hired that he would "try him out," though he hadn't actually "tried anyone out" in quite some time. He made do with even the most incompetent employees because he was afraid that their replacements would only be worse. He rarely fired anyone.

When Charlie left, John walked up to the front of the store. As he passed the produce department, he automatically reached out and removed an overripe orange.

After a few steps, John stopped short. He thought about how he had almost instinctively reacted to the overripe orange. He knew the fruit was bad and he had removed it. "Why was it so easy to pick out an orange that wouldn't sell and so difficult to spot an applicant who wouldn't work out?" he wondered.

Then John remembered that the produce operation hadn't always run so smoothly. He recalled the running battle he had had with Joe, the produce manager, about the "garbage rack" which Joe had insisted upon setting up every day.

The problem of the produce display was quickly solved because it was easily recognized. Joe needed some guidelines and together, John and Joe set up standards for oranges. They graded oranges from one to five, depending on their size, color and firmness. They even established different standards for different types of oranges. Oranges with a low, one rating were removed from the display and oranges with a five rating were sold at a premium.

When John removed the overripe orange, he had responded to an established set of standards. There was almost no guesswork involved. He admitted to himself that he knew more about selecting oranges than he did about selecting people. How much easier his job would have been had he devised standards for people as he had for oranges. If John could develop a list of characteristics that successful carryout clerks had in common, he would be able to predict, with a reasonable degree of accuracy, which applicants would perform the job more efficiently.

Specific Qualifications

John proceeded to set up a list of specific qualifications for carryout clerks, based on his own observations and past experience. He detailed the characteristics he had observed in high-quality carryout clerks during his five years as manager. He broke the job down into its basic parts, including such functions as greeting customers, bagging, carrying-out, stocking groceries and sweeping. He jotted down the traits and abilities that were required to perform each specific function efficiently.

John's list of specific qualifications for carryout clerks appears in Table 1. Special situations could be added to the bottom of the list. For example, if John's carryout clerks also filled-in as cashiers during peak periods, John should add cashier qualifications to his list. In such a case, the applicant would have to have some skill in arithmetic as well. Or, if the clerk were required to lend a hand in the produce department, John should include additional requirements relating to that function.

TABLE 1
Job Qualifications for Carryout Clerks

Duties	Qualifications
Bagging	*Intelligence* Bright enough to learn this and other routine tasks; enough education and average intelligence. *Strength* Strong enough to do moderately heavy physical work for several hours without interruption. *Coordination* Coordination required to bag carefully and at a reasonably fast pace with both hands simultaneously.
Carrying-Out	Except for coordination, same as for bagging.
Customer Contact	*Personality* Outgoing, friendly, but not too "gabby." *Courtesy* Good manners. *Appearance* Neatly dressed and groomed.
Sweeping and Cleaning	*Health* No dust allergy.
Stocking	Same as for bagging.

John did not want to base his decision on what the applicant would say during the interview but, rather, on what he was likely to do on the job. He also wished to indicate how much the applicant must bring to the job and how much he could learn on the job. Of course, everyone wants experienced clerks, but how much should John be prepared to pay to get them? How much of a trade-off should he make? How much recruiting time, energy and cost should he invest? How long should he tolerate "floaters" or incompetent workers, even those who have had years of experience? Because John was willing and able to train a new employee, and because this job required little training time compared to most, he omitted experience as a requirement for carryout clerks.

General Qualifications

Over and above the specific job requirements that John had listed, the general characteristics common to above-average employees must also be outlined. Experience has shown that there are certain qualities that all good employees have in common and that these are at least as important as an individual's ability to handle the specific job duties.

Availability for work: An employee should have a reasonably good mode of transportation to and from the store. Competing activities, such as another job, school, athletics, clubs and other such extracurricular activities may limit the applicant's availability. People with small children may have excessive absences unless arrangements have been made to care for them during working hours.

Willingness to work: The ability to do a good job is quite different from the willingness to do it. Many youngsters have never been involved, day after day, in a disciplined working situation. They themselves do not know how well they will react to such control. Will they come to work every day? Will they be on time? Will they volunteer for other assignments whenever they are idle?

Pride in work: Employee attitudes frequently determine whether or not a store will enjoy ordinary or extraordinary profits. The best employees want to perform each task properly; they are the opposite of the "just-putting-in-my-eight-hours" group.

Ability to get along with co-workers: Every year many employees are fired because of their failure to get along with fellow workers.

Good health: The most able and willing employees cannot perform their jobs competently if they are continually sick. Even if they do come to work, they cannot perform efficiently if they are not physically up to par.

Honesty: The temptation and opportunity to steal are considerably increased in a store full of merchandise. Indeed, internal thefts are more common in retail industries than in most other industries and, in a supermarket, employee thefts can be a major drain on the store's annual net profit. Therefore, honesty is one of the most important traits which an employee can possess. Employee honesty does not only mean remaining within the bounds of the law; it also refers to good moral character. For example, can the employee's word be trusted? Will he or she lie or cheat to get ahead on the job?

Of course, one cannot reasonably expect to hire only those people who rate extremely high in each of these categories. But the person who fails to meet the minimum requirements for each specific and each general job qualification should not be considered. And, needless to say, the person who approaches these ideals will make a better employee and will improve the quality of the store.

Setting up specific and general requirements for hiring employees is one of the best ways to build a top-quality, productive staff. Requirements can be outlined for each function, for low- or high-level jobs in grocery, dairy, produce, meat, deli, bakery or any other department. Different jobs call for different abilities. The job requirements for a cashier and a meat wrapper, for example, are not the same. Yet, in one company, the same specifications were used to hire people for both jobs. The requirements were determined by the employee's sex rather than by the job function.

Basic Selection Tools

Though everyone talks about trying to choose the best qualified person, many store and district managers tend to deceive themselves. Too many of the worst selections are made because store or district managers are pressured by customers to hire certain people or because managers assume that anyone can perform those jobs for which no previous technical training is required.

It is important to use a series of selection devices which provide the information that will permit the store manager or personnel department to choose the best possible employee. The six best selection tools recommended for store use are:

1. Employment application
2. Interview
3. Written examination
4. Reference check
5. Medical examination
6. Probationary process

After the specific and general requirements for a particular job have been determined, the selection tools should be used to check whether or not the applicant fulfills each of those requirements. Table 2, which can be modified to fit particular job requirements, shows how five of the six tools are used to evaluate the specific and general qualifications of carryout clerk applicants. The sixth selection device, the probationary process, may be used only after the selection has been made, and it has therefore been omitted from the chart.

TABLE 2

Selection Devices to Be Used to Evaluate the Specific and General Qualities of Carryout Clerks

Qualities	Employment Application	Interview	Written Examination	Reference Check	Medical Examination
Specific					
Intelligence	✓	✓ *	✓ *	✓ *	
Education	✓ *	✓ *		✓	
Strength		✓		✓	✓ *
Outgoing, Friendly Personality		✓ *		✓ *	
Courtesy, Good Manners		✓ *		✓ *	
Personal Appearance and Grooming		✓ *		✓	✓
No Dust Allergy	✓ *	✓			✓ *
Experience	✓ *	✓ *		✓	
General					
Availability for Work	✓	✓ *			
Willingness to Work		✓ *		✓ *	
Pride in Work		✓ *		✓ *	
Getting Along with Fellow Workers		✓ *		✓ *	
Good Health	✓ *	✓		✓ *	✓ *
Age (need for working permit)	✓ *	✓			
Honesty		✓		✓ *	
Moral Character		✓ *		✓ *	

*The selection device that *best* evaluates the particular quality.

Employment Applications

There are two basic types of employment applications: the short form and the long form. Both provide such identifying information as name, address and Social Security number, and, to varying degrees, give information that can be used to help predict success or

FIGURE 1
Employment Application/Short Form

PRELIMINARY APPLICATION FOR EMPLOYMENT

Date_____

Name_____

Address_____ Phone_____

Kind of   Have you ever worked   ☐ Yes
Work Desired_____   for (company name) before?   ☐ No

                                                 Last Grade of
                                                 School Completed_____

Names of Relatives Employed by Company_____

Present   How long have you worked for your
Employer_____   present employer? ___ Yrs. ___ Mos.

Address_____

Last Previous   How long did you work for this
Employer_____   employer? _____ Yrs. _____ Mos.

Address_____

failure on the job, including details about the applicant's education, work experience, or previous job stability.

The Short Form.   The short application form is generally printed on a 3″ x 5″ or 5″ x 8″ card, similar to the one shown in Figure 1.

This short application is initially used to screen applicants. Later, it serves as a written record to document compliance to such federal and state requirements as anti-discrimination laws, by noting that rejected applicants were turned down for legitimate reasons like inexperience, insufficient education and others. Also, if an opening should later develop for which the applicant is qualified, or if job requirements have been lowered, the short application form serves as a handy reference through which the applicant can be re-evaluated and recontacted.

The short application briefly covers only the most vital information that would enable the interviewer to predict job success or failure. This type of application, coupled with a several minute interview, should indicate to both the interviewer and applicant whether or not each is interested in further dealings with the other. Only when this stage has been successfully completed should the longer, more detailed form be filled out. If either party is no longer interested, a lot of time has been saved. What is more, it is better public relations to have obviously unqualified people fill out a small card than to tell them there is nothing for them. All applicants are customers or potential customers.

The Long Form.   The long application form is generally printed on both sides of an 8½″ x 11″ sheet of paper. It requires much more detail on education and work experience and asks questions in many other areas, some quite personal. Figure 2 is an example of a detailed long application form used by one chain. It is legal in the state in which this company operates; however, other states may have different requirements.

Applicants often do an incomplete or sloppy job of filling out the long form. Sometimes, answers are accidentally omitted. After all, many good store clerks do not like to do paper work. Moreover, some questions are occasionally deliberately neglected because applicants think they are more likely to be hired if they do not answer or if they only partially answer certain questions. It is, however, very important that the application be properly completed before the interview begins. During the interview, particular attention should be paid to the information given when the applicant is requested to answer those questions that previously had been completely or partially ignored. The answers to such questions may provide the key to evaluating the applicant's ability to perform the job.

Work Experience: Figure 3 shows how one applicant completed the Work Experience section of the long form. What does this completed section reveal about the applicant and, equally important, what crucial information necessary to making a clear and proper decision does it fail to reveal?

Upon reviewing this section of the application, the interviewer should ask himself such questions as the following: Can this applicant's employment activities be consistently traced from 1984? When did he enter and leave the Army? Did any time elapse before and after Army service? If so, why? Where did he work between the Acme Metal Manufacturing Co. job and the Red Wing job? Or did he really work at those jobs? And what happened between his Red Wing job and his National Trailer job? Why are some dates vague (like the termination date at National Trailer), while others are specific (like the Red Wing termination date)? Though January 30 at first appears to be a natural termination date, a calendar check shows that it is neither the end of that month nor the end of that workweek.

FIGURE 2
Employment Application/Long Form

	DATE
Application for Employment	STORE

THANK YOU FOR YOUR INTEREST IN OUR COMPANY – PLEASE COMPLETE ALL ITEMS NEATLY

NAME		SOCIAL SECURITY NUMBER	TELEPHONE NUMBER

ADDRESS: Street		City	State	Zip Code

| HOW LONG AT ABOVE ADDRESS? | No. YEARS | DO YOU HAVE ANY IMPAIRMENTS, PHYSICAL, MENTAL OR MEDICAL, WHICH WOULD PREVENT YOU FROM PERFORMING IN A REASONABLE MANNER THE ACTIVITIES INVOLVED IN THE JOB OR OCCUPATION FOR WHICH YOU HAVE APPLIED? IF SO EXPLAIN: | ☐NO ☐YES |

HAVE YOU EVER BEEN CONVICTED OF A CRIME? YES / NO

| DO YOU OWN A CAR? | NO / YES | IF NO, HOW WILL YOU GET TO WORK? | ARE YOU PRESENTLY EMPLOYED? | YES / NO | WILL YOU GIVE A NOTICE? | YES / NO |

WHAT DATE CAN YOU START, IF YOUR APPLICATION IS FAVORABLY CONSIDERED?

POSITION APPLYING FOR		FULL TIME	TOTAL HOURS PER WEEK
		PART TIME	

Please indicate below the hours you are available for work (be specific for each day):

DAY	SUNDAY	MONDAY	TUESDAY	WEDNESDAY	THURSDAY	FRIDAY	SATURDAY
FROM							
TO							

Please indicate any previous experience below:

	RETAIL EXPERIENCE		OFFICE EXPERIENCE			ADDITIONAL EXPERIENCE
1	CASHIER	13	CLERK TYPIST WPM	24	REAL ESTATE
2	BAGGER	14	CLERK GENERAL	25	SALES/BUYER
3	GROCERY STOCK	15	BOOKKEEPER	26	TRUCK DRIVER
4	PRODUCE	16	STENOGRAPHER	27	FORK LIFT
5	DELICATESSEN	17	SWITCHBOARD	28	WAREHOUSE
6	MEAT CUTTER	18	CALCULATOR	29	MAINTENANCE MECHANICAL
7	MEAT WRAPPER	19	ACCOUNTANT	30	MAINTENANCE GENERAL
8	BAKERY	20	DATA PROCESSING	31	ELECTRICIAN
9	NON-FOODS	21	KEYPUNCH	32	PLUMBER PIPEFITTER
10	DRUG STORE	22	DICTAPHONE	33	DRAFTING
11	SPECIALTY SHOP	23	OTHER	34	PRINTING
12	MANAGEMENT EXPERIENCE			35	OTHER

Are there any other experiences, skills, or qualifications which you feel would especially fit you for work with our company?

WERE YOU PREVIOUSLY EMPLOYED BY US?	YES / NO	WHEN?	WHERE?

DO YOU HAVE ANY FRIENDS OR RELATIVES, EXCLUDING SPOUSE, EMPLOYED WITH US?		YES	NO
NAME	RELATIONSHIP	STORE OR LOCATION	
NAME	RELATIONSHIP	STORE OR LOCATION	

COMMENTS BY APPLICANT

FIGURE 2 (CONT.)

EDUCATION			
ELEMENTARY SCHOOL		CITY	STATE
HIGH SCHOOL		CITY	STATE
SUBJECTS		SPORTS, ACTIVITIES, ETC.	
CIRCLE LAST YEAR COMPLETED 1 2 3 4		DID YOU GRADUATE YES NO	
COLLEGE		CITY	STATE
MAJOR/MINOR		GRADE AVERAGE	
CIRCLE LAST YEAR COMPLETED 1 2 3 4		DID YOU GRADUATE? YES / NO	DEGREE
OTHER SCHOOLING		CITY	STATE
SUBJECTS/MAJOR		DID YOU GRADUATE? YES / NO	DEGREE

U.S. MILITARY SERVICE YES / NO	BRANCH	RANK	DATE FROM	DATE TO	TYPE OF DISCHARGE

WORK EXPERIENCE / PLEASE LIST PREVIOUS EMPLOYMENT	LAST EMPLOYER	NEXT TO LAST EMPLOYER	SECOND FROM LAST EMPLOYER	THIRD FROM LAST EMPLOYER
COMPANY NAME				
ADDRESS				
CITY AND STATE				
KIND OF WORK				
DATE STARTED MO. & YR.				
DATE LEFT MO. & YR.				
SALARY-START				
SALARY-LAST				
NAME OF SUPERVISOR				
REASONS FOR LEAVING				

PLEASE READ CAREFULLY: I authorize investigation of all statements contained in this application. I understand that misrepresentation or omission of facts called for is cause for dismissal. I understand that any employment by this company will be on a 30 day probationary basis.

APPLICANT'S SIGNATURE	DATE SIGNED	LOCATION SUBMITTED TO

INTERVIEWER COMMENTS AND SIGNATURE

FIGURE 3
Long Form/Work Experience Section

PLEASE LIST PREVIOUS EMPLOYMENT	LAST EMPLOYER	NEXT TO LAST EMPLOYER	SECOND FROM LAST EMPLOYER	THIRD FROM LAST EMPLOYER
COMPANY NAME	National Trailer Co.	Red Wing Grocery Co.	Acme Metal Co.	Army
ADDRESS				
CITY AND STATE	Cicero, Illinois	Chicago, Illinois	Chicago	
KIND OF WORK	Helper	Head Stock Clerk		Infantry
DATE STARTED MO. & YR.	4/10/90	3/24/87	10/84	2 years
DATE LEFT MO. & YR.	1990	1/30/90	2/85	
SALARY-START				
SALARY-LAST	$830	$7.60		
NAME OF SUPERVISOR	Bad Deal			
REASONS FOR LEAVING	no opportunity for advancement	not enough money		discharge

WORK EXPERIENCE

What sort of progression is indicated by his series of jobs? What significance does it have for supermarket work? Why didn't he list his salary rate for each job? Once these rates have been ascertained, do they follow a trend? Is that trend consistent with the reasons he lists for leaving previous employment?

Are this applicant's reasons for leaving his previous jobs acceptable? Are they true? How do they stack up with telephone reference checks to his former employers? Why doesn't he list his supervisors? Is that a deliberate omission?

In a tight labor market, when so many marginal applicants lack any retail food industry background, this claim of three years' head stock clerk experience looks inviting. But is it fact or fiction?

What kind of a discharge did this candidate receive from the Army? Again, during tight labor markets in big cities, a number of ex-servicemen applying for food store employment have discharges that are either "Without Honor" or "Dishonorable." Should those men be trusted who claim "Honorable" discharges?

Some of these questions may be answered by insisting upon more thorough application information; others by the job interview and reference checks. But it would be foolish for a manager to hire an applicant solely on the basis of the information contained in this application.

Interviews

Two basic types of interviews are used to select store employees. Like the employment application, one is short (several minutes), and the other is long (twenty to thirty minutes). Both types of interviews serve two fundamental purposes: They enable the interviewer and the prospective employee to size each other up as persons ("I like him," "I feel comfortable with him," and so forth); and they permit the company to learn certain things about a candidate that can best be discovered through an interview rather than through other selection devices. The long interview also gives the applicant some insight into the job and the company and enables the company to make a sales pitch, which is especially important in a tight labor market.

The interviewer should note how the applicant reacts in a person-to-person situation: how he talks, how alert he is, and significantly, how he sees himself—the kind of person he believes himself to be.

Short Interview. Despite its limited duration, the short interview serves a hard business purpose. It attempts to match the most easily recognizable, yet most important hire-or-don't-hire characteristics of the applicant with the most obvious requirements of the job or of future jobs. Good short interviews are never random, casual discussions.

If, at the end of the short interview, both sides are still interested in considering each other, the applicant should fill out the long application form. He or she should then be interviewed at some length later that day or some other day. But it is never wise to hire solely on the basis of the short application and short interview, no matter how sure one is.

If both sides show no interest in pursuing the matter further, the applicant should be graciously thanked for taking time out to come to the interview. Such courtesy is always good public relations. Then the application card should be filed. An applicant should by no means be encouraged with false hopes if there is no intention of considering him or her further.

Long Interview.   The long interview is the high point of the selection process. In fact, the store's long-range profits may be directly affected by the manager's skill in using the long interview to identify and to win over the capable employee.

During the long interview the applicant must reveal a great deal of comparatively personal information. He or she must feel free to talk without restraint. Therefore, the long interview should be conducted in private. It is desirable, but not necessary, for both people to sit. Generally, this can be accomplished by putting two chairs in a private corner of the backroom. The front office is not an acceptable location unless privacy can be guaranteed.

Indeed, every store should have a private interview place available, even if it means rearranging a few boxes in the backroom to build a temporary partition. Stock clerks should be temporarily reassigned to some other tasks in order to get them out of earshot of the interview. The interviewer should tell whoever answers the phone that, barring an emergency, he or she is not to be called or contacted for anything during the interview. All too often, interviewers have been interrupted just as they were on the verge of really getting an applicant to open up. A change in mood is liable to deprive the interviewer of the chance to learn what needs to be known.

Good and Bad Practices.   Neither short nor long interviews should be conducted until the applicant's corresponding short or long application form has been received. It should be completely filled out; the interviewer should have read it, made notes of discrepancies and red-flagged any areas in the applicant's background that should be pursued.

The purpose of an interview is to obtain real insight into the applicant's everyday behavior. The candidate should do almost all of the talking.

Successful interviews are conducted in a friendly, sincere and unhurried atmosphere. The manager welcomes the candidate, makes him feel at ease and gives him his complete attention. Effective interviewers work hard at establishing confidence and cooperation, at understanding the applicant's point of view. They use a vocabulary and a rate of speech that the other person can understand. They realize that most applicants are nervous, so they open the interview by commenting favorably on some point mentioned in the application.

Being a Listener: Every interviewer must be a good listener. Listening carefully is second in importance to knowing what information must be elicited in an interview. Many people hear only what they want to hear and tune out anything else. Other people don't really listen because they are either thinking about what they should say next or have already decided what they are going to say and are just waiting for an opportunity to speak. Good listening means that all energies are focused on hearing and interpreting what the candidate's words really mean.

Good interviewers deliberately test themselves to see how long they can hold off reaching a decision on whether or not to hire the candidate. A number of studies have conclusively shown that poor interviewers reach decisions far too quickly, in the first four or five minutes, and then spend the next half hour trying to justify their hasty conclusions. Good interviewers, on the other hand, silently remind themselves during the interview to wait, to hold back, to refuse to make a decision until they really have gathered enough information.

Responding on Cue: A good interviewer leads the candidate by gently directing the person to do most of the talking on the right subject, at the right pace. Simultaneously, the interviewer continually looks for, and sensibly responds to signs and cues from the candidate. The interviewer's frown or smile, stiffness or friendliness, impatience or patience are all very important. A critical, unfriendly, "And why did you do that?" by an impatient manager will usually freeze a candidate right in the middle of an interview.

Framing Questions Properly: A well-trained service station attendant smiles and says: "Shall I fill it up, sir?" rather than "How many gallons?" The question is skillfully worded to get a "yes" answer. A good interviewer, on the other hand, does not ask questions that can be answered with a simple "yes" or "no." But some managers almost plead for a "yes" when they lead the applicant with: "Don't you think you'll like this work?"; or "You'll be able to get to work on time, won't you?"; or "You finished high school, didn't you?"; or "Your health is okay, isn't it?"; or "Did your last boss treat you okay, Jack?"

Such leading questions should not be asked during an interview. Rather, questions like "Describe your boss to me," or "Why do you want to work here?" should be posed. Key words like "describe," "why," "tell me about," will usually draw out the required information.

Even when the interviewer talks, he or she does not need to say much. After starting an interview, highly skilled interviewers can often sit for five or six minutes without saying any more than "Yes," "Uh-huh," "Mmmm," "And then?" or "I understand." Another good response is "Tell me more about your thinking on that." Many times a smile of understanding, a nod with a light in the eyes or a thoughtful silence, not only permits, but clearly encourages applicants to let down their guard, to forget their Sunday School behavior and show what they are really like.

The good interviewer searches for true feelings more than for hard facts, though both feelings and facts are, of course, necessary. For example, when the applicant says, "My grandmother brought me up," the skillful interviewer keeps things in low key by replying, "Your grandmother?" without too much pressure or question in his tone. The untrained interviewer, on the other hand, puts the candidate on the defensive when he replies with such a tough, obvious question as "What happened to your parents?"

Silence is another favorite device of the adept interviewer. Silence is more uncomfortable for the applicant than it is for the interviewer. After the interview has been underway a few minutes, if the interviewer restrains his questions, a candidate will often blurt out information that is on the tip of his tongue, thus completely abandoning the mask he wanted to hide behind.

Tolerance: Good interviewing is a delicate art, not so much because special techniques are used but because a special point of view must be taken. That point of view is one of open, evident tolerance. Only through tolerance will an interviewer succeed at getting an applicant to vividly describe, for instance, "how lousy his or her last boss was." But if the interviewer displays a lack of tolerance the applicant might just as quickly say: "Oh, my last boss was okay." His guard is up; he wants the job. The interviewer stands between him and the job, and he'll play the game according to the rules in order to get it.

Poorly-skilled interviewers often concentrate so hard on studying the other person that they tend to permit one outstanding trait (either a positive or negative characteristic) to influence their judgment about a candidate's other traits. Interviewers should always make sure they have touched on everything they need to know to reach a good decision. As they discuss each aspect of the candidate's background and the job, they should ask themselves such questions as "Am I judging this person fairly in this area?" or "Am I starting each question from scratch so that my judgment of the applicant in one area does not influence my judgment in another?"

Past and Present.   A person's work history usually represents a major portion of an adult's life, and not only indicates the ability to do certain jobs, but also provides many clues about social behavior, emotional stability and leadership capacity. The manner in which a person has worked is often the best single source of information about the individual's personal strengths and weaknesses. The best indicator of what an adult will do in the future is what he has done in the past.

If an applicant has not had extensive working experience, the interviewer should ask the person to briefly describe his last job, then his first job and any succeeding jobs. This approach provides an overall view of such a candidate's work background and indicates the gaps which must be filled with more information. When the applicant has worked extensively in more than one company, he should be allowed to tell his story from the beginning. This approach provides continuity and, thereby, reflects the candidate's development or lack of development on the job.

Skilled interviewers always encourage an applicant to give a full account of his previous work experience, even when that experience has been quite different from the kind of work he is now seeking. A person's attitude toward work in general, as well as his feelings about a specific type of work, often reveal a great deal of meaningful information to the interviewer.

Ending the Interview.   An interview that runs smoothly will answer the questions of both interviewer and candidate. Toward the end of the interview, the interviewer should always ask the candidate whether he or she has any questions which have not yet been answered. At this time, the interviewer should also obtain the full names and telephone numbers of persons who can provide references. The interviewer should also receive the applicant's permission to check references with each previous employer.

The applicant should not be hired immediately, no matter how well the interview has proceeded. Other selection devices must be used and their findings considered in order to make the best possible decision.

Written Tests

The use of psychological tests or basic skills qualification tests has almost disappeared in the supermarket industry. In 1968, more than half of the chains participating in the turnover study used psychological tests to screen full- or part-time or manager applicants for store level positions. In the 1983 turnover study, only four of the 25 chains reported using such tests, and three of the four restricted their use to manager applicants. In the 1990 turnover study, not a single chain reported use of such tests to reduce their turnover problems.

Basic skills qualification tests were used by three-fourths of the chains participating in the 1968 turnover study. In contrast, among the 25 chains participating in the 1983 study, one stated it uses a "basic checkstand skills" test for part-time applicants; two chains said they use a "basic math" test for full- and part-time cashier applicants; and a fourth chain was, surprisingly, the only one of the participating companies that reported using the Food Marketing Institute (FMI) test for cashier applicants.

A major reason for the decline in testing in recent years is that federal, state and some city governments have forced American businesses to be more careful than heretofore in using tests to screen employees. Federal law now permits employers to test applicants only with a "professionally developed" aptitude test. It is very likely that the federal government will continue to put pressure on companies to develop or use testing programs that are fully professional in design, administration, interpretation and use. It is, therefore, essential that any store manager who administers tests be familiar with and understand any applicable federal, state or local regulations relating to testing.

Some aptitude tests and most psychological tests present another danger: the tendency to place too much importance on the test results in relation to other selection tools. Every manager has been conditioned since childhood to believe that a score of 85 on a test is superior to a score of 80. An untrained manager will find it difficult to rid himself of the notion that numbers are absolute. But the fact is that such tests are simply not that precise and a difference of five points, by itself, is usually of little significance. Indeed, many trained personnel people fall into the same trap.

A skillfully conducted interview will provide more valuable and more accurate information about an applicant than any other single selection tool. Professionally trained personnel people use tests as supplementary tools in making employment decisions, often giving them no more than a 10 percent weight in the final decision.

Why Test? Success or failure on the job may depend upon how quickly a person can learn to do new work and solve new problems. For those people who read and write at the high school level or above, written tests can measure their general intelligence.

Written tests can also identify, with great accuracy and speed, those people who are able to solve problems in arithmetic. Such tests would not help select a stock clerk, but if the person will be used as a relief cashier or will ever be considered for promotion to a checkout manager's job, a passing score on a test in arithmetic would show that the individual at least meets that requirement. Written tests, then, can be used to measure certain abilities needed by store employees to perform entrance jobs and/or jobs to which they might be promoted.

Administering Tests. Unfortunately, written tests are not easy to administer in a store. They must be administered under standardized conditions (sitting down, no interruptions, exact instructions, precise timing for some tests and control), and interpreted for specific selection needs. Even if a group of stores could enjoy the services of a professional testing specialist it would still be hard pressed to find a suitable place in the store itself to administer the test properly.

Written tests differ in how complex they are to administer and, in particular, in how much professional training is required to interpret the results. Before they agree to sell their tests, publishers generally require that a company have people with a certain level of training in administering and interpreting tests. However, intense specialized professional training is not necessary in order to administer and interpret most tests used in the store-level selection and promotion of employees.

Performance Tests

Every experienced store manager very quickly discovers that candidates' descriptions of their work skills do not always match their actual performance. Accordingly, some companies have developed standardized performance tests for experienced applicants for certain skilled jobs. Each journeyman meat cutter candidate, for example, is given several different beef primals and told to break them down into retail cuts. Or, each person claiming produce experience is given a crate of lettuce to trim. Standardized performance tests for fork lift truck operators have also been used for years to help select warehouse employees.

Of course, instructions for performance tests should be standardized, preferably written in advance and read or shown to each candidate. This procedure guarantees that everybody receives the same test assignment and prevents misunderstanding about such matters as the comparative importance of speed and quality. Scoring is also standardized on a specially designed check sheet. Each person's performance is judged for quality, speed, skill and safety.

Performance tests are valuable not only for initial selection, but also for job placement and training forecasts. For example, the way an individual scores on a standardized performance test can provide a realistic guide to his actual work skill and can eliminate conflicts over starting wage rates. It quickly becomes apparent whether the applicant is a novice, a semi-professional or a professional, and how much training he will require to meet company standards.

A company that does not have a qualified personnel selection specialist to develop and administer a performance testing program should solicit advice from outside competent professional help, from a qualified consultant or from The American Psychological Association, Washington, D. C.

Reference Checking

An applicant's future performance is more predictable when accurate, complete and pertinent information about his or her past performance is obtained from reliable sources. A great many applicants look better on paper and in interviews than they do on the job. A check with previous employers will provide insight into how a candidate will perform in a new job.

Reference Sources.   Each person establishes a personal record in many areas of life, including friends, church, school, athletics and work. But when an individual is being considered for a job, a work experience record will provide the best information on how the person is likely to perform in another job. If the applicant has never worked, school, scouting or other records will provide useful insights. Ideally, however, a combination of both work and school records should be consulted, especially if the applicant has not been out of school for more than approximately two years.

First-hand, personally disinterested sources of information will provide genuine insight into the applicant instead of mere verification of basic information. Such sources include, above all, the applicant's present, or former immediate supervisor, as well as close work associates. They also include such persons as a school counselor, homeroom teacher, coach and scoutmaster.

Record-keeping information sources, on the other hand, are primarily useful for verification. For example, the personnel department or the principal's office will usually be able to confirm information given on the application or during the interview. However, unless the applicant is personally well-known to them, they will be unable to provide an in-depth evaluation. Therefore, such sources should never be used to the exclusion of first-hand references.

Requesting and checking an applicant's personal references is a waste of time. Such people are invariably close friends or relatives. No applicant knowingly will give a personal reference who will have something negative to say. Only disinterested third parties, such as former employers, school counselors, etc., who can be trusted, should be contacted for reference checks.

What Information Should Be Obtained?   The reference sources should be encouraged to discuss everything that will enable the interviewer to make a good hiring decision. They should contribute information about the applicant's attendance, dependability, honesty, quality of work, productivity, accident rate, personality, cooperation and relations with others. The candidate's chief strong and weak points, reasons for leaving and whether the former company would rehire the person if it could, should also be ascertained. If problem areas or special weaknesses have been uncovered, more information should be obtained. The applicant's position at the beginning of employment, position and wages at the time of departure and the starting and ending employment dates should be verified too. The reference sources should also be encouraged to comment freely, to draw a complete portrait of the applicant.

Methods of Contacting Sources.   Person-to-person contacts are actually the best way to get the "low-down" about a candidate, but such communication is seldom practical. Mail reference checking, on the other hand, is not only slow, but also extremely unreliable. Very few people will fully and frankly put down on paper uncomplimentary facts about a former employee. Moreover, most people are busy and unwilling to take the time to write an evaluative letter. Therefore, the best that can be expected is for the former employer to tick off yes or no answers to information requested on a check list. Mail reference checks should probably be limited to situations where verification in writing is required by the company.

The best and most practical method of checking references is by telephone. Most people, if interviewed skillfully over the phone, will provide most, if not all the requisite information. Sometimes a sticky question is asked and the reference source on the telephone hesitates, uses a different voice inflection or clears his throat. Such a sign of concealment or embarrassment might reveal almost as much as a direct response. It is also worthwhile to make a long-distance phone call to check the references of an applicant from out of town. Saving several dollars by not calling is a foolish way to scrimp.

Ideally, the reference check should be made by a trained member of the personnel department, or by a trained store manager or other supervisor. He or she should always be a person who has had interview training because telephone reference checking is, in many ways, similar to face-to-face interviewing. For low-level store jobs, checkout or department managers can be trained as competent reference-checkers.

Telephone Checking: The interviewer should take notes throughout the reference-checking telephone conversation. At the top of the page, he should enter the applicant's name, the company's name, phone number, and the name and position of the person contacted. When the reference check has been completed, the paper should be dated and signed.

A good telephone reference check depends on getting across to the person who is called and on having all questions openly answered. The discussion should open with an introduction, for example: "This is Louis Rogers, manager of X.Y.Z. Supermarket over on Main Street. I'm calling for a reference check on Joe Evans. Joe states on his employment application that he worked for you as a grocery clerk. Were you his supervisor?"

At this point, some people will try to cut the conversation short with such a curt comment as, "Yeah, he worked for me. He was okay." This type of person seldom responds well to a plea like, "What else can you tell me about Joe?" But many people will open up if they are quickly involved in a question that requires some detail, for example: "Joe told me that the two of you used to put up the best displays in town. Is he really that good a display man, or is he pulling my leg?"

The important thing is to ask a "warm-up" question before the actual reference check. These personalized questions should be planned in advance and tossed in when the reference source appears to be cold or in a hurry. Phone reference checks are becoming increasingly common and, with time, will be more and more difficult to make successfully because more people are taking up the time of supervisors with such calls.

In most smaller communities, reference checking is done by people who are acquainted with each other; this is rarely true in larger communities. If the reference source hesitates, or openly states that he is not really sure he is speaking with the store manager, he should quickly be asked to call back on the business phone. If the person still hesitates, he should be told that the store's telephone number is in the phone book on such and such a page, and that he would be helping a great deal if he called back at the store just as soon as it was convenient. If such responses are given unhesitatingly, all but the most skeptical persons will start talking immediately. It is always a good business policy to answer the store's telephone with the company name, but it is imperative when receiving returning calls on reference checks. If one of the carryout clerks answers the return call with "Hello," the reference source may be lost.

Obviously, precautions should always be taken when an employer is asked for a reference check on a former employee. Neither the manager nor store staff should ever give out any information without making certain that the caller has a legitimate business purpose. If there is any doubt about the authenticity of the caller, the listing should first be checked in the phone book and then the call back should be made.

Synchronizing Standards.   One of the most difficult tasks in evaluating people is to compare the standards of different evaluators and the yardsticks they apply. For example, if someone reports that a boy ran a fast one hundred yards, it is difficult to determine exactly how fast he ran. But if it is known that he ran it in ten seconds flat, there can be no doubt about his rate of speed. A similar situation often occurs when two people compare opinions of a third person. The information that someone is a fast meat cutter or a slow cashier still does not provide a good yardstick for measuring his or her capability. The word fast or slow should be translated into distinct measurable units of quantity and/or relative quality.

In a telephone reference check, one store manager volunteered that a cashier who had resigned had been absent "a lot." But how much is "a lot?" After several minutes of conversation, the manager making the inquiry learned that to the other manager "a lot" meant four days during the last year. In her own mind, however, "a lot" meant more than ten days. This type of confusion could have been avoided by asking, "About how many days was he or she absent last year?"

Watching for Fraud. It is especially important to check the backgrounds of applicants who claim they worked for a company that is now out of business, were self-employed, worked for a close relative or were on an extended vacation. They may be telling the truth, but since reference checks have become widespread, people with bad records occasionally use deceit to counteract the employer's detection skill. Those applicants claiming self-employment, for example, should, when there is room for doubt, be required to present such evidence as business forms, blank checks, invoices, or any other proof of the existence of a business. However, less embarrassing means of checking on such applicants (contacting former employees, clients, landlords or others) should be used when possible. It is also quite proper to phone the home of a former employer who, according to the applicant, has retired.

Other Sources. Two other reference check sources that are often useful are credit companies and police departments. They are both sources of negative information and each produces data that must be considered. The credit check will reveal whether or not the candidate is buried in debt. This information, when combined with other data, may be just enough to indicate that the candidate is a bad risk.

The information received from a police department must be carefully weighed and interpreted. Arrest without conviction is not proof of guilt and a misdemeanor conviction often is not significant unless it has occurred frequently and reflects a personality trait that could affect the employee's performance on the job. An important factor to consider is the length of time that has elapsed since the arrest or conviction.

Unfortunately, police departments usually search only the records within their own political subdivision. Large urban centers with a maze of suburban communities often have numerous police departments, unless they are set up on a county-police department basis. In areas where there's a good working relationship between management and the department, police checking is often a routine matter. Where a good relationship is not established, checking the records is often bogged down by red tape.

Medical Examinations

Sufficient strength, energy and freedom from disease are obviously quite necessary if an employee is to work regularly and do well. Every business needs employees in good physical condition, but it's particularly important in the retail food industry where there is real danger of infecting employees, customers and of contaminating the food itself.

Both full- and part-time employees performing strenuous work should be required to pass a medical examination for a number of reasons. First, almost all store employees perform moderately strenuous physical work all day long. Store work is not like office work where the employees sit most of the day. Store employees must have the physical stamina to perform capably.

Second, most store work requires frequent lifting of moderate to heavy weights. Physicians are best qualified to discover whether employees have, or are prone to, back conditions. Chronically weak backs are especially widespread in the industry. In one case, management in a store with a strong union had been required to keep a produce man in his job classification and at his regular pay rate despite a severe back disability. Because an agreement had been reached whereby this person would not have to lift any filled crates or other heavy objects, additional manpower, at additional cost, was required to set up and take down the produce rack.

Third, state Worker's Compensation laws make it imperative that candidates do not bring disabilities to the job and that they be physically and mentally capable of handling the work. Employers, after all, are faced with the possibility of paying two very costly bills: (1) the cost of the time lost when an employee is off the job, and (2) disability benefits. Today, compensation is not only awarded to employees claiming physical on-the-job injuries; in some cases it is also given to those claiming such disabilities as job-caused emotional disorders. Although compensation laws vary from state to state, companies are directly responsible for all accidents arising out of, and in the course of, a worker's employment. Accident-prone personnel should not be hired. Information about an employee's accident record should be obtained during reference checks.

A final reason for insisting upon medical examinations is the increasing cost of fringe benefit programs, often including payment for hospitalization, sick leave and early retirement. These expenses necessitate the hiring of persons physically capable of doing their assigned tasks.

The Probationary Process

The probationary process is the final step in a selection system and the best of all the selection devices if properly used. The probationary test is designed to determine whether the employee can and will perform adequately on the job. In order for it to work, there are certain requirements that must be fulfilled:

1. The probationer's supervisor must provide a detailed explanation of the job duties, including the "whys" and the "hows."
2. The job duty explanations must cover the probationer's relations with customers and fellow employees, as well as the purely physical aspects of the job.
3. The standards expected of the probationer must be spelled out.
4. The probationer must be adequately motivated.

Today, few store executives have a clear conception of how well a new employee is supposed to perform in order to keep a job. The demands of different managers in the same company often vary substantially. Except for cashiers, very few companies in the food industry realistically and consciously measure their new store employees against any kind of standard. As long as the new employee creates no problems and doesn't really "foul up," he or she remains on the payroll.

Some companies claim that low employee turnover means good hiring decisions, though this is not necessarily true. Indeed, one can hire good people and keep them; on the other hand, one can also hire incompetent people and keep them. If a company rejects almost no probationary employee, it either has a superb hiring process or it is not properly using the probationary period as a selection device. Properly administered, the probationary process guarantees that the new employee's on-the-job performance has satisfied those standards, written or unwritten, against which the supervisor has measured the person.

If the probationer has not measured up by the end of the probationary period, the supervisor must have the courage to follow-through on his findings. At that point, he may (1) work with the probationer to try to bring him up to standard, although this problem should have been recognized and action steps taken before the end of the probationary period; (2) transfer him to a position where he may succeed; or (3) terminate his employment. There is no real answer to the problem, but incompetence should never be tolerated.

The employee who is just below the normal standard—the one who is a little slow to learn and who has almost caught on by the end of the probationary period—is the one who creates a difficult decision-making problem for the supervisor; and the problem is compounded in a tight labor market. Frequently, managers will rationalize in this way: "If I terminate him I may not be able to replace him—at least not right away. If I do replace him, it will have to be with a green recruit, and one who may not be better anyway." The manager may also be aware that he will be short an employee if he fires the person immediately, and he may feel that he cannot afford to be without sufficient help. Nevertheless, if the manager is lax and reluctant to make the proper decision, he may be saddling himself with a poor employee for quite a while. In a unionized company, if an employee is allowed to remain on the payroll one day past the end of his official probationary period—even if only because of an oversight on the part of a manager who had actually intended to fire him—he is fully protected by the grievance system, which normally permits discharge only for a serious, proved cause.

Companies with fixed probationary periods need a pending file with a rating form for each probationary employee. This form should be given to the store manager at least one week before the expiration of each employee's probationary period. Performance evaluation techniques, which are discussed in Chapter 13, should be applied to probationary employees at this time. In any case, it is necessary to appraise the performance of the new employee by the end of the designated probationary period. In non-union companies such a procedure is highly desirable; in companies with unions it is essential and must have the full support of top management.

5 | Inducting New Employees

The indoctrination and orientation of the employee to his new surroundings are referred to as the induction process. During induction, the employee is introduced to the company, the store and to his or her job. The best recruitment and selection programs will not reduce employee turnover if the induction procedure is mishandled.

When a new employee reports to work on his first day, he is apt to feel uncertain and apprehensive. He does not know what to expect. He is not familiar with company or store policies. He is concerned about the kind of boss he will have. Other employees are strangers. He must learn a new job, or if he is experienced, work under a new set of ground rules. The entire atmosphere is unfamiliar and seems threatening. He faces a period of sharp adjustment.

The first few days are particularly crucial in developing the new employee's attitudes. How he is treated by the manager during this initiation period leaves a lasting impression that will affect his attitude not only toward the manager but also toward the company and his fellow employees. His morale, his ability to learn quickly, and his willingness to cooperate will also be affected. The way in which a person is treated on his first day of work often spells the difference between having a promotable, long-term employee, or one who will resign within a few days or weeks.

Voluntary Separations

As was noted earlier, there has been a significant increase in the hiring of part-timers in the past 21 years. The percentage of part-timers increased from 48 percent of total store staff in 1968 to 57 percent in 1983 to 65 percent in 1990, and the trend seems to be continuing. Indeed, four of the companies participating in the 1983 turnover study—all regional or national chains—reported that they were hiring only part-time store employees. The remaining companies estimated that over 90 percent of their new hires were part-timers. From all indications, this practice continues today. Full-time store employees today are typically individuals who were promoted from the part-time ranks. So, when the question of tenure is examined, it is disturbing to learn that more than 24 percent of part-time separations in 1990 occurred during the first thirty days of employment, and the overwhelming majority of these separations— 77.4 percent—were voluntary resignations.

Here are a number of typical examples of what occurs in many supermarkets every working day:

A young, talented and ambitious apprentice meat cutter, rated an excellent prospect, suddenly gives notice after only two weeks on the job. The apprentice is leaving for a similar job at the same rate of pay with a competitor who offers a more promising future.

A store manager walks into the backroom for a last look around before closing. The new cashier, who reported to work only that morning, comes in and announces: "I'm through. I can't stand the job."

A hard working young high school graduate, tabbed by the personnel department as a potential department manager, puts in two weeks as a grocery stock clerk. On Monday of the third week the clerk tells the manager: "I'm not cut out for the supermarket business. I'm leaving at the end of the week."

A deli clerk, after only three weeks on the job, has quickly developed a high degree of skill in dealing with customers. On Tuesday of the fourth week she calls in to say she has taken a job with a nearby discount store.

Similar incidents abound. Hundreds of supermarket employees with less than thirty days' service walk off their jobs every day. Why?

In every case, separation interviews with each of the above employees traced the cause of resignation to poor induction procedures at the stores. Probing elicited such comments as: "Nobody seemed to know I was here"; "The people who work here are unfriendly"; "I felt lost. No one told me what to do"; "Everyone seems to be going in different directions"; or "I don't know how to answer customers' questions."

Cutting Turnover

An effective induction program can drastically reduce the sort of turnover that has its roots in employee dissatisfaction and bewilderment during the early days of employment. One regional chain, for example, decided to do something about its extremely high annual employee turnover rates which, excluding department and store managers, averaged 32 per 100 full-timers and 98 per 100 part-timers. Within one year of training its managers in proper induction methods, this chain had reduced its annual turnover rates to 11 per 100 regulars and 46 per 100 part-timers.

Michael J. O'Connor, while Executive Director of the Super Market Institute, reported on the experiences of another chain that introduced a new orientation program:

> This company had been having extremely high turnover in warehouse employees. By establishing a three-day program of orientation, which included trips to the store to see how merchandise was received and how important the warehouseman's role was in the total scheme of things, the employee turnover in this warehouse dropped by more than 70 percent, and efficiency increased sharply.[1]

Another attempt at implementing and evaluating new programs of employee induction produced equally successful results. After careful studies identified anxiety as a major problem among new employees in a Texas manufacturing plant, a one-day job orientation program was developed. The program was designed to give employees a clear picture of their jobs, exactly what was expected of them, facts about people with whom and for whom they would be working, and what their relationship with them would be. The company also took care to give the new employees confidence in their own ability to succeed. This program produced the following five results: (1) total training time was reduced by half; (2) training costs dropped to one third of their previous levels; (3) absenteeism and tardiness dropped 50 percent; (4) waste and rejects due to faulty workmanship

[1] In an address before the C.I.E.S., New York City, 1967.

were reduced by 80 percent; and (5) costs were cut by as much as from 15 to 30 percent.[2]

Handling the Induction

In order to encourage learning and teamwork, the induction process must give employees a sense of belonging, a feeling that they are one of the group. A cordial welcome serves to relieve their fears and anxieties. The induction must also provide employees with the information they want, need and are entitled to have. The essential information about the company, store and job must be presented in a tactful, friendly manner. Whether employees will develop a favorable attitude and a sense of belonging or, on the other hand, a sour outlook, is largely influenced by the induction process.

There are three basic parts to an effective induction program:

1. Company induction
2. Store induction
3. Job induction

The personnel department or the store manager, depending on who does the hiring, should handle the company induction phase; the store manager should personally handle the store induction phase; and the department manager should handle the final, or the job induction phase. But it is always the store manager's responsibility to make sure that at least the second and third phases, and often the first as well, are properly carried out.

Company Induction. A planned company induction program provides the employees with background information about the firm they are joining and puts their own job into perspective. Company induction information includes details about the firm's history, development, organization, policies and regulations. It also includes general facts about the firm's operation, number and location of stores, warehousing facilities, and manufacturing facilities, if any. Company practices are also spelled out with regard to terms of employment, disciplinary policies and procedures, as well as employee benefit plans and opportunities for advancement. In short, the company induction phase gives new employees some insight

[2] Earl R. Gomersall and M. Scott Myers, "Breakthrough in On-the-Job Training," *Harvard Business Review*, Vol. 44 (July-August, 1966), pp. 62-72.

into the company and informs them of what is expected of them and of what they may expect in turn.

Many firms, including smaller chains, publish or sometimes mimeograph booklets containing all, or most of the induction information. Printing this information guarantees that the facts will be presented as intended and reduces the possibility of misunderstanding. What is more, the new employee will have a chance to study the information at leisure, and not simply listen as it is quickly described and, too often, just as quickly forgotten.

Once the new employee has studied the information contained in the induction pamphlet, he or she should be encouraged to ask questions about it. Indeed, despite other time pressures, the manager should make a practice of reviewing the material periodically with the entire staff, particularly the details on benefit plans, advancement opportunities and the importance of each job to the team effort of the store. Even when the company induction process is handled by company employment personnel, the store manager is still obliged to follow-up. Centralized company induction does not relieve the manager of the responsibility of checking to determine whether or not the employee has received, read and understood the pertinent material.

Store Induction.   The store manager should make the most of his first session with the new employee. He should put the employee at ease by being sincere, friendly and honest. When a manager sympathetically inquires about an employee's interests, ambitions and family, the newcomer senses that someone cares about him as a person, not only as another pair of hands. Such an approach diminishes an employee's fears and anxieties. The initial discussion must be a dialogue, not a series of statements by the manager. Many of the principles of good interviewing (outlined in Chapter 4) should be followed by the store manager as he conducts this phase of the induction.

This informal breaking-in period should be used to highlight the general nature of the new employee's work, the department in which he is to work, his job title, and the contribution he will be making to the total success of the department and store. An employee needs to feel that his job is important and this can be accomplished by explaining to him just how his work ties in with the store effort.

A manager who is courteous during the store induction phase will set a pattern of courtesy which will govern the behavior of the new employee. Courtesy is contagious. A door politely held open for the next person approaching the entrance leads to what may be described as an epidemic of courtesy as each person, in turn, holds the door open for the next. Discourtesy is also contagious. If one person releases the door to slam in the face of the next in line, the latter will usually follow suit. Similarly, the store manager must open the courtesy door and set the example and standards. And, to be sure, the courtesy of every employee has a direct bearing on the store's success. Courtesy is a particularly valuable asset in cashiers, baggers and service department employees, who have the most frequent contact with customers, but all other employees should be courteous as well. Courtesy among employees also improves the working atmosphere in a store and tends to breed a high level of morale.

The manager should resist the temptation to have someone else tour the entire store with the new part-time or full-time employee. During the tour, he should point out where various types of merchandise are stocked and sold, as well as the location of such things as time cards, rest rooms, lockers, drinking fountains and bulletin board. He should also introduce the new employee to the other employees they encounter on their tour.

The tour ends when the store manager presents the employee to his department manager and to each co-worker in the department to which he is assigned. Before he leaves the new employee in his department, the store manager should encourage him to feel free to ask any questions that occur to him. What is more, the store manager should invite the newcomer to drop by his office at the end of the first work day, just to chat briefly on how things went.

Job Induction. The department manager picks up where the store manager leaves off. As the direct superior of the new employee, he has the responsibility to introduce him to his job and to his role in the department. To perform this induction properly, the department manager should stop what he is doing and give his undivided attention to the newcomer. Too often the department manager is busy when the new employee arrives and in order to get back to his own work, quickly gives the new employee something to do. In such a case, the job induction by the department manager often merely consists of a gruff, "Check with Joe over there. He'll tell you what to do"; or "When Bill gets back from the office, he'll get you started"; or "Report to Mary Smith. She'll tell you about your job." The new employee, who has met 27 people in the last fifteen minutes, does not know Joe or Bill or Mary Smith from Adam, and his fears and anxieties mount. As a result, the time and effort expended by the store manager to start the new employee off on the right foot are in danger of being wasted.

The department manager must understand the uncertainties and fears of the new employee, as well as the means to overcome them. He must realize that a warm and friendly greeting, a smile, a handshake and a word of welcome, will go a long way to giving the new employee the confidence he needs. The department manager should ask the new employee for his given name or nickname and should make sure that the other employees know it too. On no account should he talk down to the new employee. Rather, he should let him know that the department needs him and is glad to have him. The new employee's attitude, morale and desire to cooperate will improve in consequence of such a cordial greeting.

The session with the department manager should ordinarily last no more than ten minutes, but it is the heart of the job induction. After he has greeted the new employee, the department manager should use the time to discuss the job, covering each of the following ten points:

1. The new employee's co-workers and their tasks.
2. The general nature of the tasks he will perform during the first few days.
3. What is expected of him the first week in terms of quality and quantity of work.
4. The employee who is responsible for his training in the department.
5. The importance of his work to the success of the department. (This should be emphasized.)
6. The daily starting and finishing hours during the first week.
7. His schedule of morning and afternoon breaks and of his lunch hour. (One of the other employees should be asked to accompany the new employee at break and lunch times; better still, the department manager should do so himself.)
8. His hourly rate and when he will receive his first pay check.
9. Where to store his personal belongings.
10. Location of apron, jacket, uniform or other supplies.

Like the store manager, the department manager should ask the new employee to stop by before leaving. There are two reasons for having the new employee check with the department and store managers at the end of his first day: (1) to allow the employee to ask questions that may have come up, and (2) to re-emphasize that these managers are genuinely interested in helping him. In fact, the department manager should make himself available to the new employee whenever questions arise. The new employee is usually given a great deal of information on his first day, often far more

23D

than he can retain. It is therefore important that he have an opportunity to ask questions during the first few days and weeks of employment.

Reviewing Employee Progress

At the end of the second week, the store and department managers should meet to review the progress of the new employee. They
should consider his attendance, punctuality, the quality and quantity
of his production, his learning speed and attitude. After they evaluate his performance with regard to each of these factors, they should
invite the new employee to their meeting and review with him his
progress to date. They should criticize him constructively, candidly
and specifically, praising him only when praise is deserved. Any
criticism should be designed to correct a problem, not to condemn
the individual. They should make the point that a mistake itself is
not important; what is important is that the employee know how
and why to avoid such a mistake in the future.

During this end-of-the-second-week review, employee benefits
and future opportunities in the store and company should be discussed in detail and the employee should be encouraged to ask
questions. He should also be advised at this time that the two managers will review his progress with him near the end of his first thirty
days on the job.

Table 1 contains a summary of the induction process. It is organized as a check list to guide store and department managers in
conducting effective induction programs.

TABLE 1

Employee Induction Check List

I. Company Induction (Personnel department's and/or store manager's function):
   A. Give friendly welcome.
   B. Briefly review the following information:
      1. History, development, organization and management of company.
      2. Company policies and regulations.
      3. Company operations, including manufacturing, warehousing, transpor-
         tation, number and location of stores.
   X 4. Employment facts, including terms of employment, disciplinary policies
         and procedures, employee benefit plans, opportunities for ad-
         vancement.

TABLE 1 (Cont.)

Employee Induction Check List

C. Describe the following:
1. What the company expects from the employee.
2. What the employee can expect from the company.

D. Issue employee handbook.

E. Ask for questions.

F. Plan for follow-up by asking employee to stop by the store manager's office at end of first day.

II. Store Induction (Store manager's function):

A. Do the following:
1. Put employee at ease.
2. Make discussion informal.
3. Let employee do much of the talking.

B. Explain the following:
1. General nature of the new employee's job.
2. Importance of new employee's job to the total effort and success of the department and store.
3. Value of courtesy and practices expected of the employee.
4. Administrative facts, such as employee parking area, time cards, employee lockers, rest rooms, drinking fountains, bulletin board and others.

C. Take employee on tour of store; introduce to other employees and to merchandise layout.

D. Turn employee over to his or her department manager.

III. Job Induction (Department manager's function):

A. Greet new employee:
1. Smile, shake hands and give a word of welcome.
2. Give employee undivided attention.

B. Introduce employee to all department co-workers.
1. Use first name.
2. Arrange for someone to take employee to breaks and lunch.

C. Discuss following facts relating to job:
1. General nature of work during the next few days.
2. Work standards (quality and quantity).
3. Employee to whom he or she will be assigned.
4. Importance of new employee's work to success of department.
5. Work schedule, including starting and finishing times, breaks, lunch hour.
6. Hourly rate and pay days.

TABLE 1 (Cont.)

Employee Induction Check List

   7. Storage of personal belongings.

   8. Location of jacket, apron, uniform or other supplies.

D. Ask for questions.

E. Follow-up at end of first day by asking employee to stop by before leaving for a brief discussion and to ask questions.

IV. Induction Follow-Up (Store manager's and department manager's function):

  A. Check and re-check with new employee for questions, problems and progress at the following times:

    1. End of first working day.

    2. End of second working day.

    3. End of first week.

  B. At end of second week, constructively criticize performance of new employee with regard to following matters:

    1. Attendance and punctuality.

    2. Quality and quantity of work.

    3. Ability to get along with co-workers.

    4. Attitude and cooperativeness.

    5. Review the following:

      a. Employee benefits.

      b. Opportunities within the company.

      c. Questions employee may have.

  C. Plan to review employee's progress again at the end of first thirty days.

Inducting Part-Timers

According to the findings of the 1990 turnover study, the annual rate of separations of part-time employees was four times higher than that of full-timers. There is little doubt that a major cause for this wide disparity is the way in which part-timers were treated during their first few days on the job. Often, no real attempt was made to introduce them to their jobs. Here is an account of the complete orientation that store managers gave to part-timers, as observed in stores of three different companies:

"Your starting pay is $4.25 an hour. You'll find an apron in the linen closet in the backroom. Get one on and come back up front and bag for Lucy."

"Damn. You're five minutes late on your first day at work. Where have you been? Find McCall, the assistant manager. She'll tell you what to do."

"Ruth, you can report to Mary, the cashier there on the third checkstand. She'll teach you how to operate the terminal."

"Frank, you're going to be our new produce trimmer. We fired the other one this morning. Find Mr. Salvatavello; he's our produce manager. He'll put you to work."

"I don't need a bagger, but I'm putting you on because I'm fed up with the two I've got. Go take Sam's place and tell him to report to me."

"Here. Fill out this application and give it to Marilyn in the office. Then report to the meat manager for training."

There was no evidence in any of these three chains of a program designed to introduce the new employee to the company, store or job. In each case, a "don't bother me, can't you see I'm busy" attitude was evident. With such receptions, it is easy to imagine the attitude that these new part-timers developed toward their jobs, their managers, the store and the company. It is no wonder that turnover rates among part-timers in these companies was exceptionally high.

Ironically, many store managers who do a fair job of inducting full-time employees all but ignore part-timers. They forget that on the first day of work, the part-timer is just as anxious, apprehensive and uncertain as the full-timer. The part-timer, too, requires a friendly welcome and information.

One store manager recently remarked, "Part-time bagger-carryout clerks are a necessary evil. To me, they're just hands and feet to get the dirty work done." Nevertheless, this manager complains regularly about his inability to find and hold good part-timers. He accuses the younger generation of being spoiled and lazy. Of course, his own attitude, more than anything else, inspires the poor attitudes and low performances of part-time employees.

Another manager wondered whether it is really worthwhile to put 25-hour-per-week part-timers through induction programs. She forgot that her part-timers, most of whom work in the checkout area, are on duty when traffic is heaviest and come into contact with far more customers than do her regular employees. She also overlooked the fact that customers do not usually distinguish between the regular employee and the part-timer. The customer is just as deeply impressed by the courtesy or rudeness of a part-timer as of a full-timer. And, finally, she forgot that almost all of her full-timers, including her department managers and *she, herself,* started as part-timers.

Is Induction Worthwhile?

The high incidence of voluntary separations in the supermarket industry suggests that an effective employee induction program might contribute substantially to reducing the turnover rate. The cost of turnover, though difficult to measure in dollars and cents, represents a very real expense. The industry's average turnover cost of $42,795 per year in the typical $9.0 million a year supermarket means that a substantial reduction in employee turnover can increase profits significantly.

Thirty minutes well spent on an induction process can substantially reduce turnover. To be effective, the store manager must spend approximately twenty minutes on company and store induction; the department manager must spend only about ten minutes on job induction. In addition, a few minutes of follow-up time must be invested by each manager. This is a small price to pay for an improvement in employee attitudes and for the reduced turnover rates that can result from an organized and effectively carried out induction program.

6 | Training Store Employees

A few years ago, a prominent businessman who had previously served as head of training for a major corporation, was elected to the board of directors of a large supermarket chain that was suffering from low profits. When the new director examined the chain's store-level training program, he was dismayed to learn that the personnel department, responsible for training, limited its efforts to developing procedure manuals; that store employees (meat cutters, produce trimmers, stock clerks, cashiers and others) were not trained at all but, rather, learned through osmosis, happenstance or imitation; that the company had neither the awareness nor the use of professional modern training techniques; and that there was a 60 percent annual turnover of store personnel.

As an experienced trainer, the director knew that productivity, morale, absenteeism, accident and turnover rates are directly related to the quality of employee training. It seemed incredible that so large and respected a supermarket chain could function at all without an effective employee training program. After further investigation, he was convinced that the lack of adequate training was in large measure responsible for the chain's declining profits.

Under his influence and guidance, the chain developed a strong training program. Over a thirty-month period, every supervisor, store and department manager was taught the fundamentals of modern training. Within three years after this training program was instituted, the chain's profits rose to the highest level in its history, far above the average for the industry.

Training the Trainer

In the supermarket industry, learning through osmosis or imitation is by far the most common form of training. Indeed, the industry's staffing problems stem largely from the lack of strong, formal training programs. The popular but erroneous belief that training is a simple task which can be performed equally well by all managers has, in turn, resulted from the misconception that each manager has certain innate qualities which make the individual an expert trainer.

In reality, there are very few expert trainers in the managerial ranks because most managers have not been exposed to modern training principles and techniques. Competent trainers are made, not born. Just as managers must acquire skills in such areas as merchandising, scheduling and ordering, they must also develop training skills. And ultimately, all store and department managers are responsible for the training of their employees.

The Need for Better Definitions

Few supermarket companies have defined their training needs and goals or have evaluated their training programs. In consequence, chains differ widely in their approaches to training programs. A study of four regional supermarket chains shows a wide disparity in the amount of off-the-job and on-the-job hours devoted to the training of employees in the same positions. Moreover, there is little relationship between the length of the training period and the difficulty of the skill being taught. For example, each of these companies lists more on-the-job training hours for a produce or grocery clerk than for a cashier on a 10-key electronic register terminal, even though the cashier's job is far more complex. (See Table 1.)

In reality, the on-the-job training hours that are listed do not represent any real training at all; rather, they signify hours during which the employee is hopefully learning through osmosis.

TABLE 1

Training Time by Job Classification in Four Companies

Position	Training in Company A		Training in Company B		Training in Company C		Training in Company D	
	Off-the-Job Hours	On-the-Job Hours	Off-the-Job Hours	On-the-Job Hours	Off-the-Job Hours	On-the-Job Hours	Off-the-Job Hours	On-the-Job Hours
Cashier	8	40	16	2	20	80	0	16
Bagger	0	40	0	1	4	24	0	2
Apprentice Meat Cutter	0	4,160	0	2,400	0	1,040	0	520
Produce Clerk	0	240	0	1,200	14	320	0	80
Grocery Clerk	8	240	0	2,400	0	no set time	0	40

But the amount of time devoted to training is not the only factor that contributes to a successful training program. Proper tools and techniques are also required. The first step in developing a workable training program is to approach the problem systematically, to seek answers to the following questions:

1. How much training is needed and for whom?
2. How much should training cost and what should it accomplish?
3. Where should training be done and by whom?

Establishing Training Needs

In order to determine its training needs, a supermarket company should survey, gather statistics on and evaluate its current productivity, gross profit, shrinkage, accidents, grievances, morale, customer complaints, turnover, absenteeism and personnel audits. Analysis of such data for a given store or group of stores can often pinpoint the weak spots and dictate the areas where training efforts would result in better performance.

Basically, training needs may be identified by using either of two simple formulas, both of which identify needs in terms of measurable quantities and qualities: (1) Desired Performance *minus* Present Performance *equals* Training Needs; or (2) Job Requirements *minus* Present Skills *equals* Training Needs.

Too often, training is limited to new employees while the needs of experienced people are ignored. For instance, a manager in one store became concerned about the increasing errors which appeared as net losses on his cash over-and-short reports. He suspected that the problem was caused by the three new cashiers hired and trained during the past six months. But an examination of the records showed that 95 percent of the net losses were traceable to experienced cashiers. As a result, the manager set up a retraining program for experienced employees, and within a month, his store's cashier losses were decreased by more than 40 percent.

Job requirements, on the other hand, include far more than simple mechanical skills. Attitude, morale, and the employee's ability to work as a team member are equally or more important. Modern training techniques tend to emphasize the employee's total adjustment to the job.

Training Part-Timers

Part-timers are rarely trained adequately. Even those companies that have central programs in off-the-job training schools often limit enrollment to full-time employees. The part-timer is trained on the job by a department manager or by an experienced employee who has had no formal instruction in training. In companies where all the training is done at store level, there is a similar tendency to ignore the part-timer.

In many companies, however, more than 80 percent of the regular employees were once part-timers. The part-timer usually works when the store is busiest, and generally comes into contact with more customers than does a regular employee. One company with two part-time cashiers for every regular cashier noted that its part-timers averaged twenty hours a week and its regulars, forty hours, so that the total hours worked by both groups was about the same. Yet an investigation by this chain showed that the part-time cashiers, who worked mostly in the evenings and on weekends, rang up 71 percent of all sales.

Some executives contend that they can't afford to train part-timers. Others maintain that the lower pay earned by part-timers is the reason for their scanty training. But, in fact, the gap between the wage rates of full- and part-timers is rapidly closing, and in many areas there is no significant difference. Another excuse given for neglecting the training of part-time employees is the high turnover rate of this group. However, effective training reduces turnover.

Establishing Goals and Budgets

The president of a small supermarket chain recently said: "We have no training programs so we have no training costs." But every supermarket has training costs, even if it neither analyzes nor recognizes them. Most employees are not hired with the skills and interests required for the job. Instead, they must acquire skills while they work, and as they learn (even as they learn bad practices), the company must foot the bill. Ultimately, training costs are reflected in low productivity and high labor costs.

To justify training costs and effort, it is necessary to measure the improvements in performance that result from training. Therefore, an integral part of every training program must be the establishment of goals which specify exactly what the training is designed to accomplish. Training goals should be specific, tangible and measurable.

A training goal such as "to do a better job of produce managing" is vague and, consequently, unacceptable. A better statement of a goal is "to improve produce gross profit in this store by next June 1 from 1 percent below, to 1 percent above produce gross profit in the company." The effectiveness of a training program may be evaluated and its costs justified only if concrete, measurable goals have been established.

One large chain measures its training costs in terms of the productivity of experienced employees. Its studies reveal, for example, that the productivity of the average experienced meat wrapper using soft film and proper wrapping methods, is 280 packages per hour. This, then, is the company's performance standard for meat wrappers.

A study of 23 meat wrapper trainees in this company showed that their average production during the first twenty hours on the job was 100 packages per hour, or a total of 2,000 packages. At the experienced meat wrapper's rate, the 2,000 packages represent only 7.1 hours of work. Training costs are computed as follows: The twenty hours paid for minus 7.1 hours of work produced equals 12.9 nonproductive hours or the actual production time lost; the 12.9 hours multiplied by a wage rate of $7.00 per hour puts the company's training cost for each meat wrapper at $90.30 for the first twenty hours on the job. Total training time is 120 hours; the training cost is $182.70 for the complete training period. (See Table 2.)

Comparison of trainee performance with standards established for experienced employees is one meaningful way of measuring training costs. Other factors, however, should also be considered, including cost of employee fringe benefits, time and expense of the

TABLE 2
Measuring Training Costs for Meat Wrappers

Training Hours	Average Productivity per Hour Packages	Average Productivity per 20 Hours Packages	Productivity of 280 Packages per Hour Hours	Production Loss Hours	Cost of Training Dollars
First 20 Hours	100	2,000	7.1	12.9	$ 90.30
Second 20 Hours	175	3,500	12.5	7.5	52.50
Third 20 Hours	225	4,500	16.1	3.9	27.30
Fourth 20 Hours	260	5,200	18.6	1.4	9.80
Fifth 20 Hours	275	5,500	19.6	0.4	2.80
Sixth 20 Hours	280	5,600	20.0	0.0	.00
Total Cost per Trainee					$182.70

trainer, cost of the training room (or rooms) and equipment, and cost of product spoiled or of materials wasted during the training period.

Comparing performance figures before and after training is one way of evaluating the training program. Another method is to set up control groups by comparing the performance figures of stores or departments with training programs with those of stores without them.

Types of Training Programs

Training programs are often simply classified in terms of where the training is given, as follows:

1. On-the-job training
2. Central or off-the-job training
3. Model department training

The great majority of supermarket employees learn on the job. Some larger chains and a few smaller ones do give cashiers at least some formal training centrally but, in general, less than one out of twenty supermarket line employees is trained centrally.

On-the-Job Training.   On-the-job, store-based training avoids the artificial classroom-like atmosphere of central training. There is no need for the student to re-adjust from the controlled situation of the classroom to the reality of the store. Moreover, during the training period, the trainee makes some contribution to production. At least on the surface, such a training program seems to be more economical and the responsibility for training is placed on the shoulders of those who stand to gain most from it—store management.

On the other hand, on-the-job training requires that a recruit be trained by someone who is certainly not a professional trainer and who may be a poor teacher. The store or department manager, who is usually given the job of training newcomers, may be so overloaded with work that he or she lets the training slide. When emergencies arise, the trainee is all too often pulled off the training program and used to plug the gap; the temptation to use trainees in this fashion must be overcome if on-the-job training is to succeed.

Central Training.   One of the major advantages of central training is that learning is not affected by the inevitable distractions and interruptions that occur in the stores. Standardized instruction can be given by trainers who are carefully selected and well-equipped to teach. Better control assures that the employee will receive more thorough instruction, as well as a better induction.

But centralized training usually costs more than other forms of training and may be impractical when stores are spread over a wide geographic area. Furthermore, when training is conducted centrally, there is a tendency for store and department managers to feel relieved of all training responsibilities. Some managers fail to realize that central training is really pre-job instruction, and that a great deal of on-the-job training is still necessary. Thus, the most serious disadvantage of central training is that it encourages a pass-the-buck attitude among store and department managers which may, in turn, lead to an inefficient working staff and to low employee morale.

Where central training is instituted, it is vital that store and central training people agree on the same standard practices; when they do not, confusion and inefficiency result. The following incident illustrates the need for genuine agreement between store and central training personnel.

During eight hours of central instruction in trimming methods, a produce trimmer had been correctly taught to remove outer, discolored lettuce leaves before trimming the butt. But on the first day at the store, the veteran "know-it-all" produce manager chewed the trimmer out for not trimming the butt first and then removing the outer leaves. "It's easier and faster this way," the manager said.

The new trimmer explained that the other method was taught at the company school because it gives the customer a better quality product, simplifies retrimming and reduces product shrinkage.

At this, the produce manager blew up. "I don't care what they taught you in school. You're working for me now and you'll do it my way."

This type of disparity between central training and store practices finally led to a complete collapse of the company's central training program.

Model Department Training.   Training in model departments is designed to combine the virtues of on-the-job and central training. This fast-growing innovation has been catching on rapidly in the supermarket industry. A model meat department in one store may serve as a company's training base for all apprentice meat cutters in from five to ten stores located in one geographic area; a model produce department in another store might serve as the training ground for produce clerks. Indeed, many companies have set up models for all departments.

The department is carefully selected and is made to serve as a model in every respect. Here, all company policies and standard practices are installed and followed to the letter. The department manager is thoroughly familiar with modern training devices and techniques, and in some companies is given a bonus for the extra time and effort that is put into training new employees for other stores. The department manager should possess the personal characteristics of a good trainer, and should have a friendly and cooperative staff as well.

The size, volume and layout of the model departments should be similar to those of the corresponding departments in the stores for which the employees are being trained. There must also be space available for classroom training. The model department and the store in which it is located should be above average in such vital statistics as gross profit, shrinkage, wage and supply expenses. In these respects it again serves as a model, to be imitated by other stores in the area.

Some companies use the model department to train department managers as well as new full- and part-time employees within a given area. In other companies, model department training is limited to new meat and/or produce and/or non-foods employees. In some model departments, the trainee serves as a regular department employee, rotating from job to job until thoroughly trained. In some cases, the trainee is treated as a regular employee and the trainee's salary is charged to the department payroll. In several companies, however, to make the training burden more acceptable, the department is charged with a portion of the employee's pay, while the balance is charged to a training account. In fact, in a growing number of companies, the entire trainee's salary is charged to training.

Pros and Cons of Model Departments: As in central training, standardized instruction in model departments can be provided by trainers who are well prepared to teach. On the other hand, model department training resembles on-the-job training in that training is conducted under actual operating conditions, trainees contribute to production and line employees gain training experience.

However, model department training also contains some of the disadvantages of central and on-the-job training. For one thing, distractions are present and interruptions occur. Also, store and department managers in non-model stores tend to feel relieved of any responsibility for training and follow-up. And finally, policies and operating practices may differ from store to store and the procedures of the model department may not faithfully reflect those followed in the various stores.

Despite these real disadvantages, training in model departments is usually far more comprehensive than on-the-job training and often more thorough than central training. A good model department program allows the trainee sufficient time to establish the best work habits and to become at least partially adept in using newly learned skills. Most companies that use the model department approach are convinced that it produces the best trained employee at a reasonable cost.

The Model Store.   In a few companies the model department concept has been expanded to a model store plan. Here, all new employees in an area are trained in one store. In effect, every department in the store becomes a model department. The model store approach allows for more concentrated and therefore more easily controlled training. However, the burden of training all full- and part-time employees for several stores usually is more than a single store can handle. In addition, it is rare to find a store where all the department managers are capable of becoming skilled trainers.

The Need for Modern Training Techniques

No matter which training approach is used, every store and department manager must gain an intimate working knowledge of modern training principles and techniques. Such knowledge is necessary to control training costs, shrinkage, customer complaints, absenteeism, accident and turnover rates, and to improve productivity, accuracy, gross profit and employee morale.

Learning through osmosis is not only inefficient and costly, but also usually results in learning poor methods. Even those employees who are given pre-job instruction centrally must receive follow-up training on the job. In short, the effective training and development of subordinates is a primary responsibility of every supervisor, store and department manager.

7 | Training Principles

The purpose of training is to effect a specific change in an employee's behavior. If behavior does not change, the training program is either unnecessary or a failure. Furthermore, no matter how elaborate or progressive a training program may appear to be, it is doomed to failure if sound training principles are not followed conscientiously.

Training principles may be divided into two groups: (1) principles of learning, and (2) principles of teaching. A training program cannot succeed if either the learning or teaching principles are misunderstood or improperly applied.

Principles of Learning

Every trainer must be aware of the factors that influence a trainee's ability to learn. Learning is affected by the following:

1. The trainee's capability and attitude.
2. The trainee's background, previous training and experience.

3. The nature of the task being taught.
4. The instruction methods and techniques that are employed.
5. The capability and attitude of the trainer.

Capability and Attitude of the Trainee.   It is a waste of time to train people who lack either the ability or the desire to learn. An applicant's capability and attitude should be explored in depth during the selection process because an employee's ultimate success is dependent on both. The importance of the combination of ability and desire may be illustrated by an example.

A teenager with very poor eyesight and reflexes has his heart set on becoming a major league baseball player. He practices throwing and batting every day, and does everything he can to overcome his physical handicaps. But no matter how much effort he puts into it, he can't even make his own high school team, much less the big leagues. He has the desire, but not the ability. On the other hand, a natural athlete with all the physical attributes needed to become a star won't make the team either if he has neither the interest in playing baseball nor the desire to succeed at it. He has the capability, but lacks the desired attitude.

An employee's attitude and, as a result, learning ability, depend a great deal on whether he or she is properly motivated. Motivation, which is discussed later in this chapter, means that the individual has an inner drive or desire to accomplish something. In order for a new employee to be effectively motivated, goals and objectives should be clear and achievable. The trainee should be encouraged to understand the "why," as well as the "how," of the task at hand. Learning should be conducted in a friendly, stimulating and competitive environment. The trainee should be able to measure his or her performance against a standard and the trainee's achievements should be recognized and commended.

Because people differ in their capabilities and attitudes, their progress and learning speed will also differ. Standards set by the company or trainer must be flexible enough to accommodate such differences. Fixed training periods are wasteful to the company and unfair to the more capable trainee, yet such inflexible training schedules are common among supermarket companies.

For example, a store manager trainee in one company is required to spend six months as a stock clerk, seventeen weeks as a produce clerk, and thirty weeks as an apprentice meat cutter. The store manager trainee who has a knack for meat cutting must put in the same thirty weeks as the trainee who has little aptitude for the work. The rigidity of this time schedule eventually causes interest in the job and morale to decline sharply, sometimes to the point where the trainee resigns. Any qualified training director will attest that an unusually capable trainee can often become skilled in half the time required by a trainee with low capabilities.

The Trainee's Background and Experience.   The trainee's ability to learn a given job is influenced by the individual's background, previous training and experience. A produce clerk trainee who has had previous experience working in a wholesale produce warehouse would enjoy a learning advantage over one who has not. An apprentice meat trainee who had previously worked in a packing plant would have a similar learning advantage. Previous experience in a different department in a supermarket would give a trainee an advantage over one who has had no supermarket experience. Nevertheless, experience is only one guideline. Though its value should not be underestimated, an individual's inherent learning capacity contributes more significantly to the person's ultimate success or failure.

The Nature of the Job.   The simplicity or complexity of the task to be learned is another major influence on learning. More time is required for a trainee to become a skilled cashier than to become an efficient bagger. And, of course, it takes more time for a trainee to become a proficient store manager than an effective department manager. The difficulty of the task to be learned, coupled with the capability, attitude and experience of the trainee, dictate such aspects of learning as the required frequency and length of practice and rest periods.

Instruction Methods.   A company must develop production standards based on the average performance of typical trainees. Unless such standards are established at various points in the training period and the trainee's performance is measured against those standards, there is no way for the trainee to know how he or she is progressing. Without some guidelines, trainees cannot set their own performance goals. Furthermore, without such standards the effectiveness of the trainer and the training program cannot be fully evaluated.

For example, how many chuck primals is the trainee expected to break per hour into retail cuts after five hours of training and practice? After ten hours? How many ringup error corrections does the average cashier make during the first day on the job? The second day? The fifth? How many boxes of lettuce should the produce clerk trim and wrap per hour at various stages of training? How many cases per hour should the new grocery clerk price and stock during the first day of work? The fifth day? The tenth? Without such standards against which to measure performance, everyone, trainer and trainee included, is working in the dark.

Measuring employee performance during training allows the trainee to compete, not only against the standard, but also against other trainees. The development of a friendly, competitive atmosphere can do much to instill enthusiasm, to motivate the trainee and, thus, to stimulate learning. In addition, measuring employee performance provides an objective tool for recognizing an individual's progress and achievement. When performing on a better than average level, the trainee should be commended. Deserved recognition of achievement is a strong motivating force.

The trainee must also be made to understand everything about the task being learned. The trainer should answer such questions as: Why is the task necessary? Why must it be performed in a certain way? Why is it performed at a particular point in a sequence? The trainee must also recognize how the task fits into the overall picture. Once the trainee thoroughly understands the purpose and objective of the task, the learning process is reinforced and the trainee is apt to make fewer mistakes. The importance of understanding the reasons why a task is performed in a certain way may be illustrated by the following example.

It was Friday morning, the fourth day of cashier training for Mary Heath. Trainer Jean Kern had turned her loose, and Mary was anxious to make a good impression on her customers and store manager. She rang up the purchases of the first customer, added the tax, and was ready to take a final subtotal and announce the amount due for the purchase. Suddenly, she realized she could save one complete step by totaling the purchase, thereby eliminating the final subtotaling operation.

The register drawer opened and she announced the amount of the order to the customer. After receiving payment she made the correct change, gave it to the customer, completed the transaction and closed the register drawer. She tried the same procedure on the next order, and again everything went well; she had really found a better way. "The manager and Miss Kern will both be proud of me for finding a short-cut," she thought. "I'll have to tell them about it the first chance I get." She went on using her "improved" method for the rest of the day.

That evening at 8:45, just before the store closed, Mary totaled the order for a customer and announced the amount. As she waited for the payment she pushed several checked items down the counter before bagging the order. She had her back to the register for only a few seconds, but in that brief time a man in the adjoining aisle reached into the open cash drawer, grabbed eleven twenty dollar bills and fled from the store.

Mary's "better way" had cost the store $220. She really could not be blamed because she did not know any better. The trainer had failed to explain why a final subtotal must precede ringing up the total. Mary should have been told that the reason is to avoid leaving her cash register unprotected. The "why" in the training process had been omitted.

Successful training methods include active trainee participation. The key to successful trainee participation is the degree to which instruction is interspersed with practice. Since the trainee tends to forget most rapidly immediately after instruction, learning is most effective when it is immediately followed by application. Practice reinforces memory and the trainer must create frequent opportunities for trainee practice. Ultimately, the development of any skill requires repetition and practice.

Capability and Attitude of the Trainer. One can talk forever about enlightened training principles, but if the trainer is not a suitable teacher, or if the methods the trainer uses are slipshod or do not follow sound principles, the entire program will be a waste of time and money. Moreover, if the trainer is not well-motivated, is impatient, uninvolved and unconcerned, the supermarket will continue to lose one of its most valuable potential assets—the trainee with promise.

The Qualified Trainer

A bright meat department manager was selected to be his firm's meat trainer. When asked if he'd like to take the job, he jumped at the chance in the belief that it would be an interesting challenge. He was somewhat crestfallen to learn that he could not step right into the job and begin teaching. Before he would meet his first apprentice, he would have to work approximately eight months to prepare himself and the training program. He simply could not understand why such a delay was necessary. After all, he knew the retail meat business and he had been training apprentice meat cutters for the past three years.

Two months later he realized that training is really a well-planned, well-organized approach to developing skills in others. He had failed to recognize that the thorough preparation of the trainer is an absolute prerequisite to instituting a training program for apprentice meat cutters. He had assumed that he would learn to teach as he progressed, through trial and error.

He discovered that the trainer's instructional methods and techniques have an immense effect on learning, but that without the proper ability and attitude, no trainer could succeed, no matter how progressive his methods or techniques were. A qualified trainer needed a familiarity with modern training methods, as well as a thorough knowledge of the subject he was teaching. He had to possess the capacity to express himself coherently, to communicate with others, to recognize employee needs and to plan and organize efficiently. In addition, he required an understanding of what motivates learning and a constructive attitude toward trainees and training.

Principles of Teaching

Training results depend in large measure on whether the program is thoroughly planned. Advance planning must take into account six basic principles of teaching or training employees, as follows:

1. The simple tasks must be taught first.
2. The task must be broken down into its basic components.
3. Only the correct method should be taught.
4. Teaching cycles should be short and should be immediately reinforced by practice.
5. Skills should be developed through repetition.
6. The trainee must be motivated.

The workplace and training area must also be properly arranged in advance of the training session. Good lighting and ventilation are important. The workplace should be organized exactly as the trainee would be expected to maintain it. Tools, materials, supplies and training aids should be in place and ready to use.

Precautions should be taken to eliminate interruptions and distractions. The trainer should advise someone to answer the phone, and stress that there are to be no interruptions while instruction is taking place. Quiet surroundings are conducive to learning, while interruptions and distractions reduce effectiveness and lengthen training time. While instructing cashiers or baggers in the sales area, the trainer should close off a check-stand and put up a sign informing customers that the stand is temporarily closed in order to train new employees.

Teaching Simple Tasks First. The trainee must first be well-grounded in fundamental, simple tasks. The sequence in which jobs are performed in a department is seldom the best sequence to follow in training. A meat apprentice trainee, for example, should not start to learn the meat business by first writing a meat order, then by receiving, breaking primals into retail cuts, traying, wrapping and displaying. Though this procedure may represent the actual sequence of tasks on the job, it is not the best sequence for efficient learning. Similarly, a grocery clerk should not be taught how to order before learning how to price mark and stock. Rather, training should begin with simple tasks and gradually progress to the more complex tasks. The introduction of complex tasks at the beginning of a training program may confuse the trainee. Self-confidence could be destroyed if the trainee is unable to succeed at performing these complex tasks. Teaching should never progress to the next, more complex step until the trainee has thoroughly understood and practiced the simpler material that had just been covered.

Breaking Down Each Task. Though major tasks may be taught out of sequence, the basic steps in a single task should be taught in the sequence in which they occur. In bagging customers' orders, for example, the location of bags by sizes should be taught first. Then the trainee should learn, in turn, such matters as the correct use of each size, how to grasp and open the bag and where to place it before bagging. While teaching the successive steps of a given task, the trainer should refer to a written list. This list should contain the following information: (1) each step of the task in its proper sequence; (2) the key points in each step, including details that are particularly important about the step or that are likely to cause the trainee trouble; and (3) the reasons why the step is performed in a particular way.

Here is an example of the breakdown prepared by one trainer for a small portion of the bagging operation:

Steps	Key Points	Reasons Why
1. Obtain proper bag.	1. Grasp lip with left hand.	1. Saves transfer from right to left hand.
2. Open bag.	2. Insert right hand into mouth of bag, reach to bottom, spread fingers.	2. Snapping bag open can hit or frighten the customer or tear the bag.
3. Position bag.	3. Place on bagging shelf.	3. Shelf is at optimum height to reduce fatigue.

The trainer must determine the exact number of steps in an operation, and map out the sequence and purpose of each. In order to pin down these details, the trainer should slowly perform every task, listing the successive steps and analyzing each step by noting its key points and the reason why each is important. The trainer, who performs the job almost automatically, while teaching is apt to omit one or more of the many steps that make up a particular job unless the steps are listed very carefully and in detail. What may be natural and easy for the trainer may be awkward, confusing and difficult for the trainee. By preparing a training outline of every step in a task, the trainer not only insures thorough coverage of the job but, equally important, provides the trainee with an understanding of what is being taught.

Teaching the Correct Method Only.   Recently, a trainer was instructing a produce trainee in trimming methods. First, she demonstrated the correct method of trimming corn. She did not, however, point out the key points in each step or the reasons for following a certain procedure. Then, in rapid succession, she demonstrated three incorrect methods of trimming corn.

At that point, the trainer was called to the telephone. "Practice the correct method I showed you first," she said. "I'll be right back." When she returned fifteen minutes later, half the box of corn had been trimmed incorrectly and the trainee's left index finger had been cut to the bone.

As it is so often the case with inept trainers, this one blamed the accident on the trainee. When she returned and saw the mess, her comment was: "This would not have happened had you paid attention. I told you to do it the way I showed you the first time."

But if the trainee has not learned, it can be assumed that the trainer has not properly taught. The trainer's demonstration of one correct and three incorrect methods had thoroughly confused the trainee. The trainer must realize that a procedure cannot be described in one fashion and performed in another. To the trainee, the demonstrated way is the right way, regardless of what is said. If the trainer demonstrates a task in a sloppy way to show how it should not be done, the trainee is likely to learn the sloppy method of performing the task.

Errors committed during practice must be corrected immediately, before they solidify as bad habits. A bad habit is developed through repetition. The longer it is practiced, the more natural it becomes and the more difficult to root out. Errors that occur during the performance of a task are often due to the trainee's desire to work too rapidly and, thus, to make a good impression. The trainer must emphasize that speed is a product of practice and that the trainee should initially concentrate on accuracy rather than speed.

Short Teaching Cycles.   A meat trainer in one company followed an excellent outline, demonstrating each successive step of a task, stating its key points and the reasons why each is necessary. The trainer showed how to break beef primals from the forequarter into retail cuts. He began his demonstration by cutting a chuck into retail cuts on the power saw, and followed immediately by breaking a rib into retail cuts, and then a shank and a plate. It took 45 minutes to complete the demonstration, including working up the trimmings. When he finished, he handed the trainee a knife, pointed to the power saw and four new forequarter primals, and told the trainee to go to work and break each one into retail cuts as he had just done. It is not difficult to imagine the predicament of the trainee.

Though the trainer had followed an excellent outline and had provided the proper explanations, he made the mistake of giving the trainee too much to digest at one time without the opportunity to practice each step in succession. Such an approach never succeeds because the trainee requires time to assimilate what he has been told and shown. He can retain the information only if it is presented to him in small units and if he is allowed to practice each short cycle immediately after it is demonstrated. Each cycle should contain three to six steps, depending on the complexity of the steps. For example, the meat trainer should have first explained and demonstrated how to separate the brisket from the shank and trim it into a retail cut. Then he should have asked the trainee to practice this cycle on several shanks, before proceeding to the next cycle. Likewise, the balance of the retail cutting operation should have been presented, demonstrated and practiced in short segments.[1]

However, the trainer should also take time out to describe the total job. For example, before beginning instruction on the breakdown of a primal, he should briefly discuss the total forequarter break-down, identifying the various primals on the carcass. Such a summary enables the trainee to visualize and understand the end result and to relate each successive step to that result.

Repetition Builds Skill.   The retention of information and the development of skills are directly related to the amount of practice the trainee is allowed. In the early stages of training, the apprentice

---

[1] When stores receive beef broken down into subprimals, the trainer should begin with the subprimal that is easiest to process into retail cuts, and end the training phase with the most difficult subprimal.

usually retains three to four times the knowledge, and retains it longer, if he is allowed to practice a task twice instead of once, or four cycles instead of two.

Immediately after the initial demonstration, the trainee should repeat the cycle until he performs it correctly, without hesitation or false movement. When he repeats a segment of an operation for the first time, he should be permitted to continue working undisturbed at his own rate of speed as long as he is performing correctly. If he recognizes a mistake himself, he should be allowed to correct it without interference. On the other hand, if the trainee fails to recognize his mistake, he must be interrupted immediately and corrected in a friendly manner, preferably in private because no one likes to be corrected in the presence of others. To make sure he understands the correct method, the trainee should be questioned about the key points of the step or steps he had performed. Moreover, the trainee should be praised whenever he performs the job properly.

The amount of repetition required will vary from trainee to trainee and from job to job. However, at the time of initial instruction, each cycle should be performed a minimum of three times before proceeding to the next cycle in the task. But even such a procedure does not guarantee that the trainee will master every step, and further practice is sometimes necessary. In any case, the training program must provide sufficient time for practice. The amount of time that is allotted depends on the number of steps to be learned, the complexity or difficulty of the task, and the ability of the trainee. And after each of the cycles in an operation has been individually mastered, the trainee should be guided through the complete operation and permitted to practice until he can perform it accurately and completely, without hesitation or false movement.

The Motivated Trainee

A trainer or anyone else who credits himself with being an excellent motivator of people does not understand the dynamics of motivation. A trainer can motivate himself, but not others. Motivation comes from within the employees and cannot be imposed on them by the trainer. Motivation can be compared with the growth process in a child. A trainer cannot motivate a trainee any more than a parent can force a child to grow. The parent can provide nourishment and an environment conducive to growth, but the growth comes from within the child. So, too, does motivation come from within the employee. The most a trainer (or a manager) can do is to provide an environment or climate in which the trainee *wants* to learn and perform. (See Chapter 11, Motivation and Morale.)

There are several things the trainer can do that will encourage trainees to want to learn and perform. The trainer should: (1) emphasize the importance of each task being taught; (2) learn what the trainees' attitudes and needs are, and encourage employees in ways that will satisfy those needs; (3) compliment trainees when they learn and perform well; and (4) have them set their own learning goals and keep them informed of their progress toward those goals.

If It's a Job, It's Important.

A young person, newly employed as a part-time bagger-carryout clerk, was recently asked by a neighbor (who was also a store customer) what his job was. "I'm just a flunky," he replied. "I bag and carry-out orders." The youth had not been trained to understand the significance of his work. He had not been taught the importance of his role as the final contact between store and customer. His poor attitude no doubt lost many customers for the store.

There is no such thing as an unimportant job in a supermarket. Though the required skills, strength, dexterity and leadership capabilities may vary from job to job, each job is significant. Just as a supermarket cannot stay in business without a meat cutter or produce manager, so it cannot continue functioning without a part-time bagger, parking lot cleanup person or grocery stock clerk. Therefore, no matter what job is being taught, the trainee should be made aware of its importance so that the trainee will be proud of it and want to perform it well.

Encouraging the Trainee.

The trainer must capture the trainee's undivided attention and gain his or her confidence and cooperation. Because almost everyone is apprehensive and nervous when confronted with new tasks, the trainer must first put the employee at ease. When they first meet, the trainer should greet the trainee in a friendly manner. After a brief welcome, the discussion should be directed to questions about the trainee's previous experience. The trainer can thus discover precisely what the trainee already knows about the task to be learned and can, moreover, estimate the amount of time needed for training. Encouraging trainees to talk about themselves also helps them to relax.

During this first meeting, before formal training actually begins, the trainee should be told what he or she will learn and, without excessive detail, given an overall preview of the entire job. Since learning is improved by the promise of rewards, the trainer should explain how the trainee will benefit from the learning experience.

The trainee should also understand that no one expects perfect performance on the first day and that speed will come with practice.

The trainer must watch closely for clues which will identify and perhaps explain the trainee's needs and attitudes. One trainee, for instance, may lack self-confidence and need more reassurance than another who is self-confident. A second may require closer supervision. A third trainee may be frustrated and concerned over how well he is doing and his learning ability might consequently be impaired. Such anxiety may be avoided if the trainee is kept informed of the nature of the job he is learning and of his progress. When he finds the motivating key, the trainer should use it to unlock the trainee's talents. A self-motivated trainee will learn faster and better than one who is not motivated.

When a trainee learns slowly, some trainers tend to become impatient. Though the job now seems simple to them, such trainers forget that it was not so simple when they had first learned it. A trainer should avoid showing impatience either in word, deed or facial expression. Any expression of impatience makes the trainee nervous and apprehensive, and further retards his learning ability.

A self-confident trainee, who is encouraged to ask questions and offer suggestions, will often come up with ideas for improving the job. The questions that a trainee asks also help to identify those weak spots in a training program that may need correction. Often a new trainee with a fresh outlook can recognize opportunities to improve or to step-up an operation that even the skilled trainer has missed.

The trainer who is satisfied that the trainee knows how to perform an operation should gradually allow the trainee to work alone. Over-supervision or "snoopervision" tends to kill initiative. Nevertheless, the trainee should occasionally be checked and watched, particularly for the repetition of mistakes that might have been made earlier in training.

Praising Good Performance. The chairman of a very successful regional supermarket chain, who is nationally respected and admired, once said: "The greatest neglect among top executives in this industry, including myself, is that we spend too much time and effort identifying problems, finding fault and criticizing mistakes, and too little time identifying successes and complimenting people for good performance. This is a weakness that is widespread at all management levels in our company, and I suspect the same is true in most other companies. It is a weakness that we must address and correct if we expect to have a high level of morale, motivation, loyalty and excellence in performance among our people ... the four basic ingredients of success."

This prominent executive was not speaking in clichés. Indeed, he was most perceptive in recognizing a fundamental weakness that has destroyed more than one supermarket chain; the same weakness that undoubtedly is a major factor in employee and manager resignations.

Like any good manager, the trainer must continuously be on the lookout for opportunities to praise the trainee for good performance. When a trainee properly performs for the first time a task that the trainer has explained and demonstrated, the individual should be complimented for a job well done. Every person appreciates recognition and praise for learning and performing well. This creates the type of environment in which self-motivation takes root.

Discussing Performance Progress.   The trainee should continually be kept aware of his or her performance progress. Periodically, the trainee's productivity and accuracy should be measured against those of the average trainee. In order to accomplish this, it is necessary to establish average performance figures for various stages in the training period. These figures may easily be computed for a new training program by averaging the performances of the first trainees at specified intervals during the practice period, and regularly revising the figures as more trainees are processed.

One meat trainer, for example, recorded the time required by each new trainee to cut saw-ready loins of beef into T-bone, porterhouse and sirloin steaks, and to scrape, bone, trim and tray these steaks. For each of the first twenty trainees to go through the initial program, he recorded and averaged the time required by them to process the third, fifth, tenth, fifteenth, twentieth and twenty-fifth loins. On the basis of these averages, he established learning standards for processing loins up to 25 cycles. He recorded and drew charts of the same information for other major activities in the training program. The figures were posted in the cutting room of the training store. Each trainee was encouraged to compare his or her performance with the average for third, fifth, tenth, fifteenth, twentieth and twenty-fifth cycles. As additional employees were trained, the trainer revised the average performance figures.

This is an excellent way to keep trainees informed of their progress. Guesswork and opinion are removed from performance evaluation, as trainees are repeatedly reminded of their progress. The establishment of standards for various stages in the learning process also permits the trainees to set their own learning goals on the basis of the progress they are making. Self-imposed learning goals are particularly effective in creating the environment in which the average trainee becomes a motivated employee.

As will become evident from the review of goal setting in Chapter 14, employees react differently to goals that are set for them, and those that they set for themselves. The difference is in attitude and the degree to which the employee is committed to the goals. Self-motivation and commitment are far more in evidence when employees set their own goals than when the goals are handed down from above. So, after the trainer has explained and demonstrated a given task, the trainee should be made aware of the average units per hour, or minutes per unit, or some other such measurement that has been achieved by previous trainees on the specific task. The trainer should then encourage the trainee to set goals against that average. When the trainee sets realistic, challenging goals and reaches or exceeds them, performing the task correctly, of course, he or she should be rewarded with a compliment.

Testing the Trainee

The trainer should not take it for granted that communication with the trainee has been successful or that the lesson has been understood. The trainer should never rely on an affirmative answer to the question, "Do you understand?" In fact, questions that beg for "yes" answers should never be asked because many trainees consider a negative response to such questions a sign of stupidity and would prefer to say that they do understand when they actually do not. To ascertain whether the trainee has, indeed, understood, the trainer must test the person both verbally during instruction and practice, and in writing following the learning period. Testing removes any doubt about whether the trainee has grasped the material. It also keeps the trainer informed of his or her success or failure in communicating with the trainee.

When teaching manual skills, verbal tests should be given while observing performance. After the trainer has explained and demonstrated a cycle of a task for the first time, the trainee should repeat that cycle immediately. The trainee should follow the proper sequence of steps and repeat the key points of and reasons for each. When such mistakes as omitting a step or missing a key point or reason are made, the trainee should be corrected immediately. When the trainee repeats the instructions, the trainer should be especially careful to check that technical terms have been completely understood. Many terms in supermarketing, though familiar to most veteran employees, are strange to newcomers.

While taking a meat training course many years ago, I learned the names of the various parts of the beef carcass. After boning out many rumps, I became quite familiar with what was called the "H" bone. I assumed this rump bone was so named because it was roughly shaped like the letter "H." But the word is actually *aitch*, and is derived from the French word *nache*, meaning buttock. A clear explanation of this term during training would have spared me some anxious and embarrassing moments many years later, when I wrote the term incorrectly on a blackboard before an audience of meat experts.

Programmed Instruction

No discussion of training principles would be complete that did not recognize the potential value of programmed instruction. Well-designed programmed instruction incorporates the major ingredients of good learning and good teaching. It is a teaching technique designed to improve the quality and effectiveness of training.

After the trainee reads a small bit of information he is asked to respond to a question relating to that material. He writes his answer down and is immediately advised whether or not he has responded correctly. If he is correct, he proceeds to the next item, or "frame," reads the next bit of information and answers the related question. If he has made a mistake, he re-reads the same information and answers the question again. He does not move to the next frame until he has answered the preceding question correctly. The trainee's response is usually made by selecting an answer from among two or more alternatives, or by filling in one or more words to complete a sentence.

Information presented in the successive frames gradually becomes more difficult. Each step contains additional information, but the trainee advances to new and more complex material only when he is ready to do so. In effect, the simpler material becomes the firm foundation upon which he can build by adding more complex information.

One of the reasons why programmed instruction has been so successful is that it requires the active participation of the trainee in every frame. Unlike learning through lectures or in typical classrooms, the trainee simply cannot sit back passively and relax.

Because the material is presented in <u>small units</u>, any mistakes made are also small. Errors of this sort can be corrected and unlearned more readily than large ones. On the other hand, when the trainee is immediately informed that he has answered correctly, his self-confidence increases and, as a result, his learning ability is reinforced. Programmed instruction also allows the trainee to pace himself, to proceed as fast as he can. The slow learner is not rushed and the fast learner is not retarded. Properly administered, programmed instruction reduces training time by from 20 to 50 percent. The trainee tends to learn more and to retain knowledge longer than when he is taught by conventional methods. Moreover, the training is standardized.

However, programmed instruction does not solve all training problems. It is no substitute for practice or repetition in developing manual skills and it tends to impersonalize the relationship between trainer and trainee. It is also costly and difficult to develop; skilled professional technicians are required to produce a desirable product and the cost of developing such a program may therefore be prohibitive for a small company. On the other hand, if a program can be standardized for a job classification common to a large segment of the industry, the cost of the program per employee can be reduced considerably.

During the past few years, excellent programs have been developed and used in such areas as grocery price marking, bagging orders, training cashiers, instructing trainers and training managers and supervisors in certain managerial skills. The initial results of such programs have encouraged the rapid development of additional programs in other areas of supermarketing as well.

Summary

In comparison with the costs of a conventional osmosis-type training program, the application of sound training principles in a structured training program can, according to several supermarket chains, reduce training time and costs by from 50 to 75 percent. Such savings can be realized by teaching managerial skills to manager trainees as well as by training the new employee in manual tasks.

8 | Developing a Training Program

An Eastern chain had developed a fine cashier training program, but had no structured, formal program for training its other store employees. It set about determining its training priorities. By forecasting its employee needs, preparing a personnel inventory and establishing training requirements, the company discovered that its most pressing and immediate problem was to train apprentice meat cutters. Next, it needed to identify the meat policies and procedures to be taught and the teaching methods to be used. The problem was all the more complex because the large number of meat department policies that had been developed over the years were still incomplete, and current operating procedures varied from store to store.

The executives recognized that (1) a single Standard Practices Manual had to be developed which would spell out exactly what would be taught to new apprentices; and (2) before new apprentices could be trained, these practices had to become standard procedure in all stores or a trainee might be taught a job by one method and find the job performed differently at the store. The first step, then, was to establish standard meat practices. Next, these practices had to be taught to present meat managers and instituted throughout

116

the company. Unless these preliminary steps were taken, any attempt at instituting an apprentice meat cutter training program would probably end in failure.

Developing Standard Practices

The Standard Practices Manual is the heart of any training program. It contains those departmental policies and practices that have been adopted as standard operating procedure by the company. The Manual is the guideline for what is to be taught.

Table 1 shows the subjects covered in the Standard Practices Manuals of three different companies. Company A lists standard practice subjects for the produce department; Company B, for meat; and Company C, for groceries. The Standard Practices Manual developed by each of these three chains contains the approved operating procedures, or the "how to" guidelines, for performing each task in the respective departments. The department Standard Practices Manual is the trainer's guide in the development of a strong departmental training program.

Department trainers should be given the responsibility, or at least be assigned the task of guiding the development of a Standard Practices Manual. They should be directed and counseled by such persons as the company's department head for the operation; for example, the meat department trainer should develop the Standard Practices Manual for meat methods under the direction of the meat operations head. Trainers thus acquire a vested interest in the training program. Their confidence in their own abilities and, ultimately, the respect accorded them increase.

In addition to the trainer and the trainer's superiors, department specialists and key department managers should also contribute to the development of standard practices. One recommended procedure is for management to appoint a committee of key department personnel to develop the standard practices, with the trainer or department head acting as chairperson. It is often wise to include on the committee some of the older department managers who are likely to resist the effort to set up standard practices. Once such persons have had a hand in establishing the practices, they will find it difficult to contest them. It is always good practice to recognize and credit committee members who have participated in the development of a Standard Practices Manual. Printing the names of these people on the title page of the Manual will lend it prestige, strengthen its support and increase the authors' pride in their work.

TABLE 1

Subjects Included in Standard Practices Manuals of Three Companies

Company A Produce Department	Company B Meat Department	Company C Grocery Department
1. Customer relations and service	1. Packaging	1. Space allocation
2. Handling customer complaints	A. Tray sizes for various items	A. Formulas used
3. Ordering	B. Film sizes for various items	B. Controlling system
4. Receiving	C. Wrapping methods	C. Providing cushions
5. Storing	a. Hand wrapping	a. Private label items
6. Display set-up each morning	b. Machine wrapping	b. High profit, high turnover items
7. Retrimming	2. Pricing	c. Variation by product categories
8. Display layout	A. Code dating fresh meats	2. Required items
9. Rotation	B. Case life	3. Optional items
10. Merchandising principles	C. Tare weights	4. Ordering
11. Product handling and preparation (detailed explanation of handling policies for each of 53 key items)	D. Prepackaged merchandise	A. Schedule
	a. Code dating	B. Inventory and reserve stock
	b. Returning out-of-code items	C. Ordering principles
12. Product presentation (method of overwrapping, traying or bagging listed for each of 76 items)	3. Handling price changes	D. Advertised items
	4. Displaying	E. Promotions
	A. Rotation	F. New items
13. Pricing	B. Advertised items	G. Distributions from warehouse
14. Markdowns	C. Case line-up	5. Order transmission
15. Temperature and humidity control	D. Required items	6. Receiving
16. Safety	E. Seasonal items	A. Preparation of backroom
17. Sanitation and housekeeping	F. Optional items	B. Crew size and methods
18. Customer and employee security	5. Customer relations and complaints	C. Segregation by commodity group
19. Maintenance of equipment and supplies	6. Special orders	D. Specials, distributions, promotions
20. Salvage	A. Keeping variety of servings and item thickness on display	7. Pricing
21. Inventory procedures	B. Wrapping in film	
	7. Sanitation	

A. Effect on product life
B. Cleaning schedule and methods
8. Temperature and humidity control
A. Effect on product life
B. Cooler, cutting area, packaging area, display
9. Ordering
A. Advertised items
B. Principles and guidelines
C. Inventory control
D. Weekend carry-over
E. Primal cuts
10. Receiving
A. Back door security
B. Product inspection
C. Weighing
D. Handling invoices
E. Storage of product
11. Breaking
A. Beef forequarter primals
B. Beef hindquarter primals
C. Veal
D. Lamb
12. Retail cutting—boning and trimming
A. Beef
B. Veal
C. Lamb
D. Pork
E. Poultry
13. Ground meats
A. Importance
B. Fat-lean ratio
   a. Ground beef

A. Using shelf prices
B. Location of price books
C. Case opening and marking methods
8. Stocking
A. Full cases only
B. Methods
C. Product codes and rotation
9. Merchandising
A. Building mass displays
B. Use of end displays
C. Signs and posters
D. Advertised items
E. Use of rainchecks
10. Salvage
A. Breakdown methods
B. Preparation for pickup
C. Storage
D. Use of boxes at checkstands
11. Frozen foods
A. Responsibility assigned to one clerk
B. Temperature control laws
C. Care and handling
   a. Bacteria growth at various temperatures
   b. Receiving and storing
   c. Product rotation
   d. Maintenance of display cases
D. Inventory and ordering
E. Pulling merchandise for display
F. Case opening methods
G. Price marking methods

TABLE 1 (Cont.)

Subjects Included in *Standard Practices Manuals* of Three Companies

Company A Produce Department	Company B Meat Department	Company C Grocery Department
	b. Lean ground beef	H. Handling salvage
	c. Extra lean ground beef	I. Handling new items
	C. Regrinding discolored product	J. Handling discontinued items
	14. Merchandising profitable items	12. Price changes
	15. Rehandling (rewraps)	A. Methods and procedures
	A. Rates and losses	B. Responsibility
	B. Discolored product	13. Bottle returns
	C. Torn and leaky packages	A. Refund procedures and controls
	D. Policy on markdowns	B. Balancing refunds against receipts
	E. Conversion to profitable cuts	C. Segregation and storage
	16. Cutting tests	D. Policies relating to vendor pickups
	A. Method	14. Security
	B. Frequency	A. Direct deliveries
	17. Meat inventory	a. Receiving
	A. Frequency	b. Checking-in merchandise
	B. Procedure	B. Receiving area controls
	C. Computation of department gross profit	C. Checking-in warehouse merchandise
		D. Handling employee purchases
		15. Sanitation and housekeeping
		A. Cleaning floors and windows
		B. Cleaning shelves and merchandise
		16. Customer relations
		17. Customer complaints

The committee should agree on a set of practices that are superior to those used in any one store. As a result, it will become necessary to standardize practices throughout the chain, which will usually entail the retraining of present department managers in the new practices. If the practices are just committed to paper, they will often be ignored by veteran employees who are set in their ways. But if such experienced people are properly retrained, they will generally adopt the new procedures.

Selecting Trainers

A good trainer is not just someone who is productive. The individual must, above all, be a person who knows how to train people and who enjoys teaching. The store or department manager who consistently produces the best profit may be an ineffective trainer. A good trainer must know the subject, want and like to teach, possess the ability to plan and to handle details, be patient, articulate and have a sound knowledge of training principles and techniques.

Locating the individual who could become an effective trainer often requires a diligent search within a company. Comprehensive interviews are usually needed to bring to the surface those personal characteristics and aptitudes important to a good trainer. One frequent consequence of this search is that the rules of succession are broken. The individual with the most seniority or the person who is next in line for a promotion is frequently bypassed. Some of the older employees in the company may resent the selection of a younger person. Though management should be aware of these problems, it should nevertheless fill the trainer's slot with the most qualified person, no matter where the employee stands on the promotion list. The employee finally chosen for the job should be one who can earn the respect of managers throughout the company; one whose performance can erase the antagonism that the selection might have created.

Teaching Trainers

An official announcement of an appointment does not endow a person with the characteristics of a qualified trainer. Yet some chains which set aside twelve or fifteen months to produce qualified meat cutters expect that the employee selected as trainer be immediately proficient in teaching skills. Many months are required to learn the necessary skills of a topnotch department manager, and a qualified person must similarly study and learn to acquire the knowledge and skills of a good trainer.

The various trade associations of the supermarket industry periodically hold seminars or regional meetings during which they discuss the problems of training employees. Many of these meetings provide excellent opportunities for company trainers to gain up-to-date information on new training principles and techniques. But simple exposure to training courses, publications or industry meetings does not guarantee that a person will effectively apply what has been learned. Too often, newly-trained trainers who are not properly supervised revert to their own improvised methods and techniques. There is no substitute for capable guidance and direction to insure that the principles learned are properly applied.

Selecting Model Departments

The Eastern chain described at the beginning of this chapter developed three meat training programs: (1) a program to retrain present meat department managers according to the newly established standard practices; (2) an apprentice meat cutter training program; and (3) a training program for new meat department managers. The first and third programs were similar in content and scope, but several sections varied in emphasis and duration because veteran managers were already using many of the standard practices and, for them, the retraining program was largely a refresher course.

Once the need for these three programs had been established, the company had to devise methods to implement them. It decided, first of all, to organize five model meat departments, one in each district, serving about ten stores each. These would function as training centers for apprentices and new department managers. All standard practices would be installed in each of the five model departments. The retraining of department managers would be accomplished by running a series of nine three-hour classroom-type meetings, supplemented by demonstrations and group participation. The meetings, conducted by the trainer, would be held in the various model departments during late afternoon hours. It was further decided that the new apprentice and new department manager training programs would be delayed until all present department managers had been retrained.

In selecting the stores in which the meat departments would serve as models, the company considered (1) the physical space available for setting up classroom facilities; (2) the training space available in the cutting and packaging areas; (3) weekly department volume; (4) whether the attitude and capabilities of the manager in that meat department would make him a good trainer of apprentices; and (5) the attitude of the other employees in the meat department and in the store, including the store manager. Of course, the manager of the department which had the best physical facilities was not always selected as the trainer for that district. In two districts the training manager was transferred to the store with the best facilities. In a third district, the training manager was not moved to the store containing the best facilities only because he had personal reasons for remaining where he was. In the latter case, the chain preferred the manager who was best suited to train but who worked in a department with less than ideal physical facilities. The best person for the job, rather than the best location, was properly considered the more important factor in selecting a model department.

The model departments selected as training centers must first put into practice all the standard methods and procedures which will eventually be taught. These practices should become second nature by the time training commences. The implementation of standard practices in model departments before training begins also serves as a way of testing standard practices that might be questionable and provides the model department manager with an opportunity to judge the value and practicability of each standard practice.

Developing Training Outlines

A training outline is a step-by-step guide used by the instructor to conduct a training program. It is based on the material contained in the Standard Practices Manual, and includes, among other things, questions to be asked and demonstrations to be presented. Developing the training outline is the most time-consuming aspect of preparing a company training program.

The outline can take different forms, depending on the type of training to be conducted. For example, a classroom retraining program for department managers calls for an outline which will encourage verbal participation since, here, demonstration and task performance usually play a secondary part. A training outline for new department managers usually blends both verbal participation and practice in the techniques being taught. An on-the-job training program for apprentices, on the other hand, requires an outline primarily designed to teach manual tasks, indicating each successive step to be performed, key points of and the reason behind each step. It must provide for explanation, demonstration, performance and

TABLE 2
Program Outline for Retraining Produce Department Managers

Session 1:   Receiving and storing.
Rotation in cooler.
Ordering.
Inventory control.
Inventory procedures.

Session 2:   Product handling and preparation (53 key items).
Temperature and humidity control.

Session 3:   Product presentation (method of overwrapping, traying or bagging each of 76 items).
Pricing.
Markdowns.

Session 4:   Display layout.
Merchandising principles.
Rotation on display.

Session 5:   Display set-up each morning.
Retrimming.
Handling salvage.
Sanitation and housekeeping.

Session 6:   Customer relations and customer service.
Handling customer complaints.
Safety.
Customer and employee security.
Care and maintenance of equipment and supplies.

Session 7:   Principles and techniques of training employees.

Session 8:   Planning and organizing work.
Scheduling work and people.
Developing subordinates.
Correcting and disciplining employees.
Communicating with employees and customers.

follow-up. The outline should be studied and committed to memory; in no case should it be read word for word, as a lecture, since hardly anything is more monotonous than such an unrelieved presentation of information.

Manager Retraining Outlines. The first step in developing a manager retraining outline is to list the subjects to be taught. These topics should then be tentatively combined into related subjects which can be presented during classroom sessions of two to three hours. The Midwestern chain described as Company A in Table 1 prepared a tentative outline for the retraining of its produce department managers. Its outline not only covered all the subjects listed in the Standard Practices Manual, but it also accounted for key aspects of produce managing. (See Table 2.)

Next, each subject included in a session was divided into subtopics. The key points to be made and the reasons behind each point were listed for each subtopic. Descriptions of the appropriate training aids and the accompanying demonstrations were also included. Finally, a period was set aside for questions and discussion. A detailed outline of this sort paves the way for a smooth, fast-moving presentation and pinpoints the aids and demonstrations which would make the sessions more interesting and effective.

The outline of the first session, with a stress on its first two subjects, "Receiving and Storing" and "Rotation in Cooler" as developed by this Midwestern chain, is presented in Table 3. Special care had to be taken in preparing this outline because the students were experienced produce managers to whom much of the material was familiar.

TABLE 3
Outline of Session 1 of Retraining Program for Produce Department Managers in Company A
PART A
Reference Materials and Supplies for Session 1

Subject	Handout Material	Equipment and Supplies
Receiving and Storing	FMI[1] Guide 55 S.P.[2] Manual, pp. 11-12 USDA[3] Report 129	Notebooks with S.P. Manual, pencils, paper, blackboard, eraser, chalk, FBCs[4] 1-16, extension cord, slide projector and slides 1-2,
Rotation in Cooler	S.P. Manual, pp. 12-13	chairs, tables, rostrum, thumbtacks, hole punch, six empty orange crates
Ordering	FMI Guide 159 S.P. Manual, pp. 8-10 Produce Order Form P31[5]	
Inventory Control	S.P. Manual, pp. 76-77	

---

[1] Food Marketing Institute.
[2] Standard Practices.
[3] United States Department of Agriculture.
[4] Flannel Board Card, training aid.
[5] Form for produce department.

TABLE 3 (Cont.)

Inventory Procedures	Inventory Form Number P16
	S.P. Manual, pp. 78-79
Assignment	S.P. Manual, pp. 27-43
	Written reports of action
	taken

PART B

Introduction to First Session (3:00 PM)

I. Opening remarks on retraining program delivered by the vice-president of operations:
   A. Importance of program.
   B. Support by top management.
II. Statement of purposes and objectives by director of produce operations:
   A. Background of development of Standard Practices Manual.
   B. Purpose of retraining program.
   C. Need for department managers' participation, suggestions and cooperation.
   D. Importance of reading assignments and attendance.
   E. Importance of implementing standard practices as learned.
   F. Objectives of program:
      1. Lower employee turnover.
      2. Higher ratio of produce department sales.
      3. Reduction in shrinkage.
      4. Higher gross profit.
      5. Increased productivity.
      6. Improved manager bonuses.
III. Introduction to session plan by trainer:
   A. Subjects to be covered in Session 1:
      1. Receiving and storing (FBC 1).
      2. Rotation in cooler (FBC 2).
      3. Ordering (FBC 3).
      4. Inventory control (FBC 4).
      5. Inventory procedures (FBC 5).
   B. Details of procedure:
      1. Recommend trainees take notes.
      2. Interrupt for clarity or questions.
      3. Coffee break at 4:30 PM.
      4. Adjournment at 6:00 PM.

PART C

Development of First Two Subjects of Session 1

I. Receiving and Storing (FBC 1).
   A. Preparing for delivery (FBC 6):
      Key Points:
      1. Prepare cooler (FBC 7).
      2. Prepare backroom (FBC 8).

TABLE 3 (Cont.)

3. Prepare previous night for early morning delivery (FBC 9).

Question: What are the advantages of advance preparation for delivery?

Answers: (to be written on blackboard):

1. Prevents holding up of delivery truck.
2. Eliminates rehandling.
3. Eliminates delay in setting up rack.
4. Simplifies rotation.

Aids and Demonstrations:

Slides of good and poor preparations for delivery (slides 1 and 2).

B. Unloading methods:

Key Points and Reasons:

1. Eliminate double handling (FBC 10).
   a. Use conveyor or skids.
   b. Move large unit loads whenever possible in order to save time and effort and reduce spoilage.
2. Check each item against invoice (FBC 11).
   a. To insure receipt of merchandise charged to store.
3. Inspect for quality and condition (FBC 12).
   a. To protect the department against markdowns, shrinkage and spoilage.
4. Move directly to storage (FBC 13).
   a. To protect merchandise.
   b. To conform with rules of good housekeeping.

II. Rotation in Cooler (FBC 14).

A. Discussion organized around questions and answers:

1. *Question:* What is FIFO (FBC 15)?
   Answer: First, in, first out.
2. *Question:* What method of rotating merchandise do you now use in your cooler? (Rotation by position in cooler is common present method.)
   Answer: Each person in group should demonstrate method of position rotation, using the six empty orange crates.
3. *Question:* What is the weakness of position method? (Group should criticize methods demonstrated.)
   Answer: Rotation is not assured.
4. *Question:* What method of rotation will insure FIFO?
   Answer: Code date all merchandise (FBC 16).
5. *Question:* Why should all cooler merchandise be code dated?
   Answers: (to be written on blackboard):
   a. Insures opportunity for proper rotation.
   b. Insures use of off-quality merchandise first.
   c. Provides manager and supervision with proper controls.
   d. Eliminates double handling.

TABLE 3 (Cont.)

B. Demonstration:

1. Method of code dating:

Step	Key Points	Reasons Why
a. Set code date on band stamp.	a. Today's date.	a. Band stamp gives clearer impression than dating by hand.
b. Stamp code date.	b. Upper right hand corner, label facing out.	b. Saves searching for code date and item; label identifies item.
c. Stack cases in cooler.	c. Label and code date facing out.	c. Eliminates rehandling.

2. One manager should demonstrate code dating two orange crates, repeating the key points and reasons for each step; other trainees should criticize the performance.

Table 3 is divided into three parts. Part A enumerates the subjects to be covered in Session 1, the reference materials to be distributed and the equipment and supplies required for the session. Part B lists each point to be covered by the management representatives and by the trainer in the introduction of the course. Special reference is made to Session 1 and the outline indicates where training aids are to be used. Part C details the subtopics of "Receiving and Storing" and "Rotation in Cooler," the first two subjects in Session 1. The points to be covered under each subtopic and the reasons behind each point are listed. Training aids are used liberally and demonstrations are included when practical. The outline, which in some companies is referred to as the Trainer's Manual, is designed to involve the trainee in discussion and demonstration. The company's actual training outline, of course, also includes the sequential guidelines for the trainer to follow in conducting discussions and demonstrations for all five subjects of Session 1.

On-the-Job Clerk Training Outlines. An outline for on-the-job training of clerks should contain a detailed job breakdown showing the successive steps, key points of and the reasons behind each step. The type of material needed in such an outline is similar to the demonstration on code dating in Part C of Table 3 (II B). Such a short, three-step operation usually constitutes a minor part of a manager training program, but it forms the bulk of the outline material of an on-the-job training program for clerks. Because every manual job taught to clerks must be intricately detailed, preparing such an outline is a monumental task. The practices described in the outline must be instituted in all model departments and then in all stores of the chain; in order to be effective, the outline must also be updated as standard practices are altered. But once it is developed, the outline greatly simplifies the job of training and, because it becomes the guideline for the training of all new clerks for a given department, it insures standardization of training procedures and operating techniques throughout a company.

Assembling Training Aids

Training aids are essential in a classroom training program and are also extremely valuable in certain phases of on-the-job training. They simplify learning, rendering it more interesting and effective. People tend to better understand and remember what they see than what they hear; of course, they best comprehend and retain what they both see and hear. One of a trainer's major responsibilities is to hold the trainees' interest, not only their attention. Training aids help to accomplish that end. Figure 1 illustrates the placement of training aids in a classroom.

In teaching department managers and clerks, valuable training aids include charts, blackboards, flannel boards, enlarged drawings, opaque and overhead projectors, slides, filmstrips and, in certain situations, motion pictures. A flannel board is a plywood board covered with flannel to which sandpaper-backed preprinted cards will adhere. It is an inexpensive but highly efficient substitute for a blackboard. Preprinted cards are usually more legible than the trainer's writing, and more important, they are made up in advance of the training session and can be specially designed to reinforce a point. They also save time because the trainer does not need to write on the blackboard. Moreover, the trainer can better hold the trainee's attention by facing the class instead of turning his or her back to write on the board. One supermarket trainer found that 27 percent of the training period was spent writing on the blackboard. By switching to flannel boards, the time required to cover the same material was reduced to 4 percent of total session time. For small groups, prepared flip charts are also useful, particularly when referring to tables, graphs or enlarged drawings.

The use of photographic slides frequently provides the most effective demonstrations. Meat trainers who use color slides of various meat cuts to illustrate the effects of sanitation and temperature controls on product life find that the color comparisons are quite dramatic and make the point far better than verbal explanations alone. There are numerous occasions when slides or filmstrips can

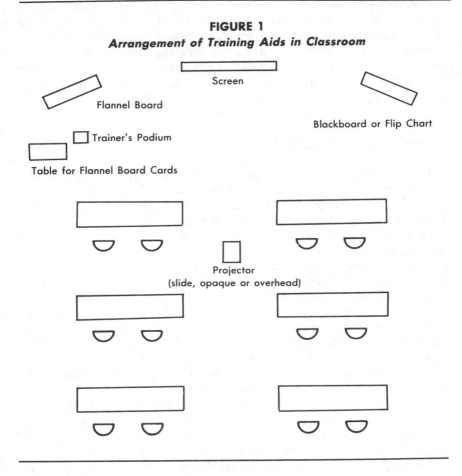

FIGURE 1
Arrangement of Training Aids in Classroom

be imaginatively used to enliven a training session. Slides are not very expensive and any competent amateur photographer can take pictures that are good enough to use in a 35 mm. slide projector. An opaque projector reflects blow-ups of printed material. An overhead projector, which reflects transparencies (up to 8½" 11") on a screen, is particularly useful when tables, forms, charts and layouts are explained. The advantage of transparencies is that the trainer can write on them when their reflections are projected. The transparency can be imprinted in advance with the form or chart to be explained; when it is shown on the screen, the trainer can fill in each entry, explain each step as it is made, draw connecting lines or otherwise improve and expand upon the printed material.

Good films, properly presented, can serve as very effective training aids. They capture the audience's attention and provide a change in routine. But they must be used judiciously because they can also be ineffective as well as costly. Because a trainee often considers movies a diversion, extra precautions should be taken to insure that a training film produces its desired results. Before the film is run, the trainee should be told its purpose and what to look for. A follow-up discussion should be developed to reveal whether or not the movie has been successful in accomplishing its objectives.

But training aids are never substitutes for training. Indeed, they increase the need for detailed and thorough planning because their use must be rehearsed in advance of each session. Lack of preparation can not only damage the presentation; it can also prove embarrassing to the trainer.

One trainer used many flannel boards during his first presentation. Suddenly, with several cards remaining, he ran out of board space. His face became red, he began to perspire and his whole presentation collapsed. After a few minutes of self-conscious stammering, unrelieved by an attempt at self-mocking humor, he finally announced a coffee break during which he collected himself. Though he had rehearsed the presentation, he had not run through the motions with the training aids. He would not have experienced such humiliation had he practiced using the aids beforehand.

Establishing Training Periods

A classroom training session should last a maximum of four hours, with at least one fifteen minute break near the middle. After four hours, the average trainee tends to become tired and the individual's attention wanders. The trainee is likely to become more interested in the hour that the session is scheduled to end than in the material being presented.

Four hours represent an ideal maximum only when the most favorable conditions exist; for instance, in the case of a retraining program where most of the material is familiar to the trainee. More training time is needed to present unfamiliar material and, moreover, such information should be presented in smaller doses. The material covered in a four-hour session with experienced department managers may require three or even four two-hour training sessions with department manager trainees.

The time interval between classroom training sessions is also important. A retraining program for department managers requiring ten four-hour sessions, for example, will be far more effective if the classes are scheduled a week apart than if they are set up every day or every other day. By spreading training over a longer period, pupils can implement and practice the various policies and procedures they are taught and also have time to assimilate the information. Of course, the more unfamiliar the material, the more important it is that classroom training schedules be broken up by practice periods.

Speed and Skill

On-the-job training for manual tasks demands frequent practice sessions too. A trainee must be given sufficient practice time to learn one task thoroughly and to be completely skilled at it before proceeding to the next. Skill means the ability to follow a motion pattern or procedure correctly and repeatedly, without hesitation or false movement. Skill is not synonymous with speed. Speed increases with practice, but skill generally does not. A person's productivity is the product of skill and speed. It takes more time for a person to achieve maximum speed than to become skillful.

Both skill and speed can be lost through lack of practice. An apprentice meat cutter who has acquired the skill of breaking beef primals will lose that skill without periodic practice. Therefore, every well-constructed training program must include flexible practice periods which will allow the trainee to retain the learned skill.

The optimum balance between instruction and practice is determined by the amount of time required to insure that the learned skill is retained. Since trainees differ in their abilities to learn and retain a skill, a flexible balance between instruction and practice must be established.

A training program which is properly designed and implemented can save thousands of dollars in training costs each year in the typical supermarket. Several supermarket executives have been amazed and pleased to learn that by applying modern training principles and techniques and by maintaining the proper balance between instruction and practice, they have been able to reduce training time and costs from 50 to 75 percent.

Over-Exposure

Learning through osmosis is a poor substitute for a planned, structured training program. More time is required for employees trained through osmosis to become exposed to the total task; and even when they have succeeded at learning the mechanics of a complete job, they will seldom understand the reasons behind each step. Moreover, since osmosis training rarely provides for measuring performance, neither the employee nor the superior can determine when the job has been learned—in other words, when the skill has been acquired. Osmosis, therefore, almost invariably leads to over-training or over-exposure.

For example, an apprentice meat cutter who is first taught to grind beef in the cooler, cut up fryers and clean up the meat department, too often performs only these duties during the first six months on the job because that is what the meat department manager did as an apprentice. Not only is such a procedure a waste of time, but it is also discouraging. Talented young people who want to learn the meat business and get ahead will not stay around long if they feel they are being asked to do the dirty work in the department for an excessive amount of time. Nevertheless, over-exposing newcomers is still common practice throughout the supermarket industry. The newest employee in any department is often initially assigned the dirty work and asked to do that work for longer than is necessary to learn the skill. Over-exposure, the inevitable result of osmosis training, leads to poor productivity, high training costs, and, perhaps most important, high employee turnover.

Modern training programs have been repeatedly damaged by stubborn and unyielding tradition. For years, unions have contended that it takes 24, 30 or 36 months for a new apprentice to become a journeyman meat cutter. That is ludicrous. Imagine needing two to three years to learn that job when, during WW II, the U.S. was able to turn farm plowboys into jet pilots in nine months or less. No sensible person could possibly believe that learning to cut meat should take twice or three times as long as learning to pilot a jet plane; but the tight grasp of tradition is hard to shake loose. To many people it is inconceivable that a new and untrained person can become a skilled meat cutter in three months, a skilled produce trimmer or grocery stock clerk in two weeks, or a skilled meat wrapper in three days. It is ironic that these training periods are often considered too short by the very companies that successfully conduct two- or three-day centralized cashier training programs to qualify a trainee to operate an electronic register. Yet a cashier's job is far more complex than that of the meat wrapper who, according to these companies, cannot be trained in three days. Effective central cashier training programs are properly designed to equip the trainee with the skill required of the cashier, but not with the necessary cashier speed. The speed must be acquired through practice on the job.

A drastic reduction in training time is possible when modern training principles and techniques are put into effect. Most companies follow these principles and techniques in training cashiers centrally far better than they do in training other employees on the job. A cashier trainer is usually a far more proficient and professional trainer than a store manager, department manager or clerk at store level who has had no formal background in training.

Learning Curves

Once training principles and techniques have been adopted, it is possible to measure individual performance at various stages of the training cycle and, on the basis of these measurements, to develop learning curves for various jobs. These curves can then be used as a basis for judging the learning progress and ability of any new trainee, and for identifying the point at which the average trainee reaches the level of the average experienced employee.

One company discovered that the productivity of its average experienced meat wrapper, using soft film, was 220 packages per hour over an eight hour day, and that the typical wrapper trainee required two weeks of osmosis learning to reach this level of productivity. The average number of packages wrapped per hour by fifteen trainees during the first two weeks on the job was as follows:

Hours Completed	Average Number of Packages Wrapped per Hour
5 hours	39
10 hours	67
20 hours	109
30 hours	144
40 hours	170
50 hours	189
60 hours	203
70 hours	213
80 hours	220

These figures are averages based on the progress of fast and slow learners, as well as of learners who have had some previous experience in other work requiring manual dexterity. Temporary plateaus were reached by most trainees at various points in the two-week learning period. There were considerable differences in trainee efficiency: three trainees were producing in excess of 250 packages per hour at the end of the two-week period; two others had failed to reach 180 by that time.

Figure 2 is the learning curve plotted by the company to evaluate the progress of its fifteen meat wrapper trainees during its conventional on-the-job training period. The slope of the learning curve in Figure 2 is rather typical; performance speed increases rapidly during the first few hours, then gradually tapers off.

A New Training Program for Meat Wrappers

After having analyzed the variations in the learning speeds of these fifteen meat wrappers trained through osmosis, the company decided to develop a meat wrapper training program by employing the modern techniques it was already using in its new meat cutter training program. First it studied the methods employed by its better wrappers, from which it learned the best ways to wrap various meat cuts. Then it broke the job down into its component parts, listing the key points of and reasons behind each step. The training program it eventually devised included four hours of explanation, demonstration, performance and follow-up by the company meat trainer, a discussion of film costs and conservation, and intermittent follow-up by the meat department manager over the next sixteen hours. During the following three-month period, thirteen new wrapper trainees, who were judged to be equal in ability to the fifteen previously trained through osmosis, were put through the program.

Figure 3 shows the learning curve based on the performance of the thirteen new trainees. They achieved the average production rate of 220 packages per hour for experienced wrappers after only 22 hours of training and practice instead of the eighty hours required by the fifteen trained through osmosis. After 35 hours, the average trainee in this group wrapped 258 packages per hour—17 percent higher than the previous standard for experienced wrappers.

These successful results were due to the (1) standardization of an improved wrapping method and (2) the change in training techniques, though it was not possible to determine the individual contribution of each of these causes to the final outcome. Later retraining of experienced wrappers, which was based on the improved standard methods, successfully raised the productivity of most of these wrappers to 258 packages per hour, which subsequently became the new performance standard for this company. The company, whose meat departments averaged $33,000 per week in sales, claimed that the new training program produced skilled wrappers

FIGURE 2
*Average Learning Curve for Fifteen Meat Wrapper Trainees
Trained by Conventional Methods*

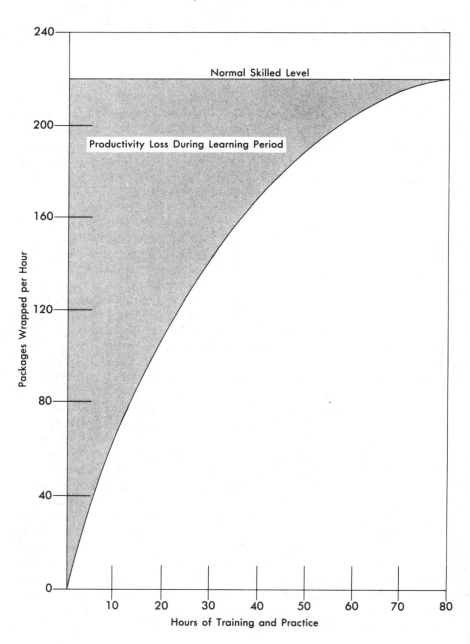

FIGURE 3
*Average Learning Curve for Thirteen Meat Wrapper Trainees
Trained by Improved Training Methods*

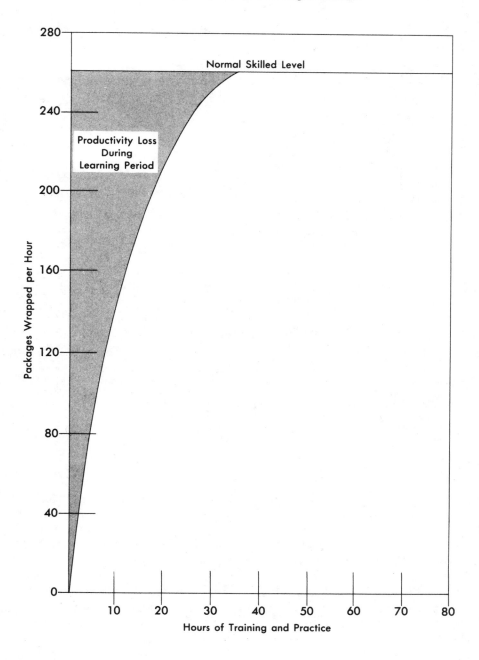

TABLE 4

Comparison of the Production and Costs of Two Meat Wrapper Training Programs

	Before New Training Program	After New Training Program
1. Average packages wrapped per hour by experienced wrapper:	220	258
2. Average packages wrapped per hour by trainee:		
A. During first week on the job:	103	189
B. During second week on the job:	200	258
3. Average hours of work produced in forty hours:[1]		
A. During first week on the job:	18.7[2]	29.3[3]
B. During second week on the job:	36.4[4]	40.0[5]
4. Average hours of work produced during first two weeks on the job:	55.1	69.3
5. Labor-hours of production lost during first two weeks on the job:	24.9	10.7
6. Cost of production loss during first two weeks on the job at $7.00 per hour:	$174.30	$74.90
7. Savings per trainee credited to new training program:		$99.40

[1] Computed on the basis of the average hourly production of an experienced wrapper. Before the new training program, 220 packages per hour equalled one hour's production; after the new training program, 258 packages per hour equalled one hour's production.
[2] Computed by dividing 2A (103) by 1 (220), multiplied by forty hours.
[3] Computed by dividing 2A (189) by 1 (258), multiplied by forty hours.
[4] Computed by dividing 2B (200) by 1 (220), multiplied by forty hours.
[5] Computed by dividing 2B (258) by 1 (258), multiplied by forty hours.

in twenty hours and fully qualified wrappers with average productivity in 35 hours.

The new training program for meat wrappers reduced the training period by 56 percent. Table 4 summarizes the production and the training costs before and after the development of the new program.

An unanticipated advantage of the new training program was discovered when three of the thirteen wrappers were assigned to a new store just prior to its opening. For the first few months, that store's film costs were lower than in other stores. Though these lower costs were initially thought to be the result of the product mix, tests proved that the wrappers were simply doing a better job of selecting optimum roll widths and controlling film overlap and waste. Ultimately, the training program was also credited with reducing film costs by 13 percent throughout the company. The many satisfying results of this training program for meat wrappers more than compensated for the planning, effort and money that were put into it.

Shorter Training Time

Thus, an effective training program for almost any job in the supermarket industry can cut training time by at least half, with a corresponding gain in productivity. As the industry gives up its outmoded traditions in favor of modern and efficient training techniques, it will turn out more productive and skilled employees in what today seem to be incredibly short training periods. Several companies have already proved that short training periods are practical and should therefore become commonplace in the near future:

Job	Length of Typical Learning Period Using Conventional (Osmosis) Techniques	Length of Learning Period Using Modern Training Techniques
Apprentice meat cutter	12-18 months	3-4 months
Meat wrapper	2-4 weeks	8-12 hours
Produce trimmer	4-6 weeks	3-4 days
Experienced clerk to department manager	2-3 months	3-4 weeks

When a trainee can perform a task correctly and repeatedly, without hesitation or false movement, he has become skilled. At this point, he should be assigned to a store as a trained, though not yet fully productive employee. He still needs close supervision by his immediate superior. Once a skill is acquired, frequent repetition will result in a gradual increase in productivity.

Records of the trainee's performance should be maintained during the entire learning period so that both the trainer and the trainee can compare his performance against the norms of each level of training. Records also allow the trainee to set his own performance goals and help the trainer to establish training objectives and budgets.

Scheduling Retraining Sessions

Retraining experienced department or store managers calls for a different program from the one required for the training of new department or store managers. When scheduling retraining sessions for experienced department managers, it is wise to provide for the participation of the store manager, supervisor and department specialist because anyone who has authority over the department manager must also be well-versed in the department's standard practices. Therefore, all superiors who are active in the supervision of the department, including the store manager, should sit in on department manager retraining programs. By attending retraining meetings with the department manager, they are exposed to the same material, and the possibility of misunderstanding and disagreement is reduced.

As previously stated, retraining programs for department managers should be scheduled over several weeks because a person can absorb only a certain amount of material in a given period of time. In addition, the trainee needs time to prepare for the sessions and to implement what has been learned. A Standard Practices Manual should be distributed to each department manager before the retraining begins. The Manual should contain lists of reference materials relating to the subjects to be discussed. Before each session, the trainee should be asked to study the standard practices and to read the materials pertinent to the scheduled subject.

Any department manager retraining program should be scheduled for a maximum of two four-hour sessions a week, which should be conducted on company time. Most chains have found it advisable to schedule these sessions on afternoons when store sales or department work loads tend to be low. Department manager retraining programs are usually of the classroom type with demonstrations worked in, and classroom facilities can be built into the backroom or mezzanine of a store. But demonstrations may also be conducted in the processing area of the model department store during the late afternoon, when most production work has been completed, without interfering with routine departmental activities. No more than 25 people should attend a retraining session, though an ideal class would be composed of fifteen persons.

Training New Managers

A training program designed to teach the department manager's job to an experienced clerk or an assistant department manager usually consists of a combination of classroom and on-the-job training. Most companies find that by slightly revising their department manager retraining programs, they can adapt them to the training of new department managers. But whereas a retraining program is usually intermittent and scheduled over several weeks, training of new department managers should be continuous. The trainees should spend all of their time in training until they become skilled.

Follow-Up

A training program is in danger of falling apart if it does not provide for careful follow-up. A few years ago, a Western chain developed a program for training new grocery clerks which included excellent trainers, well-developed standard practices and a successful retraining program for experienced department managers and clerks. What the program lacked was a follow-up plan. Chain executives simply assumed that once the training period was completed all standard practices would automatically be instituted. However, six months after training had ended, they learned that only 25 percent of the new standard practices were actually followed in stores other than those in which model departments had been established. In contrast, another chain that had developed an effective follow-up plan to reinforce its retraining program for meat department managers, discovered that six months after the completion of its program more than 85 percent of its new standard practices were in use in all stores.

Line managers and supervisors who have direct responsibility for a particular operation must be charged with performing follow-up work. Thus, the reinforcement of standard practices taught to a grocery clerk is the follow-up responsibility of the grocery department manager and, in turn, of the store manager. Follow-up on department manager training is the obligation of the store manager, as well as of the store manager's supervisor or the department specialist.

Trainers must also participate in the follow-up program. Because they usually fill staff positions with no line authority, they should see to it that a major part of their time, up to perhaps 50 percent, is spent working with, and through, managers and supervisors. They should discover for themselves the problems their trainees encounter when assigned to stores and the degree to which they adhere to established practices and procedures. Only by visiting the stores can a trainer identify areas of weakness that should be corrected by revisions in the training program. Trainees who are often reluctant to ask questions of their managers because of their fear that they may appear stupid, can also be spoken to privately and encouraged to ask their questions during the follow-up visit of a trainer. Follow-up should begin right after the first training session, as trainers observe their trainees on the job between meetings. After training is completed, they should periodically follow-up on each of their former trainees.

There are numerous techniques for obtaining follow-up information from store managers or supervisors. One of the most commonly used devices is a check list which enables the trainer to identify those stores that are following major standard practices and those that are not. Check lists can be useful, but only if they are based on personal observation and are completely accurate.

Tables 5 and 6 are two check lists used by one company to follow-up on its grocery and meat training programs. Once a month the field supervisor must complete the check list for each store in his or her district, based on personal observation, and send the completed form to the director of store operations. The latter, in a meeting of all field supervisors, reviews the status of follow-up in each store and, wherever necessary, devises corrective measures.

Setting Goals and Evaluating the Training Program

The trainer should always set tangible goals which can be accomplished by a specific date. Training costs are considerable and management is entitled to know whether its investment is producing results. The only valid way to determine the effect of a training program is to evaluate its results in terms of whether the program's goals have been achieved.

After the standard practices had been set and before training had started, one company investigated a representative sample of stores to determine how frequently each standard practice was being followed. The company then established training goals, including specific improvements in supply costs, gross profit and the ratio of meat sales to total store sales, as well as an increase in conformity to standard practices. Two more investigations conducted six and twelve months after training revealed that the goals had been reached. The improvement was attributed to the success of the training program.

Another way to evaluate the effectiveness of training is to administer tests. Tests are particularly useful in a classroom-type program for the training or retraining of department managers. Written tests on the material covered during the previous session should be ad-

TABLE 5
Supervisor's Grocery Check List

Name _____   Month _____   Date _____

Store Number: _____

Front-End Scheduling										
1. Store adjusts and re-schedules extra-hours weekly to meet forecast volume										
2. Employees scheduled according to daily sales pattern										
Shelf Allocation										
1. Allocation book kept up-to-date										
2. Shelf tags in place and correct										
3. New items worked onto shelf and tagged										
4. Discontinued items pulled when low or when space needed										
5. Allocation adjusted when items are repeatedly out-of-stock										
6. Shelf out-of-stock filled with high profit, fast turnover merchandise										

Ordering
1. Works from shelf to book
2. Uses correct method in phoning in order
3. Orders only when full case fits, except Class A items*

Backroom Management
1. Backroom area assigned and labeled into four categories
2. Inventory worked up before each order is written
3. Inventory on past promotions and errors in excess of thirty days' supply returned to warehouse (unopened cases only)

Miscellaneous
1. Store checks Night Crew Production Report for errors and takes corrective action
2. Care and charging of straddle-stackers observed

*Class A: Fast moving items (5+ cases/week).

TABLE 6

Supervisor's Meat Department Check List

Name _____   Month _____   Date _____

Store Number: _____

Display Area									
1. Area clean									
2. All products fresh—no discolored meat									
3. All products in code									
4. Packages wrapped correctly									
5. No bloody packages									
6. All required items on display									
7. No bare spots in case									
8. Packages variable in number and weight									
9. All items trimmed to specifications									
10. Ground beef fat content correct									
11. Freezer case—adequate selection—no freezer burn items									
12. Packaged deli-case adequately stocked									
13. Ad items properly displayed									

14. Sanitation standards met												
Processing Room												
1. No meat off refrigeration unless someone working on it												
2. Safety rules observed												
3. Sanitation schedule followed												
4. Refrigeration okay and air vents open												
Cooler and Storage Area												
1. No odds and ends												
2. No discolored trimming or pre-ground meat in chopper or lugs												
3. Product dated and rotated and in-code												
4. No pull backs in cooler												
5. Cooler and chopper sanitation okay												
Evaluation (check one)												
1. Excellent—no improvement needed												
2. Good—minor improvement necessary— no assistance required												
3. Fair—minor improvement necessary— needs help of specialist												
4. Poor—major improvement necessary												

ministered at the beginning of a session. Such examinations measure the amount of information retained by the trainee and serve to encourage the trainee to take notes during the session, to study those notes and to review the reading assignments. Written tests are also valuable to the trainer; a question missed by many trainees indicates that the trainer must re-emphasize or re-explain the troublesome point. In one company, meat department managers as well as their supervisors and store managers were scheduled to participate in a meat department manager retraining program. Everyone was warned in advance that a written evaluation would be given at the beginning of each session and, at the first session, the trainer urged each person to take notes and to prepare the assignments. Only the store managers and supervisors, who recognized their own lack of knowledge and were eager to learn something new, took the trainer's advice, while many of the meat managers were convinced they knew all the answers.

At the beginning of the second session, a written examination was given on the subjects covered during the first meeting. All present were surprised to learn that the supervisors and store managers scored much higher than the meat department managers. Attitudes changed rapidly and drastically, as meat department managers became furious note-takers.

Written evaluations should be carefully designed. Questions should be limited to important topics and should not be tricky. They should be sufficiently difficult so that only a very small percentage of the trainees receive a perfect score, yet not so difficult that they cause most trainees to fail. The trainer should return the test to the trainees during follow-up rounds to various stores, and should privately discuss problems or misunderstandings identified by incorrect answers. Results of tests should become permanent parts of an employee's personnel file, and should be among the many factors that are considered when openings occur and promotions are made.

Training should always have a measurable beneficial effect on employee turnover and productivity. But there are other areas in which goals can be set and the effect of training measured. Some training programs are specifically designed to improve various controllable costs; others to increase gross profit, or department sales and the ratio of department sales to total store sales; still others, to reduce pilferage and shrinkage. In every case, specific achievable goals should be set so that training costs can be justified and training results evaluated.

9 | Training Managers

It was late Friday afternoon and Harry Palmer, meat cutter at Store 16, was worried. His store manager had just told him that the supervisor was coming by to see him. The manager did not know what was up; the manager only knew that the supervisor wanted to talk to Harry.

When the supervisor arrived, he smiled broadly and, in the presence of the store manager, said: "Harry, we've been watching you pretty closely and we're impressed. You've been with us three years now and we believe you're ready for a department of your own. So starting next Monday morning, you'll be our meat manager at Store 11. You might stop by there tomorrow and have a look around."

Many similar discussions occur daily in supermarkets across the country. One day an employee is a cutter, a trimmer or a stock clerk, responsible only for his own work, and the next day he is a manager, accountable for the work of others. He is promoted because he has a good record and is well-liked by fellow workers and superiors. Suddenly, he must assume the burdens of a leader. His product knowledge and mechanical skills will no longer suffice. He is now responsible for the work of others.

Unfortunately, in most cases the new manager will be given neither training nor guidance in managerial skills. He will be left to sink or swim on his own. If he succeeds, it will only be because he is competing against managers who have also had no training in managerial skills. Indeed, it is ironic that union stewards in many companies are far better trained in modern management techniques than department or store managers or field supervisors. Many unions train their stewards in management, but many chains do not teach their own managers how to manage.

Management Training Is Growing

Almost every month, some trade publication reports that a highly respected supermarket chain has increased the responsibility and authority of its store managers which, according to industrial psychologists, is the way to attract and hold capable people and to improve store performance. Such increased responsibility must be accompanied by a program designed to train these individuals in managerial skills. Moreover, not only must new managers be trained, but especially as supermarket companies decentralize and give more responsibility to their managers, present managers must be retained.

In the late sixties, an AMA study concluded that more than 70 percent of all American companies were training their managers in managerial skills. In 1930, this figure was only 34 percent. Although supermarket companies lagged behind, this significant change indicates that "management no longer regards the supervisor as an exalted subordinate, but a first line manager with management responsibilities."[1] This progress also reflects the recognition that managerial skills are acquired, not inborn; that such skills are obtained through planned learning and practice, not happenstance, and not by attending a one-week management training seminar or a four-year college training course. Though such programs can be of great value, total dependence on them would be a mistake.

The sooner training and practice begin, the sooner is competence acquired. Training in managerial skills should be included as a basic part of a department manager's training program, to prepare the ground for advancement to store manager. The department manager must be given the authority to manage as well as the opportunity to learn from mistakes. In too many companies, a department

[1] "The Basic Principles of Supervisory Management" (American Management Association, 1968).

manager's authority is severely restricted, and he or she receives little or no management training. Such a person can only be ill-prepared for advancement.

Lack of Training Is Costly

Training in managerial skills requires a classroom-type setting, which can be costly. But the absence of managerial skills is even costlier and is reflected in such expensive ways as reduced sales and profit, high inventory shrinkage, high manager and employee turnover, low morale, interpersonal conflicts, low productivity and lack of motivation.

After having been taught managerial skills in the classroom, the trainee must be given the opportunity to practice. The difficulty is not to acquire knowledge of good managerial techniques but, rather, to develop skills through experience in using the techniques.

Much creative work has been done in the development of manager training programs, but a great deal remains to be done, especially by supermarket companies and associations. Nevertheless, there already are a great many excellent training programs, training aids and source materials available today from business associations, universities and food suppliers. Some of these will be discussed later in the chapter.

What Is a Manager?

The first step in establishing an effective training program for managers is to define the manager's responsibilities and functions. For too long, the supermarket industry has operated under the false premise that experience and a willingness to perform menial work will qualify a person for managerial responsibility. Even today, many supermarket companies have not yet really decided what they want in a manager.

Should a department manager be a skilled meat cutter who can carry out the orders of the store manager, meat specialist or district manager? Should a department manager be a talented produce clerk or grocery stock clerk who can execute the orders of the store manager or supervisor? Or, rather should a department manager be a person who can plan and organize his or her work and the work of others, who can develop and supervise subordinates?

If a manager is one who should carry out the orders of others, then the training program should concentrate on teaching the manager how to obey. If, on the other hand, the individual should be a person who can manage a department and participate in decision making, then the training program must be far more complex and sophisticated.

Managerial Skills

Therefore, before proceeding to a detailed discussion of manager training programs, it is necessary to identify those skills required for effective management. A good manager, then, whether he runs a department or an entire store must (1) be familiar with the department's and/or the store's operation; and (2) acquire the four managerial skills of planning, organizing, supervising and controlling.

Specific operational knowledge is more important to the department manager than to the manager at a higher level in the company. The further removed a manager is from an operation, the less the manager needs to know about its details and the more general supervisory skills he must possess. The following illustration indicates how the requirements differ as the manager's responsibilities increase.

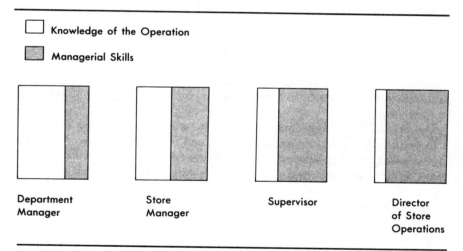

☐ Knowledge of the Operation

▨ Managerial Skills

| Department Manager | Store Manager | Supervisor | Director of Store Operations |

The differences in the roles of the various managers may be highlighted by an example. A produce manager had been receiving week-long customer complaints about the quality of the store's iceberg lettuce. The current crop just happened to be bad and the front office knew about it. The store manager had received a few complaints too, but not nearly as many as the produce manager. The problem was one that the produce manager had to cope with, based on knowledge of the operation. The produce manager might have cut back on the displays of iceberg lettuce until its quality improved and featured Boston or Romaine lettuce instead, or might have reduced lettuce space and featured other items. One thing, however, is certain: the store supervisor and director of store operations cannot be intimately acquainted with all the problems of this particular store; they know far less about the extent of customer complaints and their effect on sales than does the person at the point of sale—the produce manager.

The principles involved in the four skills of planning, organizing, supervising and controlling, however, do not vary by management level. The same basic principles apply to a department manager as to his or her store manager or supervisor, or even to the company president. The difference is just in degree. Whereas the company president may spend 90 or 95 percent of his time using management skills, the department manager may devote only 15 to 20 percent of his time applying those skills. Thus, department and store managers differ in the extent to which they need to know the operation, but they must both possess the four managerial skills of planning, organizing, supervising and controlling.

Details of Operation

The essentials of operations which should be familiar to all managers, but more familiar to department managers, may be classified in four groups:

1. *Products:* including sources, seasonality, quality, perishability, movement, pricing and markup.

2. *Standard practices:* including equipment, tools and supplies; methods of ordering, receiving, processing, packaging, rotation, price changing, sanitation, temperature control, safety, maintenance and security.

3. *Merchandising:* including impulse buying, customer traffic patterns, item profitability, product grouping, product presentation, space allocation, in-store merchandising, tie-in merchandising, inter-department merchandising, merchandising private or controlled label items, ethnic items, advertised items, promotional items, new items, seasonal items, discontinued and distress items.

4. *Service operations:* including an overall understanding of the company's service arm functions which relate to the department's or

store's operation (buying, warehousing, transportation, advertising, accounting, personnel and so forth).

Even companies with carefully planned training programs are likely to promote to department manager an employee who lacks knowledge of standard practices, merchandising and service operations and whose product knowledge is also deficient. In the training of department managers, the primary emphasis should be on operational details.

Product Knowledge. Every department manager should be knowledgeable about product source, quality, seasonality, perishability and movement, as well as about markup and item price ranges and profitability. Product knowledge is extremely important to department managers who are held accountable for customer relations, merchandising practices and gross profit.

Managers must know their products if they are to discuss serving portions, cooking suggestions and menu ideas with their customers. They will gain the confidence of their customers if they can offer helpful suggestions and speak with authority about new or unusual products in their departments. Product knowledge is important from a merchandising point of view in preparing tie-in displays, seasonal promotions and special displays.

Managers who are held responsible for gross profit in their departments must be taught the basics of cost and markup. These managers should be given markup and sales figures for their departments so that they can plan and make merchandising adjustments when necessary. Any department manager training program must include training in or review of all aspects of product knowledge.

Standard Practices. Except in rare instances, department manager trainees are generally not familiar with all the standard practices of the department. Even in companies with outstanding clerk and manager training programs, it is unusual to find a department where all standard practices are followed to the letter. Therefore, a department manager training program must include a review of all standard departmental practices.

Though a department manager is usually highly skilled in the performance of manual jobs, such skill is not vital to his success as a manager. He must, of course, know how each job is properly performed and the expected level of performance. But to manage effectively, he does not have to be capable of performing the job at a highly skilled level himself. Conversely, a person highly skilled in the performance of one or more manual tasks will not necessarily make a good manager.

Merchandising.   The subject of merchandising is neglected in most department manager training programs. The vast differences in merchandising capabilities of various stores and companies around the country can be traced, in many instances, to the almost complete absence of merchandising training programs.

A merchandising training program for any single department can be developed in five steps, each of which should be painstakingly detailed and followed:

1. The merchandising knowledge and skills that the company expects of every trained department manager must be identified.

2. The merchandising principles and the standard practices of the department must be identified and incorporated into a single Standard Practices Manual.

3. A program in which the trainee will grasp these principles and standard practices must be constructed.

4. Opportunities for the trainee to apply the principles and standard practices in the day-to-day operation of the department must be provided.

5. A follow-up system to assure successful application of principles and standard practices must be devised.

Step 1: One company properly began by identifying the merchandising knowledge and skills it required of grocery department managers. It used these requirements as the skeleton on which it built a merchandising training program for grocery department managers. Under Step 1 it listed the following:

A.   Familiarity with the research relating to impulse buying, customer traffic patterns and item profitability, conducted by du Pont, the United States Department of Agriculture, Purdue University, McKinsey and others.

B.   An understanding of how these studies influence the location of items and commodity groups with respect to aisle and shelf assignment in the store.

C.   A knowledge of space allocation and its influence on item movement, overstocks, out-of-stocks, productivity and labor costs.

D.   An understanding of the limits of the department manager's authority and responsibility with regard to in-store merchandising.

E. A knowledge of when, where and how to build mass displays that sell merchandise at a profit, and how to police and maintain these displays.

F. A knowledge of how to merchandise all items, including advertised, promotional, new, private label, ethnic, seasonal, discontinued and distress items.

G. An understanding of the value of tie-in merchandising and inter-department merchandising.

H. A knowledge of the value and techniques of using point-of-sale materials, including signs, shelf talkers and so forth.

I. An understanding of when, where and how to use dump displays, shelf extenders and special aisle displays.

J. A realization of the importance of rotation of perishable and semi-perishable items.

K. A knowledge of how to project and evaluate the results of the merchandising plans that are implemented.

L. An understanding of how to apply merchandising principles to dry groceries, dairy, frozen foods, health and beauty aids, housewares and candy items.

M. The capability of teaching others how to merchandise.

N. A knowledge of how to maintain records of special promotions and in-store merchandising efforts; of how to use these data to improve future performance.

Step 2: After specifying these as the required merchandising knowledge and skills of a grocery department manager, the company set about identifying the specific merchandising principles (the first part of Step 2) related to each of the following:

A. Product grouping.
B. Product presentation.
C. Space allocation.
D. In-store merchandising.
E. Tie-in merchandising.
F. Inter-department merchandising.
G. Merchandising items which are advertised, promotional, private label or controlled label, ethnic, seasonal, new, discontinued or distress.

Next, the company spelled out the limits of authority and responsibility in making store level merchandising decisions. It then developed a set of standard practices (the second part of Step 2) covering the following:

A. The limits of authority and responsibility in merchandising decisions.

B. The selection and ordering of all items to be merchandised.

C. The use of point-of-sale materials and other merchandising tools.

D. Product rotation.

E. Planning a merchandising program: projecting results, setting goals, measuring accomplishments.

F. Communicating merchandising plans to others.

G. Training subordinates in merchandising principles and standard practices.

Merchandising principles and techniques were then integrated into a complete Standard Practices Manual. The Manual became the foundation on which the merchandising training program was built.

Step 3: In constructing the merchandising training program, the company decided to deal with dry groceries first. Afterwards, it covered other major grocery subsections including dairy, frozen foods, health and beauty aids, housewares and candy. For each major subsection, impulse items were identified and customer traffic patterns developed and discussed. The profitability of commodity groups and of items within each commodity group was examined. Merchandising principles and standard practices particularly relevant to each major subsection of the grocery department were emphasized.

The trainer then divided the program into sessions, each covering a combination of related subjects. The trainer assembled reference materials and training aids, and detailed the classroom notes.

Steps 4 and 5: The trainer planned a program which would enable each trainee to apply the principles and standard practices in his own department. The trainer also developed a follow-up system in order to check on the application of principles and practices. Table 1 is the outline of the merchandising training program for grocery department managers as developed by this company.

TABLE 1
Outline of Merchandising Training Program for Grocery Department Managers

I. First Session.

  A. Introduction to merchandising knowledge and skills expected of grocery department managers.

  B. Dry grocery merchandising (Section I):

    1. Impulse buying:

      a. Research studies.

      b. Impulse items.

    2. Customer traffic patterns:

      a. Research studies.

      b. Trainee application of traffic study in company store.

    3. Markup, gross margin and gross profit:

      a. Definitions, methods of computation.

      b. Importance of gross profit dollars as yardstick of item performance.

      c. Computing item profitability.

    4. Commodity group and item profitability:

      a. Defining each major commodity group.

      b. High and low profitability items within each major commodity group.

    5. Principles relating to impulse buying, customer traffic patterns and item and commodity group profitability.

II. Second Session.

  A. Dry grocery merchandising (Section II):

    1. Product grouping:

      a. Analysis of arrangement of commodity groups.

      b. Logic of present arrangement.

        (1) Performance of selected commodity groups compared with industry averages.

      c. Principles.

    2. Product presentation:

      a. Ribbon display principles.

      b. Factors determining shelf position.

        (1) Item size.

        (2) Markup percentage.

        (3) Movement.

        (4) Private brand or controlled label.

        (5) Proximity of national brand or fast mover.

        (6) Principles.

    3. Space allocation:

      a. Review complete SLIM allocation and ordering system (SLIM: "Store Labor and Inventory Management," a system of handling grocery merchandise).

TABLE 1 (Cont.)

  b. SLIM control tags and control book.

  c. Principles.

 4. Product rotation.

III. Third Session.

 A. Dry grocery merchandising (Section III):

  1. For each of the following, cover merchandising and ordering techniques; examples, including results; merchandising principles and standard practices:

  ✓ a. In-store merchandising.

   b. Tie-in merchandising.

  ✓ c. Inter-department merchandising.

  2. Review responsibility and authority of grocery manager in each of the above areas.

IV. Fourth Session.

 A. Dry grocery merchandising (Section IV):

  1. For each of the following, cover merchandising and ordering techniques; examples, including results; merchandising principles and standard practices:

   a. Advertised items.

   b. Promotional items.

   c. Private label and controlled label items.

   d. Ethnic items.

  2. Review responsibility and authority of grocery manager in each of the above areas.

V. Fifth Session.

 A. Dry grocery merchandising (Section V):

  1. For each of the following, cover merchandising and ordering techniques; examples, including results; merchandising principles and standard practices:

   a. Seasonal items.

   b. New items.

   c. Discontinued items.

   d. Distress items.

  2. Review responsibility and authority of grocery manager in each of the above areas.

VI. Sixth Session.

 A. Dairy merchandising:

  1. Impulse items.

  2. Customer traffic patterns.

  3. Commodity group and item profitability.

  4. Product grouping.

  5. Product presentation.

  6. Space allocation.

  7. In-store merchandising.

TABLE 1 (Cont.)

8. Tie-in merchandising.

9. Inter-department merchandising.

10. Merchandising private label or controlled label items, ethnic items, seasonal items, new items, discontinued items, distress items.

VII. Seventh Session.

A. Frozen food merchandising:

1. Cover the same ten topics as for Dairy merchandising (sixth session).

VIII. Eighth Session.

A. Health and beauty aids, housewares and candy merchandising:

1. Cover the same ten topics as for Dairy merchandising (sixth session).

IX. Ninth Session.

A. Total grocery department merchandising.

1. Review of item ordering and selection.

2. Use of point-of-sale materials and other merchandising tools:

a. Signs.

b. Dump displays.

c. Shelf extenders.

d. Aisle displays.

3. Planned merchandising:

a. Projecting results.

b. Setting goals.

c. Measuring accomplishments.

4. Communicating merchandising plans to others.

5. Training subordinates in merchandising principles and standard practices.

Service Operations. A department manager must understand the relationship between a company's service arms and his or her own department. To this end, several progressive chains have incorporated warehouse and office visits into their department manager training programs. In one company, the trainee is instructed on the first day's training in service operations by the warehouse manager (grocery, meat or produce). They cover the following activities: receiving (rail and truck); storing merchandise; selecting and loading store orders; and scheduling and delivering store orders.

On the second day, the trainee is instructed by the department head (grocery, meat or produce merchandiser) and they cover the following subjects: ordering for the warehouse; quality control and inspection (particularly perishables); pricing (establishing gross margins); advertising (the trainee sits in as an observer on a weekly meeting of the advertising committee); selecting new items (criteria explained); discontinuing slow-moving items; and store inventories.

This type of two-day indoctrination enables the department manager trainee to become acquainted with the problems of the service departments. Perhaps more important, it enables the trainee to understand the reasons for many of the company's policies, procedures and standard practices. As a result of this service training program, the chain enjoys a relatively high degree of cooperation and understanding between its service and field operation personnel. Company executives have noted that before this program was started, conflicts between service and field personnel were frequent; today they are not.

Training Store Managers

When the boss asked a new store manager why more time was not being spent supervising the meat department, the manager replied: "I don't have the training or background to walk back there and start telling Joe how to cut meat. Sure, I spent 22 weeks in meat training, but Joe's been cutting meat for fourteen years!"

This answer reflects a problem basic to most present store manager training programs. The manager had not been taught that supervising the department does not mean "telling Joe how to cut meat." An individual must be made to understand the difference between supervising and instructing in manual tasks if he or she is to succeed at store managing.

Moreover, it should not be assumed that a person exposed to a department for a long enough period of time will become sufficiently skilled to supervise that department once he becomes a store manager. Exposure to a job and learning a skill are not the same. Too often, store manager trainees assigned to the meat department spend their training periods grinding beef, cutting chickens and cleaning the department. In the produce department they are overtrained in trimming and undertrained in merchandising. They learn the menial jobs in each department but fail to acquire supervisory skills. If, as most supermarket executives agree, it is impractical to make a skilled meat or produce manager out of every store manager, then it is futile to try.

Though most store manager training programs contain ample time for training, the time is misdirected and channeled into the wrong areas. Many weeks are wasted in useless training. Instead, this valuable time should be used to furnish future store managers with supervisory skills.

Identifying the Store Manager's Responsibilities

The store manager who must supervise the meat, produce or any other department must be trained to handle such responsibilities. The first step is to identify the store manager's role with regard to specific departments. In some chains, for example, a store manager's responsibilities in the meat (or produce) department cover the following:

1. Company policy relating to administrative matters.
2. Pricing accuracy.
3. Customer relations and service.
4. Variety of merchandise (required items) on display.
5. Freshness and appearance of merchandise on display.
6. Cleanliness as it appears to customers.
7. Security.
8. Merchandise returns.

In such companies, therefore, the training program should be built around these responsibilities. In meat training, for instance, the store manager trainee should be taught such matters as item identification and cooking methods for various cuts. The same sort of guidelines should be followed when the trainee receives produce training. Such a training program for store managers will be far less costly and time-consuming than extensive technical training and will improve relations between the department and store managers. Above all, the store manager will learn to supervise far more effectively.

Two respected supermarket chains recently adopted this more efficient approach to training store managers. One chain reduced the meat training period for store managers from 22 to eight weeks; the other chain cut the meat training period from eighteen to six weeks. The first chain also trimmed eight weeks from the produce training period (reducing it from fourteen to six weeks). The duration of the produce training course in the second chain was not changed, but its content was. Both chains have reported considerable improvement in the overall effectiveness of those store managers who have completed the new programs.

Training Store Managers in Departmental Functions

Another chain which had instituted effective training programs for grocery, meat, produce and checkout clerks, also developed department and store manager training programs. Each store manager trainee must successfully complete the apprentice and department manager training program in each department and then serve as an assistant store manager before being given a store to run.

The success of this program is based on the method of training, not on the length of the training period. In meat department training, for instance, the store manager's responsibilities are defined as follows:

A. Display case:
   1. Customer relations.
   2. Knowledge of cooking methods for all items.
   3. Making sure that required items are on display.
   4. Maintenance of proper load levels.
   5. Cleanliness of cases and floor in sales area.
   6. Maintenance of proper case temperatures.
   7. Supervising shelf life, proper code dating, product rotation.
   8. Removing discolored items, torn or leaky packages.
   9. Preventing freezer burns on frozen items.
   10. Maintaining correct prices on all items.
   11. Checking to insure that signs are on advertised items and that advertised items are on display at all times.
   12. Merchandising.
B. Receiving and processing:
   1. Receiving.
   2. Sanitation and temperature control.
   3. Making sure that merchandise is refrigerated unless it is being processed.
   4. Trimming policies (all items).
   5. Scheduling production and work loads; scheduling people.
   6. Wage expense.
   7. Gross profit.
   8. Security.
   9. Safety.
C. Cooler management:
   1. Ordering.
   2. Product rotation (particularly beef primals and other fresh meats).
   3. Sanitation and temperature control.
   4. Inventory control.
   5. Ground beef quality control (clean trimmings and no regrinding).
   6. Checking that no odds and ends are in cooler except returns of guaranteed sale merchandise.

The store manager is prepared to supervise the meat department in two training stages: (1) thirteen weeks of apprentice training, and (2) three weeks of department manager training. Both programs are intensive and include classroom and on-the-job instruction. Obviously, even a concentrated and highly-individualized training program of thirteen weeks cannot produce a very efficient journeyman meat cutter, but this is not the objective of the program. Within these weeks, the chain intends that the store manager should acquire skill, not speed. The trainee must know how to do each job correctly, but is not expected to be highly productive.

There is nothing sacred about the length of training in this program; thirteen and three weeks serve only as guides. A training course may be extended by a few extra weeks if the trainee requires more time. The controlling factor is that the trainee meet the criterion of skill established for that particular part of the program. At least twice a month the trainer meets with the trainee for a progress review and to inform the trainee of what is expected. The average store manager trainee completes training in all departments in about one year. During that time, training covers the meat, produce, deli-bakery and grocery departments and the checkout operation, and the trainee serves as assistant store manager.

Table 2 is an outline of this training program for general store managers. It should be noted that the trainee receives some management experience while still in training, by spending thirteen weeks managing the produce department. These weeks could be spent managing any department, with the possible exception of meat, where more basic training would be required. By actually managing a department, the trainee gains the opportunity to apply the four managerial skills which constitute a significant portion of a general training program for managers. The mistakes the trainee makes in planning, organizing, supervising and controlling as a department manager will not be serious enough to damage the entire store. Moreover, the thirteen weeks represent a fiscal quarter, and the trainee's performance can be measured against a previous quarter.

New Concepts in Training Managers

Most supermarket chains which are committed to developing competent managers use variations of the general store manager training program described above. But since the middle 1970s, a totally new, much more successful and far more cost effective training approach has been available to the supermarket industry.

This most notable breakthrough in the history of job knowledge and management skills training for supermarket managers involved

TABLE 2
Training Outline for General Store Managers

*Estimated Minimum
Training and Practice Time*

A.	Meat Department:	
	1. Apprentice training.	13 weeks
	2. Meat manager training.	3 weeks
B.	Produce Department:	
	1. Clerk training.	6 weeks
	2. Produce manager training.	2 weeks
	3. Manager of department.	13 weeks
C.	Grocery Department:	
	1. Stock clerk training (night crew).	6 weeks
	2. SLIM ordering, inventory control.	3 weeks
	3. Grocery manager training.	3 weeks
D.	Front-End and Office Operations:	
	1. Checkout operation.	3 weeks
	2. Checkout supervision.	2 weeks
	3. Office operations.	2 weeks
E.	Service Operations (all departments).	Simultaneous with department training
F.	Training in the Four Skills (planning, organizing, supervising and controlling).	Simultaneous with department training
G.	Assistant Store Manager.	4 weeks
H.	Total estimated minimum training period.	60 weeks

Estimated training costs to produce general store manager

A.	Salary of trainee.	$18,000—24,000
B.	Fringe benefits (35%).	6,300— 8,400
C.	Cost of trainer, training programs, materials, etc.	5,140— 9,450
D.	Total estimated training cost.	$29,440—41,850

a shift in focus from teaching by the trainer to learning by the trainee. The first experiments with the concept, conducted by a very progressive Northeastern supermarket chain, date back to the late 1960s. With respect to job knowledge, the company first documented the knowledge that a successful store manager should have. It then carefully selected a few high potential store manager candidates, and told them the job knowledge they were expected to acquire in each department on their own, and the stores in which they were to acquire the knowledge. They sent the trainees out to the selected stores with instructions to report back when they felt they had succeeded in completing the assignment.

Many executives, both within and outside the company, scoffed at the program and predicted failure. And they were right. The program failed and was cancelled after six months because it was new and untested, and management was unable to react quickly enough to the many unforeseen problems that arose. However, despite the disbelievers having been vindicated, more creative minds perceived the potential merit of shifting the primary responsibility for gaining job knowledge from the trainer to the trainees. They understood the benefits that would accrue if the trainees had to use their own initiative in seeking out the documented job knowledge from designated experts in different stores, and the advantages of having the trainees set their own schedules and work at their own pace.

Learner Controlled Instruction.   This difficult beginning to a new and creative, but drastically different approach to training in job knowledge, served as a springboard for the development of "Learner Controlled Instruction," commonly referred to as "LCI." Today, many major companies in other industries are committed to the LCI approach to job knowledge training for managers, but skeptics still abound among supermarket executives. In fact, only a handful of supermarket chains have implemented LCI over the past few years, but all with notable success.

Today, LCI is a highly refined, carefully designed program which is controlled primarily, but not totally, by the trainee. Compared to other commonly used manager training programs, LCI offers the following advantages: (1) learning proficiency is improved, i.e., the trainee learns and retains more knowledge; and (2) learning time is reduced. The basic reason for the success of the LCI concept can be traced to the fact that motivation comes from within a person. LCI provides the environment that encourages the learner to want to do his best to learn all he can in the shortest possible time. The initiative and drive shown by a majority of LCI trainees astounds their former bosses, and provides the trainees with a great sense of personal achievement. The proper climate is created because:

1. The learner has a major voice in decisions regarding (a) the *sequence* in which different parts of a specific job are learned; (b) *the amount of time* devoted to learning an individual task; and (c) *how* to go about learning a specific task.

2. The learner has a major voice in determining the point at which he has achieved proficiency on a specific task.

3. The learner is given the opportunity to demonstrate mastery of a specific task.

4. The learner is given frequent feedback on how well he is learning a specific task.

5. The learner is given the opportunity to compete with peers in a positive and constructive way.

The LCI program is built around phases, activities and tasks. A *phase* is a major segment of store operations. Each phase is composed of a number of *activities* involving one or more *tasks*. The trainee controls what he learns and the time he feels is necessary, within the program guidelines, to become proficient in each designated task. When he feels he has mastered the tasks in a particular activity, the trainee requests an appointment for an evaluation. He is evaluated on each activity by qualified personnel who are chosen on the basis of their competence in a particular area. In addition to passing an oral exam administered by the designated evaluator, the trainee must demonstrate proficiency in performing all of the manual tasks in one phase before he is permitted to go on to the next phase.

The total program consists of from five to ten phases, and 30 to 50 activities. The trainee decides the sequence in which he learns each phase, except for the first and last phases which are in fixed order. One company using LCI has seven phases covering a total of 40 activities, as follows:

1. Store Management Orientation: 7 activities
2. Grocery Management: 8 activities
3. Meat Management: 6 activities
4. Produce Management: 5 activities
5. Deli-Bakery Management: 5 activities
6. Front-End Management: 6 activities
7. Total Store Management: 3 activities

The LCI program requires an administrator who: (1) serves as the trainee's supervisor throughout the learning period; (2) establishes and maintains the company's (or division's) resource library for the trainee's use; (3) helps select the resource people, evaluators and training stores, prepares the resource people and evaluators to carry out their program duties and monitors their participation in the program; (4) maintains records on each trainee's performance and supplies division management with current information regarding each trainee's progress; and (5) counsels with and assists the trainees on scheduling their own learning activities and meetings with resource people and evaluators, and on being scheduled into the appropriate training stores.

Of course, learning and practicing effective management skills is of equal importance to gaining job knowledge, and training in management skills is usually conducted concurrently with job knowledge training in the LCI program. Usually, several hours a week of the trainee's time are set aside for learning management skills.[2]

The LCI Payoff. LCI is designed to provide store operations management with people who are qualified to step into co-manager or assistant store manager positions upon completion of the program. Typically, a graduate of the program is then "seasoned" for a year or more as a co- or assistant manager before being promoted to store manager. The LCI success stories in the limited number of supermarket chains that have implemented the program, though true, are beyond the belief of many chain executives. Store operations executives and supervisors claim that LCI program graduates are far more knowledgeable than those who went through earlier, thorough, conventional store manager training programs. And when they become store managers, their superiority cannot be challenged.

In two major U.S. chains, the time required to produce better qualified potential store managers has been reduced by 40 to 60 percent for the typical trainee in the LCI program. In one company, the reduction was from an average of 28 weeks to seventeen weeks, while in the other the reduction was from more than 36 weeks to fourteen weeks. It is rare that a chain can produce better qualified managers with any other training program, while spending fewer dollars.

One of the valuable by-products of a properly designed and administered LCI program is that material developed for the individual phases of store manager training can be adapted for LCI department manager training. Of course, some changes are necessary. The materials must be expanded in certain respects to be suitable for qualifying a meat cutter to become a meat manager, for example, or a produce clerk to become a produce manager, but the basic material is there.

The LCI program is not an "off-the-shelf" package that can be bought and installed quickly. LCI requires weeks of planning and documentation. Considerable thought and effort must go into select-

---

[2] A more detailed discussion of the LCI program will be found in Edward M. Harwell's *The Complete Manager* (New York: Chain Store Publishing Corp., 1986).

ing and qualifying administrators and evaluators, developing reference material libraries, educating top management and getting a commitment from all participants in the program. In short, it takes a major effort to get into LCI, but when properly done, it is well worth the effort.

The Four Managerial Skills

According to the 1983 turnover study, 61 percent of all store managers and almost 37 percent of all department managers who were discharged each year terminated for unsatisfactory work. Manager turnover represents a real financial loss. Not only does the company lose the investment it made in the manager, but a manager who has performed unsatisfactorily can cost a store thousands of dollars in profits through mistakes and poor decisions. Equally important is the possible lifelong damage that such discharges can have on the self-confidence and self-respect of the discharged manager.

In-depth interviews with managers separated from supermarket chains have indicated that, too often, the underlying reason for these discharges is that the prospective manager has not been trained in the four managerial skills: planning, organizing, supervising and controlling. A manager who has not been properly grounded in any of these skills is likely to fail when placed in a position of authority. The four managerial skills may be subdivided as follows:

A. Planning:
    1. Forecasting volume and labor requirements.
    2. Developing courses of action to improve performance.
    3. Establishing goals and target dates.
    4. Setting performance standards.
B. Organizing:
    1. Scheduling employees to match production requirements.
    2. Assigning primary and secondary responsibilities.
    3. Delegating authority.
C. Supervising:
    1. Checking to see that plans are successfully executed.
    2. Interviewing, selecting and inducting employees.
    3. Creating a climate in which employees are motivated.
    4. Communicating within the organizational structure.
    5. Handling grievances.
    6. Holding meetings.
    7. Training and developing employees.

8. Improving customer relations.
D. Controlling:
   1. Measuring performance.
   2. Auditing results at preplanned intervals.
   3. Analyzing problems and making decisions.
   4. Resolving conflicts.
   5. Disciplining employees.
   6. Evaluating department or store results.
   7. Following-through.

The ability to plan, organize, supervise and control is necessary to the manager if he or she is to succeed as an administrator and as a leader. These skills have a direct bearing on problems of personnel and on company-employee and manager-employee relations once the new employee has completed basic training and is working in the store. The four skills and many of their subcategories will therefore be examined in detail in several of the succeeding chapters.

Training in the Four Skills

Several programs have been developed to teach the trainee the four managerial skills. The following are the most common:

1. Industry and management association programs
2. College and university programs
3. In-company programs

Industry Programs. The Food Marketing Institute (FMI) has developed a program in which manager trainees attend seminars where they are given formal instruction as well as problem-solving situations related to everyday supermarket matters. The strength of the FMI program is that it is supermarket-oriented. Problems that are presented for discussion and solution are like those the trainees encounter in the day-to-day supermarket operation. The disadvantage of this seminar approach is the high cost of enrolling all department and store manager trainees in the program.

The American Management Association (AMA) has prepared what is probably the most complete set of training materials on managerial skills. Three of these programs are particularly worth mentioning.

1. *The Basic Principles of Supervisory Management*: This is an in-company training program that uses films, case studies, programmed instruction and discussions led by company coordinators

who have been trained to conduct the program. The program is divided into eight units: The Nature of Management; Planning; Organizing; Controlling; Standards and Appraisal; Communications; Motivation; and Improving Managerial Effectiveness.

2. *Developing Supervisory Leadership Skills*: This in-company program is similar to *The Basic Principles of Supervisory Management* and designed to supplement it. It is also composed of eight units: The Nature of Leadership; Knowing Your Employees—Individual Differences; Understanding Personality and Behavior; Improving Three-Way Communications; Maintaining Effective Discipline; Handling Complaints and Grievances; Guiding and Developing Employees; and Building Job Satisfaction and Morale.

3. *How to Improve Individual Manager Performance*: Also an in-company classroom-type program, it covers such subjects as Concepts of Management; Management Organization and Job Descriptions; Standards of Performance for Managers; Performance Appraisal for Managers; and Improving Performance through Individual Manager Development.

For each course unit in which managerial principles are discussed, general films are supplied, as well as short filmed case studies dramatizing actual problems, role playing scripts, programmed instruction texts and other materials designed for classroom and home study. Each course unit contains enough instructional materials to cover a two- to three-hour training session.

The strength of the AMA programs is their complete coverage of the subject and the technical competence of those who have developed the training materials. Their weakness is that the materials are not oriented to the supermarket industry.

In addition to the AMA's programmed instruction texts, other companies, such as the Xerox Corporation, have developed excellent programmed instruction courses for teaching certain specific managerial skills like communicating and problem solving.

College and University Programs.   Many junior colleges, colleges and universities throughout the country offer management courses in which the four managerial skills are taught. In many of these institutions, night courses are available which can be attended by employees after work. Several universities are now offering full four-year programs and degrees in food distribution, with managerial skills as part of the curriculum. Noteworthy among these are Cornell University, Michigan State University and the University of Southern California. These four-year courses provide excellent training for future key employees.

In-Company Programs.   A final approach to teaching the four managerial skills is to develop courses within the company. Obviously, this is no small undertaking. Yet such subcategories of the four skills as forecasting, scheduling, assigning responsibilities, setting performance standards, measuring performance, problem analysis and decision making should ideally be specifically industry-oriented. Some companies have used the AMA programs to teach basic principles, and have adapted company developed systems and techniques, case studies and role playing situations tailored to everyday supermarket problems to illustrate those principles.

Not only must training programs designed to teach the four managerial skills be developed, but the opportunity to practice them must also be provided. Only through exposure to situations requiring planning, organizing, supervising and controlling, can a manager gain the front-line experience needed to develop those skills. Planned follow-up to insure that managerial techniques and principles are practiced is also a vital part of such training programs. The trainees themselves, or their store managers and supervisors, can prepare periodic reports in which they discuss whether managerial techniques and principles have been put into effect. Regular group meetings of trainees can also be arranged during which they discuss their experiences and the application of the various techniques. This approach provides for an exchange of information between the trainees (now new department managers) and often leads to the exploration of new ideas and to the development of improvements in the training program itself.

Practically all management skills training programs—industry, college, university, or in-company—are conducted in a classroom atmosphere away from the job. Learning takes place in one setting while managing takes place in another. The premise is that what is taught in the classroom will simulate what happens on the job, and the program will result in changes in the manager's behavior and improvement in store or department performance. Unfortunately, what the manager learns in the classroom is useful on the job only to the extent that the organization's climate and the supervisor's predisposition allow the manager to apply what he has learned. Despite well-intentioned follow-up plans, too often a manager's behavior does not change when he returns to the store. Much of what he has learned is new and strange, and he is unsure of himself because he has had no opportunity to practice the skills that were taught. Returning to daily routines, emergencies and time-pressures, he is reluctant to test unfamiliar, untried management techniques. When this happens, the very substantial sums invested in management skills training bring no return.

As mentioned, the objective of training in management skills is to change the behavior of the manager when he returns to the job. People learn new kinds of behavior through imitation and practice. Until recently, the practice segment of the learning process has been left to the initiative of the trainee. He is expected to apply, without supervision or critique, what he has learned and sometimes seen demonstrated in the classroom. This is similar to a cashier trainer explaining and, perhaps, showing a new clerk how to operate an electronic terminal, then leaving him unsupervised to perform the task, not knowing whether he has really learned the proper methods and procedures.

Most management skills training programs include some theoretical subjects, which explain the reasons for certain types of management behavior. The logic of the theories is generally well-accepted by most trainees. But what the trainee wants, and usually doesn't get, is to learn the "how" of applying management skills. The trainee can learn *how* to communicate, *how* to interview, *how* to delegate, *how* to analyze problems and make decisions, and *how* to apply the other management skills being taught, only if given the opportunity to practice under the watchful eye of the trainer or others—just as the cashier trainee needs to practice and get feedback.

Behavior Modeling. This problem has led to the "behavior modeling" approach to management skills training. Films or video tapes are used to present a "model" properly performing a management skill in a realistic, "real life" supermarket job situation. About five or six trainees, usually peers, become involved in all phases of the learning process. A typical behavior modeling session is conducted as follows:

1. The trainer gives a brief introduction about the skill to be practiced.
2. The trainer reviews and prepares the trainees for the key points that will be demonstrated in the model film. The script usually involves a supervisor interacting with a subordinate.
3. The film, ten to fifteen minutes long, is shown.
4. The skill that was demonstrated is practiced by the trainees. One serves as the supervisor while another plays the role of the subordinate in a situation similar to that shown in the film. After each role-playing situation, the supervisor's actions are critiqued by each trainee. They focus on the key points reviewed by the trainer and shown in the film. The process is repeated until every trainee has played the role of a supervisor and has had his performance critiqued by his peers.

5. The trainer serves as the moderator. The trainer encourages the participants to create role-playing scenarios, from their own experiences, that illustrate the key learning points. The trainer compliments the role players after the critiques if they have performed well, and urges further reinforcement of the skill by encouraging them to practice back on the job.

The success of behavior modeling can be traced to the fact that it (1) focuses on letting the manager act and react in a real life situation, rather than just learning theories in a vacuum; and (2) allows the trainee to learn and practice a specific skill until he or she becomes proficient and comfortable using it.

The Food Marketing Institute and the Quaker Oats Company have produced nine behavior modeling units that are designed to train supermarket managers in a wide variety of management skills. Many of the chains that have made extensive use of these programs report that behavior modeling is far more effective than conventional classroom training in changing a manager's behavior on the job.

10 Planning, Organizing and Problem Solving

Department or store managers who analyze how they spend their time by recording their activities and how long each takes, would probably uncover some rather surprising facts. A typical manager would find that during each work day he or she spends 45 minutes on unnecessary chores, and one hour and 35 minutes on work that should have been delegated to others. With this extra two hours and twenty minutes, the manager could have been fulfilling such managerial responsibilities as planning, organizing, problem solving and decision making.

Planning

Managers commonly complain that they have no time to plan. Yet research has revealed that those who are considered by their companies to be the best managers actually perform over 50 percent more of such managerial activities as planning than do those who are considered poor managers. The more competent managers find time to plan ahead and to manage effectively by delegating non-managerial tasks to others.

Planning is not simply a way to achieve long-term goals. It also consists of foreseeing a department's or store's position tomorrow, next week, next month or even next year. In order to plan for tomorrow, it is also necessary to predict what will happen tomorrow. By predicting tomorrow's production requirements and by knowing present employees' production rates, it is possible to schedule people accurately. In general, planning consists of forecasting volume and labor requirements, developing courses of action to improve performance, establishing goals and target dates, and setting performance standards.

Forecasting.   Today, many chains are doing an outstanding job of scheduling front-end employees by using a system, developed several years ago, whereby each manager predicts store sales for the following week and adjusts his schedule accordingly.[1] Daily sales patterns are remarkably constant from week to week in most stores and a manager who studies those patterns while taking into consideration such factors as industry or government paydays, planned advertising or major promotions, can project sales and labor requirements accurately and plan accordingly. Experience has shown that the typical manager can become quite a skillful forecaster and thereby provide good customer service at a minimum cost. A manager should begin forecasting sales and labor requirements as a department manager. The competent store manager will base his weekly store forecast on those made by his department managers. Forecasting is as important in other departments as it is in the checkout operation.

In order to schedule effectively, several supermarket companies identify employee activities in departments as either variable or fixed, and measure personnel requirements by means of work sampling studies. _Variable_ activities in any department are those that are directly related to sales. In the grocery department, for example, they include such jobs as receiving, price marking and stocking. The labor-hour requirements for such activities increase or decrease in direct proportion to sales. _Fixed_ activities in any department are those that require about the same number of labor-hours, regardless of volume increases or decreases. For example, fixed activities in the grocery department include such functions as ordering, changing prices, building special displays, cleaning, supervising and others.

[1] E. M. Harwell and W. E. Kinslow, _New Horizons in Checkout Management_ (New York: Lebhar-Friedman, 1988).

TABLE 1
Variable and Fixed Activities in the Grocery, Dairy and Checkout Departments of One Chain

A. Variable Activities*	Functions Included
1. Receiving	Prepare to receive, receive from warehouse, check order.
2. Stocking	Pull merchandise to process, transport merchandise, police displays, stock, handle salvage, list shelf needs, price merchandise.
3. Checkout	Ringup, add tax, bag, take money, make change, issue stamps.
4. All Other Checkout Functions	Carry-out, return shopping carts, and all functions not listed under 3 above.
B. Fixed Activities*	
1. Receiving Direct Deliveries	Prepare to receive, receive, check order.
2. Walking	Travel empty (10 percent maximum).
3. Ordering	Take inventory, write order.
4. Clerical	Reports, mail, etc.
5. Changing Prices	Remove old prices and replace.
6. Supervising	Supervise work and attend meetings.
7. Cleaning	Maintenance inside and outside.
8. Customer Service	All customer sales floor interruptions.
9. Special Displays	Build and maintain special displays.

*Breaks are computed at 6 percent of total variable and fixed labor-hours.

Table 1 shows how one chain separated the variable and fixed activities in its grocery, dairy and checkout departments. In this particular chain, the variable labor-hours in each department were related to the sales volume of the department (total store sales for checkout) in order to develop a formula or guide to the number of total labor-hours required for different sales volume levels. The company determined that variable factors required 3.7 hours per $1,000 change in weekly sales in the checkout department; 1.7 hours per $1,000 in the grocery department; and 3.2 hours per $1,000 in the dairy department.

However, these figures pertain only to this particular company's operation and cannot be applied to stores outside this chain because every company's work sampling figures will vary according to such factors as the size and volume of its stores customer services and product mix. But managers who can accurately forecast their weekly sales can use a formula similar to the one described here to determine their personnel needs for the week. However, these personnel forecasts should always be flexible enough to accommodate an unexpected change in sales for the better or worse.

Systems for forecasting personnel requirements have also been developed for the perishable departments though, here, a workable formula is harder to achieve. In these departments, the labor-hours required are usually not based on sales but, rather, on forecasts of tonnage for various commodity groups. An example of an effective system of forecasting meat department tonnage and labor-hour requirements may be found in the Appendix.

Of course, there is less flexibility in adjusting employee schedules in some areas than in others; for example, it is more difficult to compensate for projected fluctuations in perishable departments than in the front-end operation, primarily because fewer part-timers are used in the meat and produce departments. Nevertheless, many progressive companies are hiring and training part-timers in perishable departments to provide scheduling flexibility. Moreover, departmental projections are needed because they are the basis of all planning and scheduling.

Improving Performance.   Developing plans to improve performance and altering plans to compensate for anticipated deviations require a certain element of creativity on the part of the manager. The intelligent manager is not only creative himself, but also takes advantage of the creativity of his subordinates. He involves them in searching for ways to improve performance. Subordinates who are involved in the creation of programs will develop real team spirit. Almost everyone will work harder at a program he or she has had a hand in formulating.

Another way to improve performance is by simplifying tasks. All managers should be taught the principles of work simplification. They should first receive instruction on how to break down a job into its detailed components by using a flow process chart and a flow diagram. Then they should be taught how to analyze the individual elements of the job in order to determine whether any can be eliminated, combined, re-arranged or simplified to provide for a more efficient operation. Finally, they should be taught how to apply the new methods they have developed.

It is currently standard practice in many American industries to train managers and line employees in work simplification methods. Almost every company that has trained such employees in these techniques has reduced costs and improved productivity. Much of this success may also be attributed to managers' and employees' greater readiness to accept changes they have had a part in developing.

Setting Goals.   The manager who anticipates next week's sales or tonnage and adjusts his operations accordingly, has only begun to plan. What he is saying in effect is "Here is what will happen if past performance is a reliable indicator." But a manager must do more than repeat past performance; he or she must also improve productivity by creating better methods or through better scheduling.

The manager must make long-range plans by establishing goals in each area for which he is responsible, including sales, gross profit, wage expense, supply expense, and others. The manager should base these quarterly or semi-annual goals on the specific courses of action he has developed to improve performance, and the goals should be approved by his immediate superior. The short-range goals should be compatible with long-range goals; this means that the attainment of long-range goals would depend on the achievement of short-range goals. A motorist traveling from Washington, D. C. to New York, for example, must reach such intermediate, short-range goals as the Delaware River Bridge in order to arrive at his long-range destination on time. If he hits heavy traffic in Baltimore he must compensate by altering his speed or route in order to reach New York at the projected hour.

Company long- and short-range planning resemble managerial planning except that a company's long-range goals may be projected for as much as five or even ten years. These long-range objectives are then broken down into annual and, again, into quarterly (short-term) goals. When a chain does not achieve its quarterly or annual goal, it must compensate by developing new and different courses of action for the period ahead. Both a manager's long-range goals and a company's short-range goals are often set up as quarterly targets. This means that the manager's long-range plans must coincide with the chain's short-range plans and that to establish his or her own long-range plans, the store manager must first have knowledge of the company's goals.

Job Descriptions and Performance Standards.   Job descriptions and performance standards are ingredients of both planning and organizing. The supermarket industry is perhaps the last major American industry in which few companies have developed meaningful job descriptions and performance standards. Inefficiency results when employees do not know exactly what their jobs entail and what is expected of them.

Industry associations, colleges, universities, government agencies and a few progressive supermarket chains have been improving this situation. Engineered labor standards, based on time study or basic elemental times, have been developed for various supermarket activities. Sales and gross profit projections are being computerized, taking into account such factors as product mix, advertising and sales promotion plans, merchandising plans and others. Much of this research, however, is still in its early stages in most supermarket chains and requires a good deal of technical assistance before it can be applied to a store or department. Until more sophisticated methods are readily available, however, the department or store manager can devise job descriptions and establish performance standards.

The purpose of a job description is to establish agreement between superior and subordinate on exactly what the job entails. It has been repeatedly demonstrated that the manager and employee seldom see a job in the same way. If each were to write a description of the subordinate's job, the differences in their views would no doubt be quite remarkable.

Well-planned job descriptions, then, should be developed by the subordinate and, after necessary adjustments have been made, approved by the superior. An effective job description should cover every area or activity, be clear and specific, and lucidly define areas and limits of responsibility and authority. It should provide for yardsticks to measure performance wherever possible and should specify the level at which performance is considered satisfactory.

Produce Manager's Job Description: A store manager asked a produce manager to prepare a job description. Here is what the produce manager came up with initially:

A produce manager is responsible for the following:

1. Produce sales, gross profit, wage and supply expense.
2. Checking that full displays are maintained at all times.
3. Making sure that displays are properly policed.
4. Making certain that all items are correctly priced.
5. Checking that merchandise is properly trimmed.
6. Seeing that employees do their jobs as instructed.
7. Projecting sales each Friday for the following week, and scheduling employees accordingly.
8. Keeping the department clean.

This produce manager's first attempt at a job description omitted such very important activities as inventory control, product rotation, training, customer relations and merchandising. The last three points (6, 7 and 8) were neither clear nor specific. A satisfactory performance level was not specified for any of the items. Despite its faults, however, this first attempt did succeed at forcing the produce manager to think about the responsibilities involved in the job.

The store manager tactfully pointed out the weak spots in the job description and encouraged the produce manager to try again. The produce manager's second attempt showed great improvement but still required some refinement. A third try resulted in complete agreement between the two of them. (See Table 2.)

The produce manager had prepared a job description which might be considered imperfect in many supermarket companies, but it accurately described the job and the standards of performance in the store and company in which it was developed. Store managers should have such job descriptions for each of their department managers; department managers should, in turn, have similar job descriptions for each of their subordinates.

TABLE 2

Job Description

Job Title: Produce Manager

Responsibility	*Standard of Performance*
	(Performance will be considered satisfactory when the following conditions are met.)
1. Department Sales, Gross Profit, Wage and Supply Expense	A. Self-imposed goals in these areas (which have been approved by the store manager) are reached or exceeded.
2. Inventory Control	A. All required items are on display during all the hours the store is open.
	B. Maximum weekend carry-over is 25% of weekly sales.
3. Product Quality	A. All items are trimmed as per company standard practices.
	B. Cooler temperature is maintained at 37-40°F (2.8-4.4°C).
	C. All merchandise is rotated when displayed.
	D. All merchandise is code dated on receipt, and the FIFO system is followed.
	E. No substandard product is on display with fresh merchandise.
	F. The receipt of substandard products is reported to the company produce office.
4. Scheduling	A. Sales are projected Friday for each day of following week.
	B. Part-time hours are adjusted on a weekly schedule posted Friday to insure the maintenance of $116.00 per labor-hour each week.

TABLE 2 (Cont.)

C. Best employees (John and Sue) are scheduled during peak hours of peak days.

D. All hard items are bagged for weekend requirements by 5:00 PM Wednesday.

5. Merchandising

A. At least one inter-department display is up at all times.

B. Special island display is built for feature advertised item, with high profit item alongside.

C. At least one special eye-stopper display is up at all times and changed a minimum of once a week.

D. Demand items are distributed throughout the department, as per merchandising manual.

6. Markdowns

A. No unsaleable merchandise is on the markdown table.

B. First markdown is between 25% and 50%, based on product condition.

C. Markdown table is neat and orderly.

7. Training

A. Produce standard practices are followed by all employees.

B. Assistant department manager makes decisions during the absence of the manager.

C. Assistant department manager is considered promotable after six more months in that capacity.

8. Customer Service

A. No more than three customers are in line at the produce scale.

B. Maximum weekly average is one customer complaint.

9. Housekeeping

A. No trash or product is on the floor in the cooler, backroom or display area.

B. Return cartons and boxes are stacked neatly outside receiving door.

C. Storage racks are labeled for all supplies, and supplies are in their correct places.

D. Cooler and backroom floors are swept each night; display floor is mopped before store opens each day.

E. Space in backroom is cleared out before leaving each night to receive load.

Organizing

The basic purpose of organizing is to develop a team that works well together to achieve common goals. Planning is a prerequisite to organizing, though the two activities merge at various points. But there can be no reason to organize unless goals have been established and plans developed to achieve them. Organizing consists of scheduling, assigning responsibility and delegating authority.

Scheduling.   One supermarket chain limited its scheduling activities to advising its managers that it was their responsibility to schedule employees. In effect, all it told its managers was: "Here are the figures on the dollar volume of business you do each day of the week. You have all the other figures you need. You know your store hours and the maximum number of hours the law allows each employee to work in a given day or week. Your merchandise orders for the past few weeks will show you approximately how much product you sell each day. With this information you can schedule your product and work force."

It was a produce manager in the chain who pointed out to his store manager the company's failure to establish a scheduling system. The store and produce managers decided to tackle the problem and came up with a five-step scheduling outline:

1. Develop a set of scheduling principles or guidelines.
2. For each day of the week, identify each task in the department and the sequence in which each must be performed.
3. Determine the time required to perform each of the major tasks in the department, using present methods and equipment.
4. Schedule tasks so that they will be performed by the right people at the right time.
5. Follow-through to make sure the schedule is executed or adjusted to accommodate changing conditions.

Scheduling Principles and Guidelines: The store and produce managers then developed the following scheduling principles to cover merchandising requirements:

A. Every item must be on display from store opening until store closing.
B. The produce manager must post the product preparation schedule in the backroom by 7:00 AM each morning.
C. All displays must be policed and culled prior to store opening each day.
D. Eighty percent of anticipated weekly requirements of hard items must be packaged on Mondays, Tuesdays and Wednesdays.
E. All highly perishable items must be prepared as close to the time of sale as possible.

F. Dummied displays must be used on Mondays, Tuesdays and Wednesdays and late Saturdays, but not at other times.

Next, the store and produce managers established the following guidelines for scheduling employees for maximum productivity:

A. The produce manager must open the department on Monday at 6:30 AM because of the heavier than usual culling, rehandling and retrimming work loads.

B. The manager or assistant manager must be present at 7:00 AM on Wednesdays, Fridays and Saturdays to receive and check-in the delivery from the warehouse.

C. The manager or assistant manager must be on duty Thursday and Friday nights; the manager must close on Saturday nights to take inventory.

D. The manager and assistant manager must not have the same day off.

E. The best employees must be scheduled during peak work loads.

F. The trimmer should be off on Tuesday (lightest trim day).

G. Other employees should be off on the days when they would normally have the lowest work loads.

H. In determining total labor-hours to be scheduled for the week, projected sales should be divided by sales per labor-hour goal in order to obtain the required labor-hours. Part-time labor-hours should be adjusted to insure the reaching of the goal.

I. All full-time employees should be scheduled for forty hours; overtime must be approved in advance by the store manager.

J. Each part-time employee should be scheduled for a minimum of twenty and a maximum of thirty hours per week (union requirement).

K. Wherever possible, each major function (receiving, trimming, packaging, pricing, displaying, weighing at scale station in display area) should be assigned to the employee most skilled in that function.

Daily Activities Form: After scheduling guidelines were established, the produce manager designed a daily activities form on which was entered, in proper sequence, the major tasks that had to be performed each day. The form includes a space in which the produce manager enters the initials of the employee responsible for each activity on a specific day, which the employee crosses out after completing the task. (See Table 3.)

At the store manager's suggestion, the produce manager also prepared a product requirements form for daily posting in the produce

TABLE 3
Daily Activities Form

Produce Department

	Mon.	Assigned to	Tues.	Assigned to	Wed.	Assigned to	Thurs.	Assigned to	Fri.	Assigned to	Sat.	Assigned to	Sun.	Assigned to
Before Store Opens for Business														
Receive and Check Load; Code Date, Rotate	✓													
Cull Department			✓		✓		✓		✓		✓		✓	
Pull Retrims			✓		✓		✓		✓		✓		✓	
Trim One Case of Each Item; Set Up Display with New Merchandise	✓		✓		✓		✓		✓		✓		✓	
Make Price Changes	✓						✓							
Check Prices	✓		✓		✓		✓		✓		✓		✓	
Clean Sales Floor	✓		✓		✓		✓		✓		✓		✓	
After Store Opens for Business														
Retrim	✓		✓		✓		✓		✓		✓		✓	
Post Product Requirements	✓		✓		✓		✓		✓		✓		✓	
Reset Department	✓		✓				✓							
Build Special Display	✓										✓			
Processing: Trim	✓		✓		✓		✓		✓		✓		✓	

Bag
Package
Price

Display
Prepare Hard Items for Weekend
Prepare Weekend Sale Items
Rework Hard Items Section (rotate)
Check Sale Items
Set Up Plan for Next Week
Set Up Employee Schedule
Reset Cooler
Prepare Cooler for Delivery
Inventory and Order
Check Price List and Sale Items for Next Week
Check Sales and Payroll
Review and Post Labor Schedule
Take Weekend Physical Inventory
Clean Cases
Clean-Up

backroom. This form indicates how much of various items are needed on display, the sequence in which they are required and the display method to be used. As each item is processed in the back-room and moved to the display area (or occasionally to reserve storage), it is marked through on the product requirements form. The produce manager adds new requirements to the list during the day as the need arises. About mid-afternoon, the produce manager surveys the display case and cooler, anticipates the requirements until store closing time, and adds these to the list of work to be prepared by the day crew before it goes off duty. (See Table 4.)

Job Assignments: Written primary and secondary job assignments are vital to scheduling employees in every department. A primary job assignment takes precedence over any other work assigned to the employee. A cashier's primary job assignment, for example, is checking-out customers. Any other job to which a cashier is assigned is secondary. The primary job assignment for a grocery manager on a Wednesday night might be writing the grocery order.

In many companies, the store manager must make sure that daily written job assignments for each store employee are prepared one week in advance. Department managers are responsible for sched-uling people in their departments and for checking to see that all assignments are fulfilled. Assignments may be updated or revised at any time to meet emergencies or changing conditions.

The purpose of a written job assignment is to keep employees informed at all times of the tasks and responsibilities assigned to them. Every employee should be assigned a primary job and as many secondary jobs as are necessary to cover the hours he or she is scheduled to work. Moreover, every employee, part-timer as well as full-timer, should have a unique primary or secondary responsibil-ity. Even the newest part-timer should have a unique assignment, though it be only a minor one, such as keeping the bags in all checkstands or cleaning up at the front-end. Such individualized assignments enable the employee to feel, and to actually be impor-tant, since others are dependent upon him to carry out his special function; they also give him an opportunity to prove that he can handle responsibility.

Another reason for making job assignments is to insure that all employees become skilled in performing specific tasks. Managers should therefore systematically rotate primary and secondary as-signments. In addition, job assignments enable the manager to schedule jobs for completion during the manager's absence (lunch hours, days off, vacations, and other occasions). A job assignment procedure is also a major asset to the manager's replacement during the manager's absence.

TABLE 4
Product Requirements Form

Produce Department

Note: Prepare items in sequence listed.

Item Required	Number of Cases Required	Need for Set-up	To Be Displayed in			
			Bulk	Wrap	Bag	Sleeve
Iceberg lettuce	2	X			X	
Celery	2	X				X
Cabbage	1	X	X			
Corn	2	X		X		
Green Peppers	1		X			
Broccoli	1		X			
Cauliflower	2		X			
Cucumbers	1		X			
Iceberg lettuce	4				X	
Celery	2					X

Back-up personnel from other departments should be assigned to assist in emergencies at the front-end, particularly during peak volume hours. The manager should not schedule all the grocery hours at once just because a grocery load comes in one day. That would leave a void on other days of the week, when front-end back-up personnel are needed. Primary and secondary assignments for cashiers should be tied in with the daily front-end schedule. In other departments, they should coincide with labor-hour requirements for each variable and fixed activity.

Assigning Responsibility and Delegating Authority. Assigning responsibility differs from job assignments in that an employee is given the right and the authority to make decisions and, within specified limits, to do things his or her own way. The grocery stock clerk who is responsible for pricing and stocking paper, cereal, cake mix and baby foods according to the standard practices and methods set up for the department, has merely been assigned a task. The grocery manager still orders the merchandise for the department and the clerk has been given no real authority. But employees can grow and develop on the job only when they are given some authority to make decisions and some responsibility to see that their decisions are carried out. And since a major part of every manager's job is to develop subordinates, the manager must provide them with the opportunity, guidance and encouragement that will enable them to advance. A manager must give employees a chance for self-fulfillment and, at the same time, contribute to the development of future managers. This, in turn, will free the manager for more important work.

Though a manager cannot relinquish total accountability to a subordinate, a stock clerk, for example, may be put in charge of part-timers and held responsible for their performances. Nevertheless, if the part-timers make mistakes, the manager is still accountable; delegating responsibility does not mean relinquishing it.

A good manager will not submit to the temptation to override decisions made by a subordinate to whom he has delegated authority. If he does so, he is in danger of destroying the employee's initiative and desire to grow. Too often, responsibility is rejected because initiative had been damaged by an authoritarian boss.

Delegating authority requires clear explanations, not only to the subordinate who takes on the authority, but to *his* subordinates as well. This is best accomplished with a written job description passed out to everyone involved. Each person should be made to understand the precise limits of the delegated authority and responsibility in order to avoid confusion and conflict among personnel.

Permitting Employees to Make Decisions: Many progressive supermarket companies believe that every decision should be made at the lowest possible level of employee capable of making that decision. The person closest to the problem who knows most about it should be best qualified to solve it and, in turn, decision making contributes to the person's growth and development. In operation, this means that the store manager should let the produce manager make all possible decisions about the produce department; the grocery manager, about the grocery department, and so forth.

A new but experienced produce department manager who decides to completely rearrange the merchandise in the department should be permitted to do so even if the store manager is convinced that the move would cut departmental gross profit by 2 percent, at a cost to the store of $600 gross profit for a week. Indeed, the store manager cannot really be sure that such an alteration will represent a loss to the store, and is only making an educated guess. Furthermore, chances are the produce manager is more likely than the store manager to know what will happen. The produce manager, after all, is closest to the operation and would not have planned the move had he not thought it would be an improvement. What it amounts to is a difference in opinion and, when the issue is based on opinion, the decision should be made by the person closest to the job.

Suppose, however, that the store manager, in this case, turns down the produce manager's idea. A few weeks later the produce manager returns with another proposal. "I want to rearrange the packaging equipment in the backroom according to this plan I've worked out, and it won't cost the company a red cent. With the change I'm sure we can get 10 percent more production from the packaging operation." If this and subsequent suggestions are turned down, the store manager can eventually take the credit for ruining one potentially good produce manager, for killing his initiative and for depriving him of the opportunity to develop. A produce manager who is treated in this fashion is likely to look for a job where his judgment will be relied upon or, worse, to become a "yes-man" who maintains the status quo and mediocrity in his department.

When the store manager is requested to make a decision that a subordinate should rightfully make, the manager should insist that the subordinate make it independently. A dairy manager in a large Midwestern shopping center store recently told a store manager: "Those off-brand cheese dips we got in last month just aren't moving. I'm afraid they'll all go bad before we can get rid of them. What should I do?"

The manager immediately thought of a solution but did not offer it. Instead he answered: "Look, it's 11:00 AM now. Give this matter some thought and see if you can come up with a solution. Mull over it for an hour and then come back and we'll talk about it." At noon the dairy manager returned with a plan which the store manager endorsed. In fact, as the store manager later pointed out, the solution proposed by the diary manager surpassed his own.

Of course, there are limits to the jobs that can be delegated. Managers should never delegate decisions that they must rightfully make themselves. Unfortunately, however, some managers delegate jobs that are really theirs to perform but which they find distasteful or, on the other hand, spend valuable time at menial jobs simply because they enjoy the work.

One manager of a large Eastern store spends a good 50 percent of his time stocking groceries and building displays. Though he excels at both of these jobs, his company pays him to manage. After he completes his book work and other miscellaneous details, he simply does not have time to plan, organize or analyze problems. Another manager of a large store in the South probably spends almost half her time bagging and carrying out orders. She is exceptionally good with customers, but is not being paid more than $20.00 an hour to do a part-timer's job that pays $4.50 an hour. She too cannot find enough hours in a day to fulfill her major managerial responsibilities.

When managers spend their valuable time at menial tasks which should be done by others, the store tends to drift toward mediocrity. Delegating properly carried out is a most valuable business tool; improperly handled, it becomes a major liability. Delegating authority is a primary responsibility of every manager. Because many chains believe that developing subordinates is one of the manager's most important functions, they maintain that the manager who has not delegated authority to an assistant and, thus, has not helped the assistant to grow in managerial capacity, is himself not ready for promotion. A manager's prestige is always enhanced and never reduced when he delegates authority; but in so doing he should not violate the principle that each employee has only one boss.

Problem Analysis

A manager is evaluated on the performance of his department or store. The manager's livelihood depends on an ability to analyze and identify the causes of performance problems, to come up with the best possible solutions and to follow-through to see that the problems are corrected. Running a supermarket is a complex responsibility. Because many outside factors influence performance, it is often impossible to isolate a single cause for a given change. However, even when it is possible to identify through careful analysis the causes of a change in performance, a manager often jumps to conclusions instead of systematically searching for such causes. Following are three examples of how hasty analyses lead to wrong answers.

1. The gross profit in the meat department of a major West Coast chain had been steady for several years in succession. Then, in one week it took a sudden drop from 24 to 22 percent, though the gross profit in other stores operated by the chain in the same city remained constant. During the next week the situation deteriorated and the meat department produced 3 percent less in gross profit.

The supervisor and store manager were alarmed. They rechecked the inventory, checked the receipts, billings, tonnage, movement, item prices, trimmings, bone barrels, cutting methods, security, and more; all to no avail. The situation grew worse and by the fourth week, gross profit was down 3.5 percent and no explanation could be found. After six weeks, with no sign of improvement, management grew desperate and transferred the meat manager. "Somehow, the meat manager must be at fault," was the line of reasoning. But with a new person in the job, there was still no improvement.

The cause was uncovered quite accidentally some three months after the problem appeared. Three new cashiers had been put on the payroll during the first week of the problem. These cashiers had not been taught to ring-up cheese items (considered meat items in this company) on the meat department key. Instead, each cashier assumed that cheese should be rung on the grocery key with other dairy items. The compensating improved gross profit in the grocery department did not show up until a grocery inventory was made a month after the cause was identified. A systematic analysis of the problem would have avoided the waste of hundreds of dollars spent on futile searches for causes that did not exist. Moreover, the meat manager who was transferred unnecessarily would have been spared a great deal of humiliation and anxiety.

2. In another store, grocery department sales and gross profit began to decline gradually, while meat and produce sales and gross profit remained steady. This trend continued for a year, while the store manager and supervisor hunted in vain for answers. Finally, when they were about to condemn the grocery manager, an offhand remark by a customer provided the clue to the riddle. The customer said she was tired of traveling six miles to buy dry groceries

at the discount store which had opened the previous year and which handled only dry groceries. It seems that over the past year, she and other regular customers had been buying only the advertised grocery specials as they shopped for their meat and produce in the problem store.

3. An unusual situation occurred in another store where the new manager seemed thoroughly unable to keep any cashiers. Almost every new cashier would stay a few weeks, then quit, and when the manager interviewed them, the reasons were always the same: a better job, dissatisfaction with the work, the hours, the pay, and so forth. After several months, the supervisor persuaded the company that the manager simply could not handle people and the manager was fired.

One of the cashiers finally revealed the real reason for this epidemic of resignations. It seemed that a regular cashier, who had been hired by the store at about the same time as the released manager had taken over, was addicted to narcotics and continually solicited loans from other cashiers, which were never repaid. Though the employee had a pleasant personality and got along well with co-workers, the cashier's habit and financial problems put the other people on the spot. Rather than complain to management, they quit.

Problem Solving and Decision Making

The best way to solve performance problems is to carefully follow these twelve steps:

1. *Identify the problem*: Any variance between planned performance and actual performance is considered a problem.

2. *Classify problems by priority*: The seriousness of a problem is determined by two factors: (a) the area of performance affected by the problem (sales, gross profit, wage expense, sales per labor-hour, bad check losses, shrinkage, turnover and so forth); and (b) the degree of variance between planned and actual performance.

3. *Identify controllable and non-controllable factors influencing performance*: Every known factor that might have an adverse effect on performance in the problem area should be written down.

4. *Identify the time, place, nature and degree of variance*: The selected problem area, and when and where the variance first occurred, should be noted. Then, the degree of variance to the present day should be indicated.

5. *List unusual events*: Every unique or unusual event that oc-curred at, or about, the time the variance first appeared (whether or not the event seems to be related to the problem) should be written down.

6. *Identify possible and impossible causes*: Each controllable and non-controllable factor should be reviewed and the list of un-usual events that occurred simultaneously with the problem should be examined for possible connections. Each factor that is positively rejected as a cause should be struck out.

7. *Classify alternate causes*: Controllable and non-controllable factors that are not eliminated remain as possible causes of the problem and deserve critical analyses. Each of these factors should be related to the unique or unusual events already listed, and possi-ble connections should be examined. Now, all factors should be arranged in sequence, with "most likely cause" at the top and "least likely cause" at the bottom.

8. *Develop alternate solutions*: Depending on what is considered the most likely cause or causes, alternate solutions to overcome the problem should be developed.

9. *Establish objectives*: A goal and target date, showing the amount of variance to be reduced or eliminated, should be set.

10. *Evaluate alternate solutions against established objectives*: Alternate solutions should be studied in order to determine which is the best in terms of the objectives already set.

11. *Make the decision*: The decision should be made on the basis of the best solution.

12. *Implement the decision*: Follow-through should be con-ducted to insure that the cause of the problem is removed. Periodic checks should be made to insure that planned progress is made toward the goal of eliminating the variance.

This twelve-step procedure is not really as complex as it may seem. With this plan, many problems can be analyzed and resolved in less than an hour. Each of the three problem situations described earlier could have been solved within a few hours at most, had this systematic approach to problem analysis and decision making been used. Of course, there are many supermarket performance prob-lems that are not as simple as those described in the three examples. Some problems have several interrelated causes which are difficult to separate and identify. Yet without a systematic approach to prob-lem analysis, there can be little hope of ever solving such problems except accidentally.

Problem analysis should seldom be a one-person effort. Though the manager responsible for performance in a problem area should lead the analysis and make the final decision, advantage should be taken of the talents of others, particularly those closest to the problem, to identify factors that influence performance, pinpoint unusual events, classify alternate causes and solutions, and help in the critical analysis.

Managers and Employees

An employee's performance and satisfaction with his job are in large measure dependent on the manager's skills as a planner, organizer, problem-solver and decision-maker. When a manager fails to plan, forecast and schedule carefully, the employee is often in doubt about what he will be doing next; his sense of security is threatened. The manager who does not organize effectively by assigning responsibility and authority, damages employee self-respect and team spirit, and denies his subordinates the possibility of progressing and developing. If a manager tends to solve problems and reach decisions frivolously, his employees can neither trust him nor rely on him for sound judgment. Thus, in a very real sense, a manager's competence in these areas affects an employee's readiness to do his best and, in turn, influences the total performance of the department or store.

11 | Motivation and Morale

Sometime after the turn of the century, my grandfather owned a grocery store in a small town. A small staff operated the store. My father was the full-time help and the teenage boy who came in Saturdays was the part-timer. Their roles were interchangeable; communication was direct. Though employee morale was never discussed as a personnel concept, it existed at its best in my grandfather's store.

But that was over seventy years ago. Since then businesses have expanded enormously. Today's big stores require more than a hundred employees. Departmental, store and divisional decisions flow up and down between headquarters and local stores. It is necessary to provide superlative service in what is now a highly competitive business. Because employees must work in teams to make such service available, they must be highly motivated and their morale must be excellent. They must feel that they are contributing to "their store" so that customers, in turn, will come to think of the store as "their store."

Good Morale

Good morale results when persons of different backgrounds are motivated to cooperate for the sake of a common cause which makes sense to them and which seems to be worth attaining. In supermarketing, good morale is the product of an understanding of the company's goals, the chance to share and even work out goals, and, thereby, to make a real contribution to the growth of the enterprise.

In a company that pioneered in the processing and marketing of orange juice concentrate, morale was at its highest when the company could not meet its payroll and faced bankruptcy. During that crisis, its employees stood shoulder to shoulder in support of the idea the company was developing and showed remarkable faith in management and in themselves. This company had somehow succeeded at creating an environment that resulted in an extraordinarily high morale. But even in normal situations, the level of employee morale is a fairly accurate indicator of the effectiveness of leadership and reveals how well employees respond to the requirements set by the employer. Morale, then, is not a reflection of employee capability but, rather, of the leadership qualities of the individuals who set the standards.

Trust, the Basis of Leadership

No matter how lofty and potentially satisfying a company's goals may be, the absence of trust between its leaders and members will prevent the fulfillment of its goals. The manager who employs the best techniques and has a record of outstanding accomplishments will certainly fail if his people distrust him. On the other hand, a manager whose motives are not suspect can inspire a relationship which results in effectively motivated employees. "One thing about Charlie," say his people, "he may be tough, but you can trust him. When the going gets rough, he's the one you can count on."

Employee morale is dependent on direct and personal human relations. The company and its philosophy, its carefully worked out goals, contribute only secondarily to morale. What matters is how employees interpret the boss and whether they trust him.

Employee Needs

In order to inspire employee trust and loyalty, managers must recognize individual needs and create an environment in which

FIGURE 1
Hierarchy of Needs

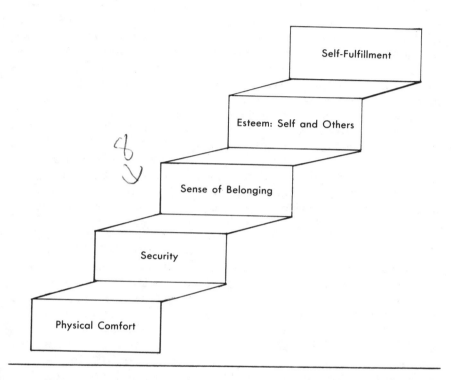

those needs can be satisfied. Most persons share certain needs, including the need to belong, to be a part of the group, to share in shaping personal and group goals, to have a voice in establishing group rules; the need to be given definite responsibilities which they can handle and which tap their skills; the need to contribute to a worthwhile cause which transcends personal or group satisfaction; the need to grow with the group and to be kept informed of the progress of the group; and the need to be supervised by good and trustworthy leaders.

According to Dr. Abraham Maslow, a well-known expert in the field of motivational research, there is a definite "hierarchy of needs" which can be illustrated by a series of steps.[1] Each of these ascending steps represents the progress of an individual from infantile dependency to a poised, mature adulthood. (See Figure 1.)

[1] *Motivation and Personality* (New York: Harper & Row, 1954).

Needs and Motivation.   An individual's morale is dependent on the degree to which his needs are satisfied. The clerk who sees his job as a chance to make enough money to buy a sports car will be content only when he achieves that goal. Another employee may primarily require a sense of security from his job at the store. He will be satisfied when his manager tells him what to do, his union protects his rights, and when he can retire with enough to get by. A third clerk may see the store, the company and its employees as a sort of family, giving him a sense of belonging which matters more to him than other needs. When another company offers such an employee a similar job with more pay, he would be likely to resist because of his deep feeling of belonging; alternatively, this sense of belonging might be detrimental to him by keeping him in one place and stunting his growth to a point where he may object to management's desire to promote him away from his accustomed store. A fourth type of employee who values appreciation and esteem has far more sophisticated needs than does the one who requires simpler satisfactions. Finally, the most mature individual will achieve self-fulfillment only in a store's or company's top job, where the rewards are more than money or security.

The manager who insists that people work for money and nothing else is taking into account only the human needs for physical comfort and security. In disregarding the equally powerful human drive to belong, for esteem and self-fulfillment, such a manager fails to tap a most significant source of motivation. As an individual matures, the prospect of self-enrichment motivates him far more successfully than do the simpler rewards of money and security. In order to enhance self-motivation, an individual's personal standard of values must be considered. An intelligent manager can have motivated subordinates by matching situations to employees' training, experience, general background and above all, to their patterns of needs and values.

Morale Indicators

Excessive employee turnover, low productivity, a continuing flood of inconsequential grievances all reflect poor morale. Poor morale can take the form of excessive absenteeism caused by an employee's desire to escape the problems and demands of his job. Low morale is also invariably demonstrated by employee rudeness and by poor service to customers. Managers and their superiors have also learned to interpret customer complaints about the store, a department or an individual as signs of poor morale among employees.

Creating Good Morale

In order to create good morale, managers must pay attention to and exploit all of the often contradictory variables which comprise the human personality. They must consistently work at building team spirit. Individuals must be motivated beyond their elemental need for physical comfort and security. Morale depends on more than slogans, cheers and group enthusiasm. Peter Drucker, in his *Practice of Management*,[2] has provided some excellent hints which the manager who wishes to improve employee morale would do well to consider. Some of Mr. Drucker's suggestions are summarized here.

If an employee is to invest his mental and physical energies in a company, he must be encouraged to understand the company's programs and goals, both short- and long-range. Among these programs and goals, he should be able to find something which appeals to him and with which he can identify his own values and needs.

Once an employee understands the philosophy and goals of the company, he should also be provided with sufficient challenge to enable him to grow to his maximum potential on his job. Management must be prepared to provide for the human needs to progress and develop.

Few things jar an employee's security and morale more than uncertainty about what his work involves. An employee must be told exactly what is expected of him. Job descriptions provide an employee with such information. It is most important to allow each employee to match the job to his own unique talents and abilities. Properly motivated, an employee will expect more of himself than his superior expects of him, and will set higher standards for himself than the job usually demands.

An employee's morale often depends upon the degree to which he is trusted to do his job without oppressive supervision. Some employees never have much of a chance to prove what they can do before a superior intrudes to offer advice and, occasionally, to take over. Though such a course of action may provide the manager with a spotless record, the employee's initiative is destroyed and his development is obstructed.

[2] (New York: Harper & Row, 1954.)

A periodic review of an employee's work should be scheduled in accordance with the requirements of the particular job. Such reviews prevent the manager from supervising excessively, while giving him a prescribed time during which he can offer constructive criticism. Even during such reviews, however, the object should not be to interfere but, rather, to share ideas, to examine together gains and losses, strengths and weaknesses, in order to facilitate progress toward individual and company goals. Nothing gives a person a more secure feeling than having a chance to do his work, to have it reviewed at friendly, unthreatening meetings designed to give him direct and meaningful help. His security and, consequently, his morale will be even further enhanced if he knows that he can feel free to ask for help whenever he needs it.

The desire to be recognized and appreciated also significantly motivates employees. Recognition, appreciation and attention represent a form of payment for which employees are usually willing to work. A business that is looking for good, promotable people should provide such recognition in the form of respect, salary and advancement.

Renewing Employee Morale

Absenteeism, turnover, grievances, low productivity and generally poor morale are not difficult to spot. They can be detected by management, reflected in complaints from customers, or revealed through attitude surveys. An employee whose morale is low and whose attitude is poor is not motivated. In order to exploit such an employee's full potential, the manager must first discover what motivates him and what he values. The employee must be presented with new alternatives to match his own values, and provided with adequate help, training and guidance. His individual ideas, skills and energies should be considered and tapped. He must be encouraged to overcome the natural fear that he will fail at his new tasks or that he will be expected to perform perfectly at once.

A manager's skill at creating an environment which produces motivated employees and high morale is as significant as his insight into the store's operation and his ability to plan, organize and solve problems. The productivity and success of the store is in large measure dependent upon whether its staff is sufficiently motivated to work as a team to fulfill store goals.

12 | Communicating

"How can I get a message through to my people?"
·"What can I do to make communication lines work?"
"How can I encourage people to speak up at meetings?"
"How can I convince people to share their ideas?"

Questions of this sort are consistently asked by people in top and middle management positions whenever they meet. When discussing the major difficulties they encounter working with people, managers always give special priority to the problem of communicating.

What Is Communication?

Communicating in business is more than simply transmitting and receiving information. In a business relationship, effective communication is a way of eliciting a favorable response. Hopefully, when the superior communicates with the employee, the result will be effective and successful action.

201

An employee examines the messages he receives in order to decide whether or not to act upon them. He perceives and interprets combinations of words, gestures, sounds, actions, facial expressions—in short, the total atmosphere of a message. Individual backgrounds and temperaments often make for a wide range of interpretations of the same message. Occasionally, the personal factor leads to so complete a distortion of the original message that it is no longer recognizable.

Communicating is much like hooking up to a two-way radio, with a speaker and receiver at both ends. When one person speaks, the other must tune in; when the other speaks, the first party must do the same. But there is always the chance that static—emotion, tone of voice, and numerous atmospheric conditions—will contribute to a misinterpretation of the words. In face-to-face encounters, gestures, facial expressions and other factors also interfere with successful communication. Even while privately reading, thinking or writing, a person's ability to receive and transmit ideas is colored by feelings, attitudes and general state of mind. Anyone who has considered the problems of communicating would no doubt agree with the person who said, "I know you believe you understand what you think I have said . . . but I am not sure you realize that what you hear is not what I mean."

Communication Guidelines

1. *Creating the right climate*: The manager who wishes to communicate successfully must first create the right climate or atmosphere so that his subordinates will be willing to share ideas and set up good communication links. An atmosphere of good will and trust must be established from the outset.

2. *Planning*: A manager, writer, counselor or meeting leader must know in advance what he wants to accomplish. If the message he wishes to transmit is not clear in his own mind, he will be unable to communicate coherently and the listener will surely fail to get the message.

3. *Organizing*: There are no easy short cuts to communicating an idea. Ideas must be thought through and organized in advance so that they may be communicated clearly and precisely.

4. *Clarity*: President Coolidge was once approached by a neighbor who missed church one Sunday in New Hampshire. "What was the sermon about this morning?" asked the neighbor. "The preacher never said," replied Coolidge. This preacher had obviously not succeeded at communicating. His sermon was obscure; he had violated

an important communication principle by addressing his congregation in an unclear fashion.

5. *Considering the listener:* Words evoke a multitude of associations in the mind of the listener. The speaker who wishes to communicate successfully with his audience must choose his words carefully. He must select those words that will elicit the desired response from the listener. He must speak in the listener's language, for the sake of the listener.

6. *Considering the speaker:* Ralph Waldo Emerson said: "What you are speaks so loudly that I cannot possibly hear what you say." Anyone who wishes to communicate effectively must take into account the preset notions the listener has about him.

7. *Patience:* When some persons obtain no result from a memo they write or a speech they deliver, they tend to condemn the listener rather than themselves. Such people are likely to conduct a meeting expecting miracles to result, and to give up when their hopes are disappointed, asserting that meetings are a waste of time. They lack the necessary patience to communicate an idea.

8. *Testing comprehension:* A speaker may ascertain whether or not he has communicated successfully by periodically asking questions and listening to answers. In this fashion he can make sure that he has been tuned in properly and that his listeners have understood his message as he wished it to be understood.

A Coaching Session

A store or department manager, like a coach, must be able to lead, counsel and discipline his subordinates in order to encourage them to do their best. He must consider each person's unique position, experience, training, temperament and nature. Like a good coach, he must praise his subordinates, but he must also offer constructive criticism in order to help each person to function better as an individual and as a team member.

The store or department manager should arrange a one-hour session every six months with each of his immediate subordinates in which to discuss the subordinate's progress. A person needs to be told how he is doing so that his self-esteem and sense of fulfillment and belonging may be reinforced. The manager who must satisfy those needs must understand what motivates people, be sensitive to individual differences, and be armed with the tools to successfully communicate with others.

Such a manager would do well to follow the eight communication guidelines outlined above. He should select the right time and place for the coaching session and then extend an invitation to the employee. With all the employee's records at hand, the manager should ask himself what the counseling session should accomplish and how its objectives should be achieved. Because a good employee is a company's greatest asset, the coaching-counseling session should be handled as carefully as decisions on merchandising or on ordering. All have the same purpose: to increase profits.

During the meeting, the manager should avoid all signs of impatience, hurry, thoughtless criticism, lack of empathy and other negative actions that block communication and eventually lose employees. The employee must be encouraged to participate in the discussion. The manager must suppress the desire to do all the talking.

The desire for change should be self-motivated; instead of telling the employee what to do, the manager should ask him for his suggestions. The manager should elicit the employee's feelings, thoughts and beliefs. Together they must decide on the positive steps that ought to be taken to insure the employee's advancement. Among the questions the manager might raise are the following: What gives you the most satisfaction here? What do you think is your real strength? What specific part of the work do you do best? Where do you think you most need improvement? What can we do to be of assistance? What is your most important short-range goal? Where would you like to be in five years?

Listening

The average manager spends approximately half his or her communication time listening. In a counseling session, the manager must not only listen with his ears, he must also listen for overtones of feeling; he must listen in an alert, friendly and sensitive manner in order to make sound judgments and appraisals. In addition to his role as a listener in the counseling session, a manager must also listen daily to problems, messages, small talk, gripes, and news of interpersonal relationships of all descriptions. He must listen to his employees, his employer and to his customers. Nevertheless, most managers are ill-prepared to listen successfully.

Emotional barriers, including patterns of authority, positive and negative feelings about a situation, different ways of seeing the same thing, abrasive personalities and impatience, often prevent good listening. The manager's anxiety to succeed, to complete a job quickly or to elicit a favorable response, can cause him to make gross errors in listening and translating what an employee says. Likewise, the employee's desire to succeed might impel him to listen only

superficially so that he can quickly get on with the work of improving his performance. Even worse, when animosity exists between
the participants, each person tunes out the other in a hurry or listens
poorly.

Some people in authority tend to listen solely for facts at the
expense of ideas. Instead of getting the total picture or concept,
they select the details that interest them. They miss what is behind
an idea, what the person is really saying and feeling; they miss the
reason why an employee says what he says and why he chooses this
occasion to say it. How the employee's conversation fits into the
general pattern of his behavior and performance is also lost to the
person who listens for facts rather than ideas. Some managers also
tend to miss the ideas of slow-speaking, inexperienced or distressed
employees and show their failure to listen patiently by interrupting
the employee with such comments as: "Now, in other words" (meaning in the manager's words); "What you really mean is . . ." (here,
the manager twists the employee's words); "Get to the point, Bill"
(the manager reveals his impatience with the employee).

A manager is likely to feel that others will understand him as long
as he understands them. However, language and job-level gaps exist
in all businesses and they widen when those involved in communication fail to recognize these gaps. When a boss tries to be a "buddy,"
his words are often translated into the voice of authority and he can
be grossly misinterpreted.

Listening requires attention. The manager who yields to all types
of distractions and is constantly handling pressing details during a
conversation with an employee cannot listen properly. A place
where distractions and pressures are reduced to a minimum is required for good listening. Internal distractions, such as the manager's feelings about the employee or his prejudices about the issues,
must also be reduced or eliminated. The manager who dislikes a
person or objects to his way of acting and speaking, will often filter
out only part of the conversation and miss the point of the employee's comments.

If a manager reacts in kind to an employee's anger, insolence,
negativism, abusiveness and rudeness, he will never hear the message or be able to help. An employee will be deeply humiliated by
his manager's refusal to hear him out and, conversely, will be truly
flattered when he receives his manager's full and sincere attention.
The manager should therefore indicate when he has received the
message by making the appropriate response or by asking the right
question. The attention a leader gives an individual can give him
confidence to speak his mind, to volunteer both the good and bad
ideas which may be accepted or rejected, but which ultimately

contribute to the growth of the employee, of the manager and of the organization.

Conducting a Meeting

The details on good communicating and listening presented above may not only be applied to individual counseling sessions, but to district, in-store and department meetings, and to all other types of communications that normally take place in a supermarket company. Communicating with a group, however, is obviously more complicated than communicating with a single individual. A group leader must satisfy the individual needs of a number of different personalities, while simultaneously achieving the goals that have been set for the meeting. In order to accomplish this, the leader must devote considerable time and thought to conducting a successful meeting.

Planning a Meeting

Planning with some of the participants: If 25 employees will be involved in a one-day meeting, progress will be insured if five of them gather with the manager beforehand for a planning session. These five will most likely provide the manager with guidance, as well as assistance in planning and working out the physical set-up of the meeting. They should be involved in the various activities that will make the meeting more effective. For example, they might be encouraged to prepare notices and materials, to set up the meeting room, to act as hosts, and even to serve as leaders for all, or part of, the meeting.

Selecting the target: Several types of meetings may be conducted, including those that merely provide information; those in which the presentation of information is followed by questions; those in which advice is sought from others, such as outside researchers; those in which advice is sought from members; and those in which people work together to solve problems. The manager must determine in advance the sort of meeting he wishes to conduct. He must set a target in terms of his subjects or problems.

Choosing the most effective methods and techniques: The manager must select a technique or a combination of techniques that will produce maximum participation from the audience. Active participation insures the utilization of the unique experiences, training and ideas of individual members. It also furthers the learning process

FIGURE 1
Seating Arrangements for Meetings

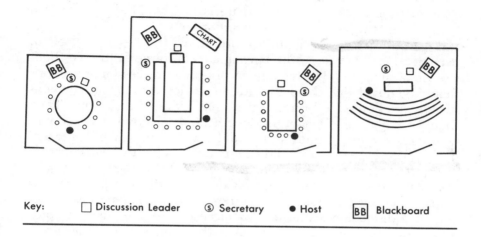

Key: ☐ Discussion Leader   ⑤ Secretary   ● Host   [BB] Blackboard

by providing an opportunity to become involved. Finally, active participation gives individuals experience in speaking up; such experience helps them to grow and develop.

Working out details of the meeting place: The physical arrangement of the meeting will depend on the target that has been set and the methods that will be used. Six boxes in a circle may be the best arrangement for a meeting of department managers in the backroom of a store. On the other hand, the right room in a hotel may guarantee a successful all-day meeting.

The arrangement of a room can have a profound effect on the atmosphere of the meeting. When less than fifteen persons are participating in the meeting, a circle arrangement is perfect. If chairs are placed in rows, as in a schoolroom or lecture hall, a chilly atmosphere is produced which stifles discussion. For larger sessions, a "U" arrangement or a square might produce the best results. Semicircles are useful arrangements for meetings that involve 24 to 100 people. (See Figure 1.)

Enlisting a hosting committee: If the meeting is formal, that is, not conducted on boxes in the backroom, a number of employees might be asked to serve as hosts. They should be responsible for the arrangement of the room, and for the preparation of such tools as blackboard, chalk, paperboards, pencils, notebooks or writing paper, and visual aid machinery. When the members arrive at the meeting place, the hosts should greet them and conduct them to their seats. They should see to it that the participants are treated with as much thoughtfulness as is accorded to invited guests. When the meeting ends, the hosting committee should be responsible for the safety of equipment and other company material. It should also make sure that the meeting room is left in good order.

Preparing questions: Sound questions are the key to successful participation. They keep the participants on target and give them a sense of direction. During a good pre-planning session, questions should be developed that will lead the participants to focus on constructive action. Good questions should be clear and brief. They should have a single target, be specific and selective. They should be framed positively; questions should never be negatively phrased. Finally, good questions should excite and involve the participants.

Employing simple discussion techniques: One of the toughest jobs of any manager is to relinquish his or her leadership prerogatives when soliciting discussion from others. The manager must be an objective discussion leader and use accepted techniques to inspire maximum participation and to cover the subject as completely as possible. The manager must stay out of the discussion by following the rules of parliamentary procedure which prescribe that the president who wishes to express an opinion must surrender the chair to the vice-president. The manager must refrain from imposing opinions, judgments and authority on the group. People who are subjected to criticism or censure will rarely discuss their ideas or problems freely. If a manager chooses to act as both discussion leader and boss, employees will think of the manager as a boss, and clam up. All comments from members of the audience should be greeted with an objective "thank you." A highly complimentary response may dampen the courage of the next speaker who fears that he or she may not be similarly complimented; a derogatory remark would be equally discouraging to potential speakers.

Finding ways for others to lead: Managers often mistakenly tend to feel that they alone should run all the meetings in which they are involved. Under any circumstances, it is not unreasonable that one of the group is a more effective discussion leader and is able to elicit better participation than the manager. Such a subordinate should be given the chance to lead. For example, the produce manager should be encouraged, after duly preparing, to run a session on tie-in sales involving produce. The opportunity to lead will give subordinates a chance to learn, grow and to temporarily assume management responsibilities.

Free Discussion

Few meetings are totally free and open. Often, monopolists take over, tempers grow hot, and a small group of articulate participants runs the session.

Free discussion is a type of meeting which requires self-discipline on the part of the members so that ideas might be shared and battles for control may be avoided. The manager or discussion leader should state the ground rules at the beginning. It is the leader's responsibility to see to it that everyone has a chance to participate and that no one monopolizes the discussion. All members should be cautioned that they have an obligation to the group to think before they speak, to organize their ideas for clarity, to speak briefly and to the point.

Members should be made to understand that the floor will be denied to anyone who has spoken too often, so that an opportunity for others to be heard may be provided. This can be done tactfully with such comments as, "I'm sorry Joe, but will you let me move around you for a minute to make sure that we share the discussion a bit more?"; or "Fred, I'm going to ask you to tell us about that Friday sale you held last week, so get yourself ready to give us a good story."

The leader of a free discussion must be alert to prevent too many digressions. He or she should keep the group on target by focusing its thinking on the basic elements of the problem. Any of the following questions might be raised to keep the discussion in line: What is the problem? Why is it a problem? How can it be handled? Who should take the responsibility? When should it be done? Where should it take place?

Circular Response

Dr. Eduard C. Lindeman developed the circular response technique, a simple discussion method that works most successfully with groups of no more than eighteen people seated in a circle. (However, if more than eighteen people are scheduled for the meeting, they can be split up into smaller groups under individual leaders.) He worked out a formula whereby each person at a meeting is given a minute to express himself.

The target of the discussion, in other words, the problem, should be phrased for the group in advance. According to the rules of circular response, each participant may speak for one minute, with no outside interruption. The discussion begins when the leader calls for someone in the circle to volunteer an answer to the question or problem. With a member of the group acting as timekeeper to restrict a participant to one minute, the leader moves around the circle, clockwise or counterclockwise, always making certain that members contribute in turn.

The circular response method resembles a poker game. When a volunteer offers his idea (bid), the man next to him has several options. He may (1) bid, with a different idea; (2) raise, by adding to an answer already presented; (3) pass, which means he cannot contribute now; or (4) ask that his minute be spent in silence so that the group may consider the subject further.

The key to a good discussion is the well-prepared question. Once the question has been established, the leader of a circular response type of discussion must list the ground rules. The leader must explain that the method provides one way of insuring that each person's right to speak is protected and that the group quickly covers an idea. Once the rules have been understood, the leader should submit the discussion question, usually by writing it on a blackboard where all can see, and then give each person three minutes to think through and write down a good answer. When three minutes have elapsed, the leader should ask each person to reduce his or her answer to ten words or less for clear reporting. The leader should then ask one of the group to act as a timekeeper and to signal when any member has spoken for a minute. As each idea is presented, it should be recorded on the blackboard for the later consideration of the group. The leader may choose to go around the circle more than once, depending on the extent to which the subject has been covered. When all of the ideas have been presented, and when it is no longer possible to elicit additional comments, the manager may speak as the leader of the group.

The circular response method is most useful in a group composed of peers. It creates an open discussion and effectively warms up a group. A manager can use the circular response technique to build an agenda by asking the group such a question as, "What subjects, if handled this morning, would help you most?" When the circular response device is used, people learn to share in discussion and the monopolists are controlled. It is also useful in summarizing a meeting and in securing a commitment from the team; for instance, when the manager-leader asks such a question as, "What is the first step you will take today to put this new store policy into operation?" In short, the circular response device can set up quick communications between several persons, and evoke ideas, advice and solutions to problems in a brief span of time.

There Are No Formulas

Understandably, managers would love to be presented with formulas to cope with the personal problems of employees, to encourage new employees, maintain the spirit of old employees, handle demotions, improve performance, improve morale, and deal with many other communications problems. But formulas or pat answers are impossible because each person is different. Each person has unique problems and possibilities which must be individually investigated by the manager. The ideas presented in this chapter represent broad principles and procedures that the manager may apply to individual situations whenever appropriate to improve communication and morale.

13 | Evaluating Performance

Today, many supermarket executives routinely apply tough business sense and computer technology to such complex problems as determining the best store location, store design and product mix. But very few give serious thought to the methods their companies use to appraise employee performance. It seems that in the opinion of many of these business people, appraising performance is either too difficult to do well or too simple to merit serious thought.

An effective performance appraisal system has two objectives: to accurately evaluate the performance of the employee and to improve the employee's future performance. The appraisal system which fails to accomplish these two objectives is inadequate. Many companies in the industry are saddled with appraisal or evaluation systems that are impossible to use objectively or that stress attributes that are irrelevant to company objectives. For example, many evaluation systems call for appraising employees on the basis of such subjective personality traits as "loyalty," "cooperativeness" or "self-confidence." Now what do such terms mean? Does everyone agree on the definition of "loyalty"? To whom or what should an employee be loyal? To an immediate superior? To top management? What if the two are in conflict in a certain situation? And how is "loyalty" measured? How important or meaningful to a company's objectives is the "loyalty" of its employees?

What exactly does a manager mean when he rates a stock clerk as "very cooperative"? Is the employee meek and submissive, taking orders with no back talk? Is such "cooperativeness" a virtue? Does it help the company to achieve its objectives? And when a manager rates an employee as "uncooperative" or "stubborn," does he effectively distinguish those traits from "assertiveness" or "self-confidence"? In fact, unless he is specifically trained for the purpose, a manager is not qualified to judge a subordinate's personality. Any appraisal system that deals with intangible traits or attributes, which are not directly related to company objectives, is dangerous and unfair.

The Need for Objectivity

A major league baseball player is certainly not judged on the basis of his personality traits. Many baseball stars, including Babe Ruth, would be considered "uncooperative," assuming the stories written about them are true. There are very firm and precise measurements for determining how well a ballplayer performs, including his runs-batted-in, batting average, earned run average, fielding average, double plays and others. No matter what his role, there are objective ways to measure his accomplishments. Though a player who breaks training rules is subject to a fine and even suspension, he is ultimately evaluated according to how well he measures up against very concise and clear-cut statistics. His measured performance, compared with the performance of other players, means the difference between staying with the team or being shipped down to the minors. The team itself, of course, is measured by its record of wins and losses, as well as by its standing in the league when compared with other teams.

Measuring Line Employee Performance

Objective standards, like those applied in baseball, are also available to supermarket managers for measuring the performances of line employees. When the score is determined by store sales and profits, line employees are the players who help to win or lose the game of retailing. The stores that score better than their competitors are among the league leaders; those that do not are in the cellar.

Still, every day someone says, "Ann is doing a good job," or "Mac's coming along." Do such statements comprise valuable performance appraisals? What information has been communicated? Is Ann *really* doing a good job? In what respect and to what degree? Is Mac "coming along" because he is agreeable and willing? Or does the speaker mean that the measured performances of Ann and Mac are above average? Because it is such a broad and general comment, it simply will not do as a precise evaluation of Ann's or Mac's performance on the job. Unfortunately, however, evaluations of this sort are still prevalent in the supermarket industry.

Suppose Mac is a grocery clerk. In that case, in order to know how well he is doing, he must be compared with other grocery clerks in the company with regard to such matters as how long it takes him to cut, correctly mark and stock one hundred cases of canned goods; how long it takes him to make price changes on thirty different items; how long it takes him to build a fifty-case soup display; his record of absences and latenesses; or how many customer complaints are lodged against him. Similarly, if Ann is a meat wrapper, she can be evaluated on the basis of the number of packages she wraps per hour and the number of rewraps she causes compared with company averages.

It is important to establish fixed appraisal techniques for a number of reasons. Both the employee and the manager must know exactly where the employee stands. Objective standards allow for the recognition of exceptional performances and for the identification of those employees whose performances are below par and who must therefore be helped rather than scolded. Good evaluation devices help to locate store problem areas and training needs, cutting guesswork to a minimum. Performance evaluation systems that are not based on objective factors are not only a waste of time, but even worse, they may lead to improper conclusions and, therefore, to costly decisions. They may also lead to unnecessary and undesirable turnover of employees who are poorly appraised.

If George, one of the company's top producing meat cutters, and Sam, one of its lowest producers, were measured on the basis of personality factors, it might be reported that Sam is "very pleasant and cooperative" while George is a "loner and shy." Clearly, such appraisals have little value when considering whether George or Sam should be transferred to a high volume store. When filling a production position, it makes no sense to hire a person with qualifications for a popularity contest.

There are objective standards of time, quality, production capacity, and even customer complaints or praise that can be set up to measure any line job in the supermarket industry. Unlike baseball, however, establishing such standards is not an easy job because no two companies play the game precisely alike. Objective standards must be tailored to each company's specific operating procedures, equipment, methods, needs and averages, and they must be pertinent to the particular job in question. But standards must always be defined if line employees are to be both properly appraised and fully productive.

Informal Appraisals

There are two basic ways to evaluate performance: informally and formally. The informal appraisal, which is used by some chains today, is really no system at all. An informal appraisal is made when a store manager tells his supervisor that "Ann is doing a fine job" or when several supervisors sit down when a job opening occurs to discuss the pros and cons of an employee. Consider, for instance, this informal appraisal made during a typical meeting between a director of store operations and three supervisors, Comden, Black and Miller:

"As you know, our new store in Northgate is due to open in a couple of months," said the director of operations, "and Stevens is to be moved from Number 11 to manage it. This meeting was called to select someone to replace Stevens. Take a couple of minutes to review in your minds the performances of those assistant managers in your stores who are best qualified for promotion. Have you got anyone who is qualified, Comden?"

"Smith at Number 2 is the best person I have," said Comden. "He's really a worker. Only yesterday I noticed he was working an hour after quitting time." The director then turned to Black and asked, "Who do you have for the job?" Black replied, "Buck at Number 7 has a real fine personality and gets along well with customers. He does everything I tell him to do with no argument. He's a company man . . . and he's ready for advancement."

When his turn came, supervisor Miller said, "I recommended Eddie at Number 23. His department has the best wage percentage in the company and also the highest sales. Eddie is bright and uses good judgment in dealing with customers and employees . . . in my opinion he has real potential.

"An analysis of this conversation reveals many interesting details. Supervisor Comden "just yesterday" saw Smith "working an hour after quitting time." Did this recent incident, which stuck in his mind, color his decision? Is Smith's willingness to work on his own time really a positive characteristic or does it indicate an inability to complete his work on time? Supervisor Black offered a number of generalizations, but also hinted that he is recommending Buck because Buck does as he is told "with no argument." Is that a valid reason for promoting someone? As a rule, good managers are not "yes-men"; they tend, instead, to think and speak for themselves. Miller's candidate, on the other hand, at least runs the highest sales and the best wage percentage in his present department. And he "uses good judgment," whatever that means. But what if Myers at Number 12 is really the best person for the job? Supervisor Black, who may know this, might not want to give Myers up because the promotion would mean losing him to a different supervisor.

These supervisors have not, point-by-point, objectively evaluated the strengths and weaknesses of each candidate. The inherent weakness of informal appraisals, in fact, is that no manager or supervisor can be totally objective. It is most difficult to completely overcome personal prejudices, or to avoid placing undue weight on recent events, or to prevent being unduly influenced by a general over-all impression or some outstanding characteristic.

Once the existence of prejudices (such as a bias against short or obese people) is admitted, the objective is to overcome them. Yet even though the influence of prejudice on actions may be reduced, it can seldom be entirely eliminated. Recent events, such as a supervisor overhearing a manager making a caustic comment to a customer or another manager showing a decrease in his wage cost of .5 percent of sales, further interfere with objectivity in appraising the performances of subordinates. Personality traits strike different people differently. Seldom will two supervisors agree wholeheartedly on all aspects of an informal evaluation. Indeed, seldom will they even agree on the basic factors that should be considered when appraising employees.

Formal Appraisals

Because of the built-in weaknesses of informal appraisal systems, some chains have adopted formal programs for judging their employees. In many cases, however, the formal system simply means writing down personal prejudices, recent events and outstanding characteristics, rather than discussing them. Even in formal reports, subjective evaluations are the rule. Though subjective ratings are better than none at all, it is important to root out as much subjectivity as possible.

The Evolution of Formal Appraisal Systems.   Formal employee appraisal systems have been used since before 1900 in government personnel work, and since 1900 in private industry. Psychologists and personnel people have tried to identify the traits required to perform certain management and non-management jobs. They have established appraisal systems requiring the superior to judge such attributes as self-confidence, trustworthiness and loyalty on a numerical scale, which implies that a trait can be measured to within one percentage point. Superiors simply marked the point at which they felt employees stood with regard to specific characteristics, on such a rating form as this:

These psychologists and personnel specialists soon recognized that the various levels of a trait could not be accurately distinguished. They then replaced the numerical scale with a degree system. At first, they used familiar ratings such as "excellent," "very good," "good," "fair" and "unsatisfactory." When these classifications did not produce the desired results, they replaced them with a set of multiple choices, as follows:

How well did the employee inspire his or her crew?
☐ To a high degree.
☐ To a moderately high degree.
☐ To a moderate degree.
☐ Not at all.

Gradually, more sophisticated classifications were developed which spelled out the main job duties and the level of performance required over a specific work period. Part of a meat manager's degree rating, for example, included a development of the question on how well he had trained his crew:

How well did the meat manager train each crew member in need of training?
☐ With the participation of each cutter and wrapper, he diagnosed training needs and developed a training plan for each crew member in need of training. He followed plans; used genuine training techniques: explained, demonstrated, observed the learner's performance, corrected and followed-up. Considering the training needs of his crew and

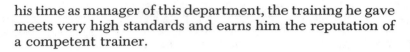

his time as manager of this department, the training he gave meets very high standards and earns him the reputation of a competent trainer.

☐ He diagnosed the training needs of each cutter and wrapper rather well and developed an adequate training plan for each member in need of training. He generally used genuine training techniques: explained, demonstrated, observed the learner's performance, corrected and followed-up. Considering the training needs of the crew and his time as manager of this department, the training he gave meets good, solid standards.

☐ He gave some deliberate training when he believed it was necessary. He encouraged experienced members to train inexperienced members. When pressed by his supervisor, he used some formal training techniques, usually accompanying his demonstrations with some explanation, but did little follow-up. Considering the training needs of the crew and his time as manager of this department, the training he gave barely meets minimum adequate standards.

☐ He gave no, or almost no, genuine training. He used the osmosis method, by having the learner gain skill and knowledge almost entirely alone. Considering the training needs of the crew and his time as manager of this department, the training he gave is below minimum adequate standards.

Fifteen to twenty years ago, such a degree rating was well accepted. Management was especially pleased because it took very little time to complete the form. It reduced arguments from the rated employee and satisfied management's conscience. It represented a workable program for employee appraisal.

But when this newly-designed form did not get the rated employee to perform any better, it was decided that it was the rater who did not know how to rate properly. During group training sessions, the rater was advised of the need to overcome the influence of prejudices, of recent events, and of some outstanding characteristic of the person being rated. The rater was also warned against other pitfalls that were described in incomprehensible technical terms.

In self-defense, the rater tried to outwit the statisticians of the personnel department. The statisticians, in turn, scrambled the degrees on the rating scale for different factors so that the rater had to be extremely careful about what he was checking. In addition, they did not allow the rater to keep a copy of his last rating of an employee because he might duplicate it on his current form. Finally, they developed a "forced choice" rating technique, which attempted to conceal from the rater whether he was giving a good or bad rating. The rater was required to select words or statements which he believed would best and least describe the employee rated. A typical pair of options was "vigorous" and "trustworthy." Though both seem to be virtues, according to this system, both good and bad performers are normally considered "trustworthy," whereas only good performers are usually judged "vigorous." Without realizing it, the rater was likely to damn poor performers with faint praise. The "forced choice" technique appealed to management as a way of eliciting honest answers from raters. However, most companies have become increasingly dissatisfied with this oversimplified appraisal device.

The Performance Review.   Most formal performance appraisal systems used in supermarket companies today include a semi-annual or annual review of the appraisal, attended by the employee and his or her superior. The purpose of the review is for the superior to point out the subordinate's strengths and weaknesses, and for both to agree on ways in which the subordinate's performance can be improved. In many companies the formal appraisal and review are also used to determine merit increases, promotions, demotions, transfers, terminations, training needs, manager development and so on.

The supermarket managers who have conducted performance reviews know the pitfalls first hand. When the manager gives the employee a low rating on a personality trait, the employee is likely to become defensive, interpersonal conflicts develop, and further communication is difficult or impossible. Managers who have had such unpleasant experiences tend to overrate employees to avoid conflicts. Such managers often try to shy away from the review or, if possible, to avoid it altogether.

If the manager is appraising performance on the basis of his own judgment rather than by specific measurements, there is often cause for disagreement and conflict. The problem is compounded when he begins to theorize by explaining poor performance as the result of lack of initiative, desire, self-confidence and so forth.

Another problem occurs when performance review is tied to salary review. Merit increases should *never* be discussed during a performance appraisal review; when they are, the appraisal and review tend to deteriorate to a justification of the decision to recommend or not to recommend the wage increase. For the employee, the primary purpose of the appraisal and review should be to evaluate performance to date and to find ways to improve future performance. This purpose is defeated when future earnings are dependent on the appraisal. When the boss's rating is not favorable, tempers are likely to flare and once again, communication is blocked so that there is little possibility that the review's primary objectives will be achieved.

Some supermarket companies using formal appraisal systems have developed elaborate training programs to teach managers how to conduct review sessions. Managers and other key personnel are taught to "overcome" personal prejudices, to avoid dominating the review with one-sided conversation, and to concentrate on past performances and improving future performance. Most such programs, however, have met with little success.

Evaluating the Appraisal System.   Much recent research and the experience of many companies condemn the traditional formal appraisal for failing to accomplish its basic objectives: accurate evaluation of individual performance, informing the employee of where he stands, and finding ways for the employee to improve future performance; for failing, also, because of inaccurate appraisals, to identify personnel inventories and training needs. The personnel director of a large, highly respected regional supermarket chain recently reported as follows:

> Until a year or so ago, we had a formal appraisal program which we considered successful. One recognized authority in the field told us we had one of the finest programs he had ever seen. Still, we weren't satisfied. We decided to make an objective appraisal of the appraisal system itself, using some outside people to help us.
>
> We studied our appraisal records at length. We focused on the review session between the subordinate and his superior, since this was the discussion that was supposed to motivate an employee to improve his performance. We used confidential personal opinion surveys to find out what our people *really* thought of our performance appraisal system; we had confidential discussions with superiors and subordinates at various levels in the company; and we attempted to relate what we defined as successful appraisals with corresponding improvements in the performance of subordinates. Here is what we learned:
>
> 1. We found no relationship between successful appraisals and improvement in subsequent performance.

2. In spite of our careful training of superiors in techniques of conducting appraisal reviews, too often there was disagreement between the subordinate and his superior over actual performance and over the subordinate's weaknesses. Sometimes the disagreements were violent.
3. One basic problem in the program was that superiors were attempting to judge the *cause* of a person's behavior. The superior's lack of qualification to determine motives was recognized by many managers and supervisors and was reflected in their expressed resentment of the program and their reluctance to discuss weaknesses and/or the final rating with the subordinate.
4. The appraisal program produced an overabundance of high ratings. We found two causes for this peculiarity: higher ratings reduced the possibility of disagreement between the superior and the subordinate; and they were needed to justify the merit increases in wages which were tied to the appraisal system.

The study we made of our appraisal program convinced us that for many years we had been näive. We kidded ourselves into believing that our program was of great value because we had developed it into a well-organized, sophisticated tool which appeared to be a precise device for appraising performance. We know now that we were wrong.

We decided that our whole performance appraisal system was doing us more harm than good; so we junked it. We are now working on a new approach to measure individual performance, and to have the subordinate set his own performance goals, which we hope will motivate our people to perform better.

This report is unique only in that it came from a supermarket chain. Similar experiences have been reported in recent years by large companies in other industries.

Factors Influencing the Development of an Appraisal System

If informal appraisal systems are of little or no value, and if traditional formal appraisal systems, at best, raise serious questions, a new and better approach must be developed. A number of factors, however, must first be taken into account in developing such a program.

1. People, unlike store fixtures, are an appreciating asset. Time must be invested to help them to do their work better. Clerks, as well as managers, produce better results when their supervisors allow and encourage them to share in making significant decisions about their work.

2. Business, by its very nature, requires periodic evaluations of the performances of employees at every level of the organization. Performance must be appraised in order to select people for promotion, for training or for executive development; to construct personnel inventories and determine training needs, and to provide the employee with the information on his progress that he wants and is entitled to have.

3. It will never be possible to entirely eliminate human judgment from a performance evaluation system; nor is it even desirable to do so. Some areas of responsibility are difficult to measure objectively, for instance, the training of employees. Results that are measured in specific terms must also be interpreted in the light of outside influences, such as a store's increase in sales when a competitor closes down.

4. In spite of the inherent problems, periodic performance reviews to keep the subordinate informed of his progress and shortcomings are a necessary ingredient of any appraisal system. During such reviews, it is important to focus on past and future results, rather than on motives or personality factors. Though merit increases should be based, at least in part, on the results of appraisals, they should not be discussed during reviews nor should they be timed to coincide with reviews. The system that is finally developed should provide for the measurement of specifics and should focus on techniques to improve future performance.

Developing Performance Standards

Who should develop performance standards? The company, the manager, or the employee? Standards established by company staff members who are specialists in measuring performance is the most common, as well as the quickest and most precise approach. But because line personnel have little or no voice in establishing the standards, this approach frequently meets with resistance and rejection by managers and store employees.

When a manager establishes standards for employees in his department or store, the standards are less precise. However, such standards have the advantage of fitting the conditions peculiar to the particular department or store. More important, when the manager is involved, the resulting standards are acceptable to him and he is more likely to exert effort to see that they are met.

Standards set by the experienced employee for his own job are likely to be more amateurish, but they usually produce the best results. The employee is far more likely to strive to reach his own goals than those set by someone else. Unfortunately, because of the high employee turnover in many jobs, it is not always practical to have the employee set his own standards. Still, even though it is perhaps a more unwieldy approach, performance standards should be set, whenever possible, by the employee, with the assistance and guidance of his manager.

Even in larger companies in which industrial engineering departments set performance standards for various store jobs, once the employee has gained experience, he should be encouraged to use his creative ability and ingenuity, and challenged to improve on the company-set performance standards.

When no company standards exist, the employee should first analyze each basic part of his job as he performs it and list the major segments that his job entails in a column on the left side of a formal standards sheet. On the right side of the form, he should indicate, in as specific terms as possible, when performance of that segment is considered to be up to standard.

It is not difficult to establish specific, measurable performance standards for most supermarket line jobs. The major task of each job can usually be measured in numerical terms, such as packages wrapped, priced or displayed per hour; cases priced and stocked per hour; cases of lettuce trimmed per hour, and so forth. Perhaps the most difficult job to nail down in specific, measurable terms is that of a part-time bagger-carryout clerk. But even here, a standard of performance can be established for many of its segments. (See Table 1).

TABLE 1
Performance Standards for Bagger-Carryout Clerks

Job Segments	Required Standards of Performance
I. Attendance	
A. Absence	A. No absences without legitimate reason and without notifying store in advance.
B. Tardiness	B. Rare latenesses and, then, only in emergencies.

TABLE 1 (Cont.)
Performance Standards for Bagger-Carryout Clerks

Job Segments	*Required Standards of Performance*
II. Bagging 　A. Quantity	A. Regularly hustles more than most baggers in most stores in the area; no excess talking or fooling around; graciously accepts and follows suggestions and instructions from cashiers; and bags nine of ten orders with both hands simultaneously after building bag foundation.
B. Quality	B. Selects correct bag size nineteen of twenty times; bags nineteen of twenty orders according to company requirements for solid foundation, square corners, solid packing, glass in center, and care of breakables, perishables, refrigerated and frozen items; and inspects bottom of each customer's shopping cart for unchecked merchandise.
III. Carrying-Out and Placing Bags in Car	Always lifts all heavy bags with at least one hand underneath; always uses care when opening and closing customers' car doors and trunks; unless otherwise requested by customer, regularly places merchandise on floor or in trunk and secures bags against movement in event car stops suddenly; causes no more than one breakage accident every three months; and never hits a customer's car with a cart.
IV. Public Relations 　A. Appearance	A. Always reports to work with clean body, shaved face, clean hands, clean, neatly-trimmed fingernails, and hair appropriately cut and combed; clean, pressed, and appropriate clothing (white shirt, tie, and all other company clothing requirements), and shined shoes; and never chews gum, eats, or smokes in a customer area.
B. Tipping	B. Never accepts a tip.
C. Complaints	C. Refers all customer complaints to the proper person.

TABLE 1 (Cont.)
Performance Standards for Bagger-Carryout Clerks

Job Segments	Required Standards of Performance
D. Customer Reaction	D. Causes no more than one legitimate customer complaint every six months.
	(At least 90 percent of the customers served by him day after day, if asked, would agree that the bagger is courteous, friendly, sincere, and happy to be of service; and that he handles merchandise efficiently, very much as the customer likes it to be handled.)
V. Returning to Bagging Duties	Always returns immediately to bagging duties, detouring only to return other carts to the store or to help shoppers who are in obvious need of assistance.
VI. Other Duties	Earns reputation with manager, head cashier and cashiers for cheerfully and readily volunteering for other work when current work has been completed, or when he can perform work for which he is urgently needed.
	Always does full share of keeping checkout area and floor clear and clean; nesting unused carts in the front of the store; and keeping store entrance clear of carts.

Note: Other duties, such as cleaning, obtaining prices of unmarked items, etc. need to be added to complete these standards of performance.

Once the performance standards have been developed and refined through repeated use, copies can be made and given to the new employee when he starts work so that he will know, in clear, concise terms, just exactly what is expected of him. After the employee becomes thoroughly experienced, he should be given the opportunity to offer suggestions to improve the standard for any of the segments of his job. Most managers would be amazed at the improvement in performance that can result by challenging even such employees as the part-time bagger-carryout clerk to improve performance in the various segments of his job.

Setting performance standards is an excellent means of evaluating the performances of store employees below the department manager level. For managers, however, the answer to evaluating performance lies in the use of a tool called goal setting, described in the next two chapters.

14 | The Case for Goal Setting

Goal setting, as a formalized program, has rapidly been gaining favor in many food companies in recent years. Properly used, it allows store and department managers to apply their own knowledge and creativity in order to set and achieve goals.

Goal setting is often confused with management by objectives. "Management by objectives" usually refers to a program whereby top management establishes the goals and imposes them downwards. This approach is based on the assumption that the creative ability and ingenuity which lead to improved performance exist only at the higher levels of supervision. "Goal setting," on the other hand, means that subordinates establish their own goals in their own areas of responsibility; thus, goals originate at store level and move upwards. Though several supermarket companies, as well as many firms in other industries, have been using many of the goal-setting principles for a number of years, it was not until the mid-1960s that some chains formalized these principles into full-scale goal-setting programs.

Challenging Tradition

Peter Drucker, in his 1954 book, *The Practice of Management*, challenged many of the traditional methods used by management to accomplish its aims, and offered new alternatives instead. His ideas started management thinking along new lines. Drucker noted that some very effective managers customarily ask each of their subordinates to write a "manager's letter" twice a year:

> In this letter to his superior, each manager first defines the objectives of his superior's job and of his own job as he sees them. He then sets down the performance standards which he believes are being applied to him. Next, he lists the things he must do himself to attain these goals—and the things within his own unit he considers the major obstacles. He lists the things his superior and the company do that help him, and the things that hamper him. Finally, he outlines what he proposes to do during the next year to reach his goals. If the superior accepts this statement, the "manager's letter" becomes the charter under which he operates.[1]

General Electric was one of the first companies to apply Drucker's "manager's letter" idea to solve a performance appraisal problem.[2]

In 1957, Dr. Douglas McGregor, writing in the *Harvard Business Review*, challenged the effectiveness of traditional performance appraisal systems. He offered a substitute approach to improve performance, based on self-imposed goals.[3] He elaborated his goal-setting procedure in his book *The Human Side of Enterprise*, a remarkable analysis of human motivation.[4]

Later in their article, "Positive Program for Performance Appraisal," Alva Kindall and James Gatza proposed a five-step program similar, in some respects, to Drucker's "manager's letter":

1. The individual discusses his job description with his superior, and they agree on the content of his job and the relative importance of his major duties—the things he is paid to do and is accountable for.
2. The individual establishes performance targets for each of his responsibilities for the forthcoming period.

[1] (New York: Harper & Row, 1954), p. 129.

[2] Herbert H. Meyer, Immanual Kay and John R. P. French, Jr., "Split Roles in Performance Appraisal," *Harvard Business Review*, Vol. 43 (January-February, 1965), p. 123.

[3] "An Uneasy Look at Performance Appraisal," *Harvard Business Review*, Vol. 35 (May-June, 1957), p. 89.

[4] (New York: McGraw-Hill Book Company, 1960.)

3. He meets with his superior to discuss his target program.
4. Checkpoints are established for the evaluation of his progress; ways of measuring progress are selected.
5. The superior and subordinate meet at the end of the period to discuss the results of the subordinate's efforts to meet the targets he had previously established.[5]

A Pilot Study

Early in 1963, before the appearance of Kindall's and Gatza's article, we began to experiment with Drucker's idea. We asked several store managers and supervisors in two major supermarket chains to prepare a letter to their superiors by following these six steps:

1. Define the responsibilities of your superior's job as you see them.
2. Define the responsibilities of your own job as you see them.
3. List the things that your superior, the office and the warehouse do to help you.
4. List the things that your superior, the office and the warehouse do to hamper you.
5. Set your goals in each area of your responsibility for the next three months.
6. List the steps you plan to take to reach each goal.

Each person was given thirty days to prepare his letter. Results in both companies were very discouraging; the responses were most inconsistent. Among four store managers who responded in one company, training was the only area of responsibility identified by all four; three of these managers cited clean operation, courteous and helpful attitude, merchandising all departments for growth and profit, and improving customer relations; two managers mentioned customer service, cutting supply and labor costs, recognizing employee efforts, improving morale, creating enthusiasm and a will to work; one reference was made to such responsibilities as cash control, store operations, maintaining store climate, providing quality merchandise, protecting the investment in the store, being a credit to the employer inside and outside the store, commanding respect for authority and decisions, checking on employee appearance, security control, satisfying customer complaints and delegating re-

[5] *Harvard Business Review,* Vol. 41 (November-December, 1963), p. 100.

sponsibility. Responses to the other five steps in the program were equally inconsistent. We concluded that the cause of the problem was our failure to be specific in our instructions to these managers.

The next step was to meet separately with each store manager participating in the program and to have him verbally identify his areas of responsibility. At this meeting, each person was given a detailed description of exactly what type of information was desired for each of the six steps. Though this approach brought somewhat better results, we were still dissatisfied. During the next two years, through trial and error, we gradually developed the goal-setting program described in the next chapter.

These early experiences taught us several valuable lessons. We learned that the major areas of responsibility for each store or department manager must be identified in advance; that performance in each of these areas must be measurable in specific, tangible terms; that the goal-setting program must be implemented at the department manager's level, as well as at the store manager's level, because the store manager is able to obtain results only through the participation and commitment to the program of his department managers; and that each man must develop the steps by which he proposes to reach his goals before he actually sets those goals.

It became obvious that an individual must first recognize his areas of responsibility and then be given the authority to use his own ability and ingenuity to improve performance in those areas. Only then should he be asked to take several days to develop steps that would lead to better results. Once he knows exactly what he plans to do, he could be expected to translate the steps into the degree of improvement he anticipates.

The guiding objectives in instituting a goal-setting program were to locate a tool which could measure performance objectively and to replace the traditional performance evaluation systems with a better program.

The Advantages of the Goal-Setting Program

Goal setting, when properly implemented, has proved to be an effective device for measuring performance objectively. But it also provides two other vital advantages at the department and store manager levels: (1) improved performance in the areas of manager responsibility; and (2) the development of the capabilities, talents and experiences of these managers.

Robert Blake and Jane Mouton, in their *Managerial Grid,* [6] have analyzed several managerial styles and have suggested that the most desirable one may best be implemented through the use of self-imposed goals. They emphasized the improvement in performance that can be brought about by educating managers and line employees in the use of various managerial styles, and placed heavy stress on candor in interpersonal relationships. Though these authors appear to consider goal setting a secondary factor in improving performance, our experience suggests that the success reported by several companies who use the Grid and goal-setting programs simultaneously is largely due to the effectiveness of goal setting.

Store Management Must Have a Voice

Numerous supermarket executives have reported that they already employ the goal-setting technique. It soon becomes obvious, however, that what they are using is the "management by objectives" device, which gives supervisors or store managers little real voice in decisions. They describe their so-called "goal-setting" program as one in which their "district managers periodically (quarterly, semi-annually or annually) meet with each store manager, and together set goals or targets for the store for the forth-coming period in such areas as sales, gross profit, and wage expense." What actually occurs is this: the district manager is first briefed on company goals for the forthcoming period; he then meets with each of his store managers, who agrees to budgets or targets for the store that reflect company goals. Often, the department manager is not even involved in the planning but, rather, is advised of decisions after they have been made. Seldom are both department and store managers asked to present their ideas on what should be done to improve performance in the various areas of their responsibility. Thus, they are really only receiving the word from the top about what is expected of them. They are not active participants in company planning.

Douglas McGregor has effectively pointed out that "the capacity to exercise a relatively high degree of imagination, ingenuity, and creativity in the solution of organization problems is widely, not narrowly, distributed in the population."[7] Any supermarket organization can point to numerous examples of improvements in methods, equipment, tools, techniques, procedures, and so on, which

---

[6] (Houston: Gulf Publishing Company, 1964.)

[7] *The Human Side of Enterprise, op cit.,* p. 48.

have originated with line employees, department and store managers. The position taken by some members of top management, that store goals must be set by supervisors because only they have access to such information as future company plans and promotions, is a weak one. The real test is: which approach leads to better performance? Experience has shown conclusively that the best results are obtained when employees participate in developing goals; in other words, when goals are oriented upwards rather than imposed downwards.

Providing Information

During the course of a visit to a store, made some time ago with one of the company's supervisors, the supervisor called the produce department manager to the office and proceeded to chastise him for the low gross profit which appeared in the accounting department's latest four-week period report. The produce manager was helpless. It seemed that he had not been advised of his gross profit each week, even though his practice was to take a weekly inventory and despite the fact that his gross profit was computed each week by the office. In addition, he had never been advised of the cost or markup of each item.

After we left the store, I asked the supervisor why the produce manager had been deprived of this vital information. His reply was: "Information is confidential; we can't tell department managers the cost or markup on each item. Suppose it got out to a competitor?" When I asked him how the company could hold an employee responsible for gross profit if it refused to give him markup information, he replied, "Each week we identify four or five high profit items and tell him to promote them."

This company, which gives no figures to department managers, seems to overlook the fact that store sales, the most valuable information to competitors, is known every day by several people in the store. In many supermarket companies, particularly smaller ones, department managers are not informed of their daily or weekly sales, which is common knowledge to the clerk in the store office. Most of the larger companies, however, and many small, progressive chains, provide each store and department manager with a complete breakdown of performance figures whenever such information becomes available.

A manager cannot be expected to make intelligent decisions unless he is given the facts on which to base those decisions. Without information, he cannot manage effectively. He is reduced to a messenger—a puppet manipulated from above. Such a manager is likely to describe his role as one in which "I must carry out the orders of my superiors." Supervisors in these companies, in turn, are likely to describe their jobs as follows: "To find replacements for employees who don't show up for work; to relate information from the office to the stores; and to transfer merchandise from store to store."

The View at Jewel

Frank Lunding, former Chairman of the Board of Jewel Companies, Inc., wrote:

> Good management ... consciously seeks growth, progress and greater net profit each year as a by-product of greater service to the public. It imbues its employees with [the] idea of shared responsibility for ever-better service to the public and inspires each to contribute his utmost to that end. Also, it does not fail to see that each shares fairly in the monetary and spiritual rewards which are the fruit of better service to the public. . . . A common shortcoming among business executives is a tendency to think they are the only ones capable of solving the problems of the business with which they are connected; to think they must generate most of the ideas and make most of the decisions themselves. Despite the current enthusiasm for suggestion systems, the notion that the only good ideas are those that originate in the boss's office is fairly widespread.
>
> However, with the right kind of encouragement, and a sufficiently broad and deep understanding of top management's plans and problems, many men who seem only "average" could share much more of the executive load than they are being asked to carry. If they are enabled to do so, they can relieve their superiors of much pressure and at the same time develop within themselves that sense of responsibility and of individual worth and dignity which to most men is the highest form of compensation.
>
> When decision-making is shared with the people in the organization their minds are stimulated and their understanding increased; they are given a sense of participation; they develop their ability to weigh and decide on the basis of facts and to judge the pros and cons of calculated risks . . . In Jewel Tea we are learning to use the sharing technique increasingly to solve all sorts of problems in all departments. Instead of *telling* our people what to do to solve their problems, we are placing ourselves at their disposal to lend what assistance we can to help them find their own solutions, and we are *asking*

them to give us the benefit of their thinking and help us solve our problems.[8]

What a remarkable contrast to the traditional approach of management by edict and authority!

Five Objectives of Goal Setting

In summary, the goal-setting program has five basic objectives:

1. To improve the manager's performance in each specific measurable area of his responsibility.
2. To develop the manager into a more capable leader; to provide him with the opportunity to prove what he can do on his own.
3. To give the manager a sense of personal achievement and an opportunity to be recognized for his achievements.
4. To provide the means to evaluate a manager's performance objectively.
5. To keep the manager informed on where he stands and on his progress.

[8] *The Sharing of a Business* (Scarsdale, New York: The Updegraff Press, Ltd., 1954), pp. 52-53.

15 | The Goal-Setting Program

A goal-setting program, when first introduced in a company, should shout start at the highest level of management. Each superior should gain experience in setting goals before asking any subordinates to do so. The president of a company should first ask his vice-presidents to set goals in each area of their responsibility; then the vice-presidents should ask each of their subordinates to set goals. This procedure should be continued down through the various levels of management.

Top management is often reluctant to wait until each superior completes the entire goal-setting cycle before implementing the program at store level. Once exposed to the advantages of the program, management usually wants to move swiftly to the department and store manager levels where the program will do the most good. Another common mistake is to immediately introduce the program on a company-wide basis. Regardless of the size of the chain, the program should first be implemented in a limited number of stores; three stores is usually a good starting point.

When the company is ready to extend the program to store level, the district manager should assemble the store managers of the pilot stores, and spend about an hour explaining the program to them. After this meeting, the district manager should meet with each store manager and the respective department managers to spend another hour describing the program to the department managers. At the end of that week, the district manager should hold two more meetings lasting approximately twenty minutes each: the first meeting should be with the store manager to discuss the steps and goals; the second meeting should be with each department manager separately, in the presence of the store manager, for a similar type of review.

If, at the end of the second quarter, the program is proceeding smoothly, the district manager should prepare to introduce it to additional stores and to conduct the same types of meetings. However, the goal-setting program should not be introduced in a newly opened store until that store's volume has been established. A minimum of three months should elapse before the store and department managers of a new store are asked to develop steps and to establish goals. It would be meaningless to ask them to set goals at any earlier date because there would be no available data on the store's past performance on which to base future improvements and goals.

The goal-setting program should not be limited to store operations. It is equally effective in such departments as the warehouse, transportation, accounting and personnel. It can be used in any department where measurements can be devised to evaluate performance objectively.

Introducing the Program

The following are the five major steps that must be taken to institute an effective goal-setting program:

1. *Identify the responsibility and authority of each department and store manager*: In most companies, areas of responsibility for department managers are defined by the company as department (1) sales, (2) gross profit, (3) wage expense, (4) supply costs, and (5) laundry expense.

2. *Provide information*: In order to plan quarterly goals, each department manager must be given the actual performance figures of the department for the corresponding quarter of the previous year, as well as the comparable figures for other similar stores.

3. *Plan steps and set goals*: Each department manager should be given approximately one week in which to independently develop

steps that would improve on last year's performance in every area of the department manager's responsibility. The department manager should then translate those steps into projected dollar and percentage figures for each period of the forthcoming quarter.

4. *Review steps and goals*: The department and store manager should meet to review and agree upon the steps and goals for the forthcoming quarter.

5. *Review performance*: The store manager should provide the department manager with the actual figures on the department's performance as soon as such information becomes available. Such figures would include department sales on a daily basis, gross profit and wage expense, which are usually available on a weekly basis in perishable departments, and so on. The store manager should go over the figures with the department manager at regular intervals during the quarter, in order to periodically review the department manager's progress. At the end of the quarter, they should meet again to review and evaluate the department manager's success or failure in achieving the goals that had been set for that quarter. After each quarterly meeting, the department manager should establish new steps and goals for the coming quarter.

Spelling Out the Limits of Responsibility and Authority

Responsibility must be defined before authority can be assigned. The company should hold department managers responsible for those factors they can effectively control. It is obvious that department managers have varying degrees of control over their five areas of responsibility; they have almost complete control over wage, supply and laundry expenses, but less control over gross profit and sales.

Nevertheless, their influence on departmental gross profit and sales is great even when prices and advertising are controlled by the main office. Gross profit, for example, is largely dependent on the kind of merchandising job they do. Similarly, the manner in which they operate their department (cleanliness, in-stock position, customer courtesy, and so on) greatly affects departmental sales.

Table 1 is a goal-setting form used by one company to detail each area of responsibility in the meat department. Alongside the five areas of responsibility, the indicators of performance are listed, as well as the controllable and non-controllable factors that influence or affect performance in each area. Indicators of performance in sales, for example, are dollar sales per week and the ratio of department sales to total store sales. Among the controllable items listed are ordering accuracy and factors relating to product display. Others, such as refrigeration, are only partially controllable by the meat department. Those items in the non-controllable column may not be altered or affected by department personnel. Normally, these are areas of authority expressly denied to the department manager and reserved by the chain for its own control.

TABLE 1
Department Manager Goal-Setting Program/Meat Department

Areas of Responsibility

Responsibility	Performance Indicators	Factors Affecting Performance	
		Controllable	Non-Controllable

I. Sales	A. Dollar Sales
	B. Ratio of meat sales to total store sales
		A. Ordering accuracy
		B. Display:
		  1. Variety of cuts and sizes
		  2. Out-of-stocks
		  3. Fullness of display
		  4. Layout of cases
		  5. Display materials*
		  6. Demonstrations*
		  7. In-store promotions
		C. Quality:
		  1. Trim*
		  2. Freshness*
		  3. Cleanliness
		  4. Refrigeration*
		D. Customer service:
		  1. Special orders
		  2. Special service
		  3. Customer relations
		E. Packaging:
		  1. Package appearance
		  2. Control of leaks, tears and seals
		F. Pilferage*
			A. Availability of product from source
			B. Retail prices
			C. Trim policies
			D. Required items on display
			E. Equipment
			F. Advertising
			G. Company-wide promotions
			H. Location of department in store
			I. Display space available
			J. Checkout ringup accuracy

TABLE 1 (Cont.)

Areas of Responsibility

Responsibility	Performance Indicators	Factors Affecting Performance	
		Controllable	Non-Controllable

II. Gross Profit	A. Gross profit dollars
	B. Gross profit percentage
	C. Cutting tests
		A. Shrinkage loss:
		  1. Cutting loss
		  2. Cutting skill
		  3. Accurate check-in
		  4. Pilferage
		B. Pull backs:
		  1. Frequency
		  2. Markdowns
		  3. Conversions
		C. Ordering accuracy
		D. Pricing accuracy
		E. Display:
		  1. Anticipating case needs
		  2. Variety of items on display
		F. Cleanliness
		G. Refrigeration*
		H. Revenue from by-products*
		I. Merchandising techniques*
			A. Cost of product
			B. Retail prices
			C. Advertising
			D. Refrigeration*
			E. Trim policies
			F. Merchandising policies

III. Wage Expense	A. Labor dollars
	B. Ratio of labor dollars to meat sales
	C. Sales per labor-hour
	D. Pounds per labor-hour
		A. Scheduling:
		  1. Employees
		  2. Product
		B. Crew efficiency
		  1. Training*
		  2. Methods
		  3. Skill
		  4. Effort
		C. Pull backs
		  1. Number
		  2. Type
		D. Film size
		E. Average value per package
			A. Space available
			B. Layout
			C. Equipment
			D. Training*
			E. Wage rates
			F. Type of film used
			G. Customer service policies

TABLE 1 (Cont.)

Areas of Responsibility

Responsibility	Performance Indicators	Factors Affecting Performance	
		Controllable	Non-Controllable

IV. Supply Expense	A. Supply dollars
	B. Ratio of supply dollars to meat sales
		A. Tray sizes used
		B. Film sizes used:
		  1. Amount of excess overlap
		C. Average value per package
		D. Rewraps
			A. Film and tray used:
			  1. Types
			  2. Sizes
			  3. Unit cost
			B. Film yield

V. Laundry Expense	A. Laundry dollars
	B. Ratio of laundry dollars to meat sales
	C. Number used:
	  1. Aprons
	  2. Coats
	  3. Uniforms
	  4. Rags
		A. Usage
		B. Waste
		C. Inventory control
			A. Service contract

*Partially controllable.

The key to designating authority is: *Any authority not expressly denied becomes the authority of the department manager under the supervision of the store manager.* A company that agrees to share its problems with its department managers must also be willing to give them the authority to make decisions in their distinctively defined areas of responsibility.

Providing Information

Once responsibility and authority have been firmly established, the department manager must be given information on the past performance of his department. Table 2 shows one of the most effective ways to detail the information needed by the meat department manager. When goals are to be set for a coming quarter, the actual performance figures of the corresponding quarter of the previous year are entered on the chart. The figures are broken down into four, five, and four week periods, to conform with the

TABLE 2
Department Manager Goal-Setting Program/Meat Department
Past Information and Projection Form

Name: Rex Davis   Store Number: 27   Department: Meat

		4 Weeks Ending 1/27/90		5 Weeks Ending 3/3/90		4 Weeks Ending 3/31/90		Total Quarter 1990	
		Dollars	Percentage	Dollars	Percentage	Dollars	Percentage	Dollars	Percentage
1. Sales—Average per Week	Projection								
	Actual	$ 28,716	XXXXX	$ 30,004	XXXXX	$ 30,983	XXXXX	$ 29,909	XXXX
2. Sales—Total Period	Projection								
	Actual	114,866	100.00%	150,020	100.00%	123,933	100.00%	388,819	100.00%
3. Gross Profit	Projection								
	Actual	26,821	23.35	34,475	22.98	28,765	23.21	90,061	23.16
4. Wages	Projection								
	Actual	12,015	10.46	15,587	10.39	13,025	10.51	40,627	10.45
5. Supplies	Projection								
	Actual	1,367	1.19	1,515	1.01	1,400	1.13	4,282	1.10
6. Laundry	Projection								
	Actual	126	.11	150	.10	136	.11	412	.11
7. Total Controllable Expense (sum of 4 + 5 + 6)	Projection								
	Actual	13,508	11.76	17,252	11.50	14,561	11.75	45,321	11.66
8. Adjusted Gross Profit (3 minus 7)	Projection								
	Actual	13,313	11.59	17,223	11.48	14,204	11.46	44,740	11.5

accounting calendar of this particular company. Listed on the left hand side of the form are the department manager's areas of responsibility: (1-2) sales, (3) gross profit, (4) wage expense, (5) supply costs, and (6) laundry expense. Item 7, total controllable expense, is the sum of items 4, 5, and 6. The adjusted gross profit, item 8, represents the difference between the gross profit (3) and the total controllable expense (7).

At the same time that the department manager is given this historical information, he should also be provided with a blank copy of the same form, on which he will enter the projected performance of his department for the corresponding four, five, and four week periods, as well as the projected total for the coming quarter. These figures, which he enters on the form in the "projection" blocks, will, based on the steps he proposes to take, become the anticipated performance of his department in each area of his responsibility.

Planning Steps and Setting Goals

A goal should be set for a given area only after steps to improve that area have been developed. The degree of improvement anticipated, and the goal itself, are totally dependent on the steps developed by the manager in every area of his responsibility.

Problem areas, or areas needing improvement, may be identified first by comparing past and current performance figures with those of similar stores in the company. Each controllable factor that affects performance should be analyzed by the department manager, and every detail of present methods and techniques relating to these controllable factors should be re-examined. Whatever suggestions the department manager makes will, of course, be subject to the store manager's approval. Nevertheless, at this stage, the department managers should not be bound by tradition, but should be daring enough to develop unique, intelligent, workable alternatives to present practices. He should also urge his subordinates to search for better ways to improve performance. In creating new ideas, he must recognize the fact that people usually resist change. Deviation from an old pattern requires courage and a willingness to face opposition from superiors as well as from subordinates. The department manager should remember that the most effective way to overcome resistance to change from subordinates is to involve them in the creation of ideas. Employees who have had a hand in the development of a program will seldom object to the changes it entails.

The steps listed by the department manager must be specific. As a step to improve sales in his department, he should not write such generalizations as "to do a better job of merchandising." Instead, he should outline exactly what he intends to do to improve his merchandising practices. He might, for example, propose that he be given the authority to display certain additional features on weekends. Or he might identify three, four or more high profit meat items which he intends to use in building special displays or demonstrations during the target period. Table 3 is a list of distinct and specific steps developed by a meat department manager to improve performance in each of his areas of responsibility.

TABLE 3
Department Manager Goal-Setting Program/Meat Department

List of Steps

Store Number _____

Areas of Responsibility	Steps to Be Taken
I. Sales	A. Increase number of traffic items on display (cube steak, chickens, and ground beef displays).
	B. Use tie-in displays with grocery and produce items (steaks with potatoes, hams with sweet potatoes, steaks with mushrooms, corned beef with cabbages, etc.).
	C. Use tie-ins of two meat items (cheese and sliced ham, boneless stew and brisket stew, franks, bacon and cheese).
	D. Offer more suggestions to customers; use more hand-out recipes, case signs and posters.
	E. Develop and keep on display new items to create impulse buying (steak rolls, wafer thin ham slices, breakfast steaks, wish bones, roasting chickens).
	F. Develop aisle and table displays using such items as cheese, salt meat and canned hams.
	G. Display a wider variety of package sizes and thicknesses of cuts.
	H. Display in-store promotions of high profit items in hot spots of case.
II. Gross Profit	A. Train new meat cutters in company trimming and boning policies to reduce waste and miscuts.
	B. Cut down on rewraps by scheduling the cutting operation closer to the time of sale; wrap packages more snugly.
	C. Merchandise more profitable items (liver, fryer parts, breakfast steaks, steak rolls).
	D. Display sale and traffic items between high profit items.
	E. Prepare high profit items first.
	F. Rotate high profit items weekly in hot spots of case.

TABLE 3 (Cont.)

List of Steps

Store Number _____

Areas of Responsibility	Steps to Be Taken
	G. Work up slow moving cuts on Saturday instead of carrying them over the weekend.
III. Wages	A. Schedule help during peak production hours; stagger breaks and lunch hours.
	B. Prepare ahead; do as many jobs at the beginning of the week as possible (price and display frozen items, cheeses and luncheon meats).
	C. Plan and watch labor-hours required each day.
IV. Supplies	A. Avoid waste (use proper size trays and rolls of film, maintain minimum overlap on each package).
	B. Store supplies properly.
	C. Use cheaper supplies whenever it is possible to substitute.
	D. Cut down on rewraps by cutting closer to the time of sale.
V. Laundry	A. Wash out towels each night.
	B. Re-use aprons and jackets when they are not soiled.
	C. Avoid wearing clean jacket or apron when opening or handling beef primals.
VI. Other	A. Conduct regular meetings to discuss other steps to achieve goals.
	B. Keep morale high to obtain greatest efficiency.

Once he has listed all the steps he plans to take to improve a specific area of his responsibility, the department manager should evaluate the effect that these steps will have on his department's performance in that area, and enter his anticipated figure in the proper "projection" block of his goal sheet. When he translates his steps into performance goals, the adjusted gross profit figure, both in dollars and in percentage, should show an improvement over the department's performance in the same quarter of the previous year.

Though the conventional target period is usually three to six months, it should always be sufficiently long to allow for periodic reports on actual performance in each area of responsibility during that period. Though sales and wage expense figures, and gross profit figures in perishable departments, are available in most companies by department and by stores on a weekly basis, figures on other

TABLE 4
Store Manager Goal-Setting Program

Past Information and Projection Form

Name _____   Store Number _____   Department _____

		4 Weeks Ending ____		5 Weeks Ending ____		4 Weeks Ending ____		Total Quarter 1990		Total Quarter 1991	
		Dollars	Percentage	Dollars	Percentage	Dollars	Percentage	Dollars	Percentage	Dollars	Percentage
1. Sales—Average Per Week	Projection										
	Actual										
2. Sales—Total Period	Projection										
	Actual										
3. Gross Profit	Projection										
	Actual										
4. Wages	Projection										
	Actual										
5. Supplies	Projection										
	Actual										
6. Cash Loss	Projection										
	Actual										

7. Bad Checks	Projection	
	Actual	
8. Light and Power	Projection	
	Actual	
9. Heat and Fuel	Projection	
	Actual	
10. Water	Projection	
	Actual	
11. Laundry	Projection	
	Actual	
12. Telephone	Projection	
	Actual	
13. Stamps	Projection	
	Actual	
14. Total Controllable Expense (Sum of 4-13)	Projection	
	Actual	
15. Adjusted Gross Profit (3 minus 14)	Projection	
	Actual	

areas of controllable expense are not usually available, except on a four-week or monthly basis.

The department manager should not sit down at a desk for two or three hours to come up with projected steps and goals. He should think about them during his working hours, while driving back and forth, from and to work, or at any time when his mind is not otherwise occupied during the week in which he is expected to prepare those steps. The steps and goals should be his own; he should not be helped by his superiors while preparing them, but should be helped by his subordinates. They should be encouraged to work together to find ways to improve performance, particularly in their own areas of responsibility.

Reviewing Steps and Goals

Once steps have been developed and translated into goals, the department manager should meet with his store manager. The store manager's responsibility is to study the steps and goals proposed by the department manager. If he considers them reasonable, he should accept them.

The store manager should never provide the department manager with new steps. This is the department manager's problem; the department manager must feel that he has had the opportunity to show what he can do. It is crucial that the department manager feel he has the freedom to implement the authorized steps. He is not likely to feel obligated to reach his goals if his authority and decision-making power are curtailed or overridden.

The key to the success of the meeting between the department and store managers is the attitude of the superior. He must make every effort to accept each goal as it is projected, even leaning over backwards to do so. As long as he maintains the attitude of assisting the subordinate, rather than the more conventional one of directing him, the chances are that a successful goal-setting program will result.

Once each department manager's goals have been accepted, the combined department goals become the store goals. The store manager adds up the agreed upon goals of the meat, produce, grocery, and any other department, to obtain the store goals for that period.

The form on which store goals are entered is similar to the form used by each department manager. However, in addition to such items as sales, gross profit, wage expense, supply costs and laundry expense listed on the department manager's form, the store manager's form includes items of controllable expense such as cash loss, bad checks, and others not allocated to each department. Figures are entered on this form that represent actual store performance for the corresponding quarter of the previous year. (See Table 4.)

The store manager also lists the steps he proposes to take to show improved performance in each of the areas not covered by the department managers. He, too, should be given a week to consider steps he might take to show an improvement over last year's figures in such areas as cash loss, bad checks, light and power, heat and fuel, and telephone costs.

The store manager is also given a blank copy of the store goals form on which to list the anticipated performance he expects will result from his proposed steps. The store manager should not list any sales, gross profit, wage, supply and laundry costs on this blank form until he has reviewed and accepted his department managers' steps and goals. The supervisor must, in turn, review and accept the steps and goals of each of his store managers; the combined figures of his stores then become his goals for the coming period.

Just as the combined goals of each department become the store goals, so the combined supervisors' goals become company goals. Invariably, however, the combined goals for all stores tend to exceed company projections (established in the typical manner by top management) by a wide margin. In one company, improvement in adjusted gross profit for all stores, when projected under the goal-setting program, exceeded by 60 percent the target previously established by the company for a forthcoming quarter.

Reviewing Performance

The store manager should keep a copy of each of his department manager's goals. When information on performance becomes available at the end of each accounting period, the store manager should enter it in the "actual" blocks of his copy of the goal chart and determine how well each department manager is doing in comparison with the goals he has set. The store and department managers should sit down at the end of each accounting period to review the department manager's progress toward each of the goals.

At the close of the final period of the quarter, the accounting department should supply the store manager with the complete information for each department for the quarter, showing the actual figures in dollars and percentages for the corresponding quarter just ended, the dollar change from the previous year in terms of actual and projected figures, and the corresponding percentage change for the present quarter. (See Table 5.)

The store manager should evaluate these figures and discuss them with each department manager, rating the department manager on the steps he had developed and on the progress he had made toward reaching his projected goals. When warranted, appropriate comments should be made on the form. In the same manner, the store manager's steps, goals, and actual performance should be evaluated by the district supervisor.

When targets have not been met, discussion should focus on ways to obtain improvement, rather than on excuses. The discussion should always be concerned with how obstacles may be removed in the future, not on why they were present in the past. The superior should encourage his subordinate to take the lead in the discussion. He should also be sure to recognize progress made by his subordinate and to acknowledge success. The meeting should conclude with a request to the subordinate to develop new steps and goals for the coming period.

When the goal-setting program is effectively carried out, strong personal relations are established between the department and store manager. As the combined department goals become store goals, the store manager usually acquires a genuine desire to see that his department managers reach their goals. Department managers and their store managers are committed to the same goals and it becomes the store manager's responsibility to assist his department managers to reach their goals. If the department managers succeed, the store manager's success is also insured.

Questions About the Program

Any discussion of the goal-setting program invariably produces a great many questions. Many of the most perceptive are asked by store and department managers when the program is first introduced to them.

The questions and answers which follow are based on a transcription of a meeting with store and department managers during a supermarket seminar that was held a few years ago. These questions and answers cover many of the major points of a goal-setting program.

TABLE 5
Department Manager Goal-Setting Program/Meat Department
Evaluation

Store 27   Quarter Ending 3/30/91   Department Meat   Manager Rex Davis

	Total Quarter 1990		Total Quarter 1991				Dollar Change*		Percentage Change*	
	Actual		Projected		Actual					
	Dollars	Percentage	Dollars	Percentage	Dollars	Percentage	Projection	Actual	Projection	Actual
1. Average Weekly Sales	$ 29,909	XXXX	$ 31,550	XXXXX	$ 32,182	XXXXX	$ 1,641	$ 2,273	5.49%	7.60%
2. Total Quarter Sales	388,819	100.00%	410,150	100.00%	418,361	100.00%	21,331	29,542	5.49	7.60
3. Gross Profit	90,061	23.16	97,410	23.75	104,297	24.93	7,349	14,236	8.16	15.81
4. Wages	40,627	10.45	42,245	10.30	41,962	10.03	(1,618)	(1,335)	(3.98)	(3.29)
5. Supplies	4,282	1.10	4,300	1.05	4,476	1.07	(18)	(194)	(.42)	(4.53)
6. Laundry	412	.11	410	.10	426	.10	2	(14)	.49	(3.40)
7. Total Controllable Expense	45,321	11.66	46,955	11.45	46,864	11.20	(1,634)	(1,543)	(3.61)	(3.40)
8. Adjusted Gross Profit	44,740	11.51	50,455	12.30	57,433	13.73	5,715	12,693	12.77	28.37

Evaluation of steps listed:
Rating   X
   Excellent   Above Average   Average   Below Average   Poor

Evaluation of manager's follow-through and results:
Rating   X
   Excellent   Above Average   Average   Below Average   Poor

Comments/recommendations: I encourage other meat managers to check this department for ideas on sales and profit. Rex is doing an outstanding job.

*Compared to actual figures of base period.

Inspiring Employee Enthusiasm for Goal Setting

Is there sometimes a negative response from managers who feel that the goal-setting program will add clerical work and otherwise take time away from their busy work schedule?

Yes, but only until such managers become convinced that in return for their time investment, they are really being given, perhaps for the first time, the opportunity to become a manager in the true sense of the word. Disbelief is the most common reaction to this program when it is first presented to a group of store or department managers. After all, in many supermarket companies, store and department managers have not truly been given the authority to manage. When a talented store or department manager becomes convinced that he will be allowed to show his true abilities, he will usually welcome the opportunity.

Companies that are already using the goal-setting program are convinced that it separates the wheat from the chaff. The managers with talent show up well and produce results; those without talent do not. A person who claims that he already has too much to do and cannot find time to set goals is saying, in effect, that he does not have time to manage.

What should be done about the individual who refuses to set goals?

This sometimes happens. In one situation, for example, a store manager, when asked to develop steps and goals, took the position that the program represented an insult to him. He asserted that he was being implicitly accused of not doing his job as a manager and that the request to set goals was some sort of trap. He refused to budge even though strenuous efforts were made to convince him that the program was by no means a trap. His company decided to let him go his own separate way, running a lone wolf operation. Today, he is the only manager in the chain who does not participate in the program. Unfortunately, his department managers are also penalized by his refusal to participate because they too cannot set goals. The manager himself has been identified as non-promotable.

Another person who refused to participate in the program was a department manager with very low mental ability as measured by psychological tests and little self-confidence. His refusal was based on reasons similar to those given by the store manager in the above case. Attempts were made to persuade this department manager to participate, but he was obstinate in his refusal. On occasion, a company may have to insist that such persons participate in goal-setting programs.

Does the goal-setting program tend to penalize the best performers?

Though it may seem so at first, it rarely turns out that way. More often than not, the best performers are those who do a better job of eliciting creative ideas from their subordinates. However, it is probably true that managers in stores which have shown the poorest performance do, in fact, have a greater opportunity to show improvement than those who efficiently manage their stores. Nevertheless, the most opportunity for improvement does not always guarantee the best results.

How can employees be convinced that the company is sincere in its willingness to delegate more authority and responsibility to them?

Sometimes it may be difficult to convince employees of the company's sincerity, particularly when the company has had a history of operating in a highly centralized or authoritarian manner. In explaining the program to subordinates, it must be emphasized that the authority they will be given will be subject only to agreement by the superior. It must also be pointed out that the delegation of such authority is a necessary ingredient of the program if it is to succeed. Beyond such encouragement, only time will prove the company's sincerity.

Any company that implements the goal-setting program quickly discovers the many advantages that are obtained by permitting subordinates to be involved in decisions relating to their respective departments. A division manager and supervisor once visited a store on the goal-setting program in order to present a preliminary remodeling plan for the store and to explain the proposed changes to the store manager. They asked the store manager to study the plan and to make any suggestions he might have for the remodeling. The store manager was stunned. "Do you mean that after 24 years, you are really going to give me a voice in the remodeling of my store?" he asked. This store manager presented the plans to each of his department managers, and they came up with a number of excellent ideas that were later incorporated into the remodeling plans. The invariable results of involving people in store programs are better performance and improved morale.

How does a company maintain enthusiasm and interest in the program?

At first many companies expected that their managers would begin to run out of ideas within a year or so. However, new employees in a given department constantly bring in fresh ideas. Also, an idea successfully employed by a department manager in one store during a given target period will inevitably appear among the steps listed by other department managers for the succeeding target period. It does not take long for word to spread that a certain step has successfully improved performance. On the other hand, there doesn't seem to be any end to the availability of original ideas.

Involving Subordinates in the Program

Should a department manager involve his or her subordinates in developing steps and setting goals?

This is the heart of goal setting. A meat department manager in one store asked his wrappers to help cut costs in the goal-setting program because the wrappers had far more control than he had over supply expenses in the department. He explained the goal-setting program in general terms to his wrappers. After showing them the film and tray costs for the department over the previous year and recent months, he asked them to think of ideas or methods to reduce such costs. The next day the wrappers suggested that if they were more careful in the amount of overlap on each package, and if they used the proper roll width in wrapping various packages, they could reduce the film cost over the next quarter by 10 percent. The meat manager accepted their suggestion, though he doubted that the costs could be reduced so extensively. He promised to keep them informed of the actual film costs whenever such figures became available. After three months the wrappers had reduced their film costs, not by 10 percent, but by an unbelievable 18 percent.

In another case, a store manager involved his cashiers in developing ideas that could reduce cash losses due to overs-and-shorts on the cash registers. His store had higher than average losses from changemaking errors. He called his cashiers together and presented the problem to them, showing each cashier her record of daily overs-and-shorts during the preceding months. He asked them to develop steps to reduce the losses.

The cashiers discussed the problem among themselves, and a day or so later suggested that the store manager keep them posted daily on each cashier's amount over or short for the previous day. At the end of the week, the store would determine which cashier had done the best job balancing out at zero. The cashier with the best record was to be awarded a bouquet to keep on her checkstand during the following week. The store manager was skeptical, but he accepted the proposal. At the end of the target period, the net loss due to overs-and-shorts in that store was reduced by 50 percent. The cost of a bouquet was about $5.00 a week.

In these two instances, the almost incredible results were attained because the steps were developed by the employees themselves. The employees, through participation, became committed to the goal in the respective areas of the manager's responsibility. Whenever the goals of line employees can be aligned with store goals, progress is bound to result.

The Importance of Information for Setting Goals

What should be done if top management is reluctant to divulge statistical data on performance figures?

The willingness to divulge performance figures to department managers is a major prerequisite of the goal-setting program. Without this information, the program cannot be implemented.

If figures from the previous year are not typical, how does a manager go about setting his or her goals?

This situation does occur occasionally. The meat manager in one store, for example, whose department had been running about two percentage points higher in gross profit than during the same calendar period of the previous year, was provided not only with last year's figures, but also with performance figures for each quarter since then. It was pointed out to him that his department's gross profit had been 22 percent for the quarter of the previous year that corresponded with the coming quarter, and 24 percent for the two quarters preceding the one for which he was now planning. A gross profit goal of 24 percent for the forthcoming quarter, therefore, could not be considered an optimistic goal, even though it showed a 2 percent improvement over the same quarter of the previous year. The meat department manager was asked to take the recent improvement in performance into consideration when setting his goals in gross profit.

How are major company promotions, which are not known to the department manager at the time goals are set, to be taken into consideration?

A manager's performance can be drastically affected by actions of this type. After such a major promotion has been announced by the office, the department manager may (1) be allowed to revise the goals, or (2) have his or her performance evaluated in comparison with the performances of the same department managers in other stores of the company.

For example, a grocery department manager may set a goal to increase gross profit from 16 percent to 16.5 percent for the target period. In the middle of the first month of the target period, the company may initiate a major price reduction campaign which affects all stores in a given metropolitan area to a similar degree. As a result of the price reductions, the grocery gross profit drops from 16 to 14 percent. If this grocery manager, who has set his goal for a .5 percent improvement in gross profit, shows a gross profit loss that is .5 percent less than the loss of the average store, he should be considered to have reached his goal.

Areas in Which Goals Are Set

It would seem that a store has a greater degree of control over maintenance costs than it does over heat and fuel, for example. Why, then, aren't maintenance costs included as an area of controllable expense and as an area of responsibility for the store?

There is no hard and fast rule on this. One company on the goal-setting program does, in fact, list store maintenance costs as one of the store manager's responsibilities. Other companies, however, do not. It is doubtful that any two companies would use identical forms or would identify identical areas of responsibility for the store manager. The way in which a company breaks down its fiscal year into periods, as well as its accounting practices, also affect the design of its goal-setting program.

Should goals be set for such intangible or difficult to measure areas as employee morale, customer service, training and development of subordinates, cleanliness, checker ringup accuracy, customer or employee pilferage and others?

Though all of these are important areas of responsibility for any manager, a goal-setting program depends on the ability to measure performance in specific terms. Methods must be devised to measure these so-called "intangibles" so that goal setting would eventually be expanded to include performance in such areas.

Some of the indicators of good or poor practices in the areas of customer relations and service include the number of complaints sent into the office or received at the store. Good customer relations are reflected in compliments received from customers. If the number of unsolicited customer complaints and compliments per month could be established, these averages might be used as a basis for measuring performance in the future. To measure the level of customer service, the number of customers waiting to be checked out at three peak periods of the week might be counted, for instance, at 5:00 o'clock Friday afternoon, 7:30 Friday night, and 11:30 Saturday morning. The number of customers who leave loaded shopping carts in the checkout area might serve as an indicator of the level of poor customer service. If the length of lines during those busy periods could be reduced without decreasing business, overall volume would be improved.

A little thought and ingenuity would serve to identify indicators in almost any area of a manager's responsibility. Indicators of employee morale might be turnover, absenteeism, tardiness, length of time taken at rest periods, sales per labor-hour, and others. The amount of improvement in sales per labor-hour might be used to measure the effectiveness of training. Employee promotions within a store, or to other stores, might be used to measure a manager's ability to develop subordinates. Cleanliness might be measured by having supervisors periodically inspect specific store tools, equipment and areas. Cashier ringup accuracy might be periodically measured by basket checks made either by the manager or by an outside service. The reduction of customer and employee pilferage could be measured by a reduction in store shrinkage figures.

Such measurements, however, are only indicators of performance. The manager who develops steps to show improvement in these indicators must translate that improvement into one of the areas of his responsibility, such as sales or gross profit, which would, in turn, show an effect in adjusted gross profit. The net results should always be an improvement in adjusted gross profit for the forthcoming period.

Adjusting Steps and Goals

When a manager's goals seem to be overly optimistic, how should they be adjusted to a reasonable level?

It can be a mistake to assume that very optimistic goals are impossible to attain. According to one supermarket executive, an employee should set impossible goals and then achieve them. With proper motivation, the seemingly impossible is often accomplished.

In one Midwestern chain, for example, a supervisor was responsible for the specialty department in various stores of the chain. The specialty department, which sold hot, prepared, take-home foods, had in the past contributed 2 percent to the total company sales. This department head was provided with information showing the past performance of the department in sales, gross profit, wages, supply and laundry costs. On the basis of this information, the department head proceeded to develop a list of steps and goals for the department for the forthcoming thirteen-week quarter.

The list of steps covered three, single-spaced typewritten sheets, and included what seemed to be far more than any one person could accomplish in a three-month period. The goals outlined seemed even more impossible. The department head had proposed an improvement in sales of 50 percent for the forthcoming quarter; in other words, an increase in sales from an average of 2 percent to an average of 3 percent of total company sales. At the same time, he had projected an improvement in gross profit of two full percentage points over the same period of the previous year, and a reduction in wage costs of one full percentage point.

When management attempted to convince this department head that his goals were unreasonably high, he became angry and adamant. He accused management of a lack of faith in him. He was persistent and determined not to give in. Finally, management decided to let him have his way.

By the end of the target period, this department head had not only reached his goals, but had exceeded them. He had spent about eighteen hours a day, six days a week, implementing his steps in order to prove to management that he was right and it was wrong. Similar experiences have convinced many companies to accept very optimistic goals when an employee insists that he can reach them.

What can be done about goals that seem to be unreasonably low?

This is a common problem. Some employees, when first exposed to the program, feel that they are purposely being put on the spot. They exhibit a fear of the program or develop unambitious goals because they believe they will be judged on whether or not they reach them. The employee must be told that his success will not be measured on the basis of whether or not he has reached his goals but, rather, by the degree of improvement he has shown in (1) his department's or store's performance in the areas of his responsibility, and (2) the adjusted gross profit in dollars and percentage over the corresponding period of the previous year.

When a subordinate presents goals that appear to be unreasonably low, his superior, after reviewing his steps (which will probably also be modest), should decide if the subordinate can do a better job of developing ways to improve performance. If the superior concludes that the goals are, indeed, unreasonably low, he should encourage the subordinate to develop additional steps which might show a greater degree of improvement. However, he should resist the temptation, in such cases, to suggest specific steps to the subordinate.

The store manager faced with such a problem should take a positive approach. He should indicate his confidence in the department manager's ability to come up with a greater degree of improvement. If, however, the department manager strongly believes that he has presented reasonable steps and lofty goals, then it is best for the store manager to accept them.

When the steps developed by the department manager show little originality or when his goals are low in comparison with those of other managers in other stores, he will soon know it. As soon as he discovers the inferiority of his steps and goals, such a department manager will usually set higher goals for the next target period.

Can an employee modify his goals if experience shows that he was too optimistic when he set them?

Yes. Any manager participating in a goal-setting program should be allowed to raise or lower his goals if and when it becomes obvious that they were incorrectly set. When store managers review the performance of each department manager at the end of every accounting period, the department manager should be given the opportunity to revise his goals, downwards or upwards, if such a revision seems in order. If the actual figures show that he was too optimistic originally, and if he is not allowed to revise his projections, he will lose interest in achieving what have become unrealistic goals.

What should be done with an employee who continues to set goals which are unrealistically high?

Nothing should have to be done. After two or three cycles, it should become obvious to the employee that his proposed steps are not producing the anticipated results. Such an employee should be reminded that the effectiveness of this program is not measured in terms of whether or not goals have been realized, but, rather, by the degree of improvement shown in each area of the participant's responsibility.

Do the goals of store and department managers become more reasonable with time?

Yes. Initially, there is a tendency for many participants to be overly optimistic, but as they gain experience with the program and learn the effectiveness of various steps, they become more reasonable in projecting the degree of improvement.

How should an employee be prevented from projecting improved performance in one area of his responsibility at the expense of another?

If, when the superior reviews the steps proposed by his subordinate, he becomes convinced that customer service, for example, might be adversely affected by a projected reduction in wage expense, he should discuss this possibility with the subordinate and, together, they should work out a solution. When a step is accepted, but the superior still fears that it might adversely affect performance in another area of the subordinate's responsibility, he should watch the operation carefully to prevent this from happening.

What should be done when a participant in the program proposes either a capital investment or an increase in labor cost to improve performance in an area of his responsibility?

Such an individual should be required to justify the expenditures. A store manager in one store, for example, committed himself to a 7.5 percent increase in store sales on the condition that he be authorized to add 40 part-time labor-hours a week at the front-end in order to provide better customer service. After computing the net gain in adjusted gross profit dollars that would result from such an action, the supervisor approved the step. It proved a worthwhile investment. Over that target period the store realized an increase in sales of 7.2 percent, which management attributed to the additional personnel at the front-end.

In another situation, a meat department manager requested that a semi-automatic wrapping machine be installed in his meat department, at a cost of about $6,300. To justify the cost, he submitted a new meat department schedule which showed how he intended to eliminate 22 labor-hours per week by replacing a full-time employee with a part-timer. His proposal was accepted, the equipment was installed, and the department, as a result, realized an increase in adjusted gross profit dollars.

If a department manager is authorized to take certain steps to improve his gross profit, and in so doing implements poor ideas, what should the store manager do?

The store manager should make sure that the department manager is aware of the error. Nevertheless, he must not overrule the department manager in any area in which he has handed over the authority to make decisions and to act. The store manager must recognize in advance that people will make mistakes and that, occasionally, he has to live with those mistakes.

One grocery manager requested and received authority to determine which grocery items were to be mass merchandised on six of the ten end displays on the store gondolas. One morning the store manager looked up from his desk to see the grocery manager and two helpers building a display, can by can, from the floor almost to the ceiling, of buffet-size vegetable items. The store manager gritted his teeth; it would obviously take the three men most of the day to build the display at the rate they were working. Though the items selected by the grocery manager were fast-moving, high profit items, and the display idea was worthwhile, the labor expended would far exceed the possible additional gross profit. Nevertheless, the store manager overcame the temptation to correct the grocery manager.

By the end of the day, the grocery manager had spent 21 labor-hours building the display. Before leaving the store that night, he admitted he had made a mistake. He told the store manager that he had thought that the display could be built in about three hours: "Next time, I'll use cut cases instead of stacking the cans individually," he commented.

In the goal-setting program, situations that involve errors in judgment are the exception rather than the rule. Far more often, originality and creative ideas result when subordinates are given the authority to develop steps and to set goals.

In the center of the grocery department of another store, in a three-foot wide display, from the top to the bottom shelf and adjacent to the vanilla wafers, there suddenly appeared a mass display of bananas. In the produce department, four different salad dressings were set out on the refrigerated display rack between the tomatoes and lettuce. The produce and grocery managers, both of whom were participants in the goal-setting program, had agreed to trade space for their mutual benefit. The increase in sales of the displayed items in each department was gratifying.

Goal Setting and Other Programs

Many companies ask their supervisors and store managers to jointly set quarterly budgets and goals in sales, gross profits, wages, and other areas. Isn't this the same thing as a goal-setting program?

No. In fact, this procedure is usually diametrically opposite to the goal-setting program. In the typical budgeting system employed by many supermarket companies, the company first establishes budgets for various areas of responsibility. It asks its district managers to come up with budgets for each store in sales, gross profits, and so on, that will bring about the realization of company goals. The process originates at the top and is fed down, through various levels of management, to store level. The goals are, in effect, top management's goals. The store manager, when he agrees to goals proposed by his supervisor is, in reality, agreeing because he has no choice; the goals are not his. This traditional system also does not challenge the store or department manager to devise his own steps and ideas to improve performance.

How does the goal-setting program supplement conventional budgeting techniques?

It does not supplement conventional budgeting techniques; it replaces them. Top management uses the combined goals of the various stores for each area identified as a department or store manager's responsibility in order to establish company goals and budgets.

Every Saturday store and department managers in one company project the following week's department and store sales and labor-hours. How does this practice fit in with the goal-setting program?

It is perfectly compatible with the goal-setting procedure. The important point is that department managers must have a voice in projecting their own department sales and labor-hours for the coming week. If the store manager did this for them, then this system would be incompatible with goal setting. As long as the department manager establishes his own weekly projections of sales and labor-hours, the practice should be continued after a goal-setting program has been instituted.

How does goal setting fit in with incentive programs?

It is difficult to imagine any incentive program which would not be compatible with the goal-setting process. Both are designed to improve performance. Most good incentive programs, like effective goal setting, are designed to show an improvement in adjusted gross profit dollars.

However, an incentive program is not necessary to encourage the participants in a goal-setting program to reach their goals. In the opinion of many people, the goal-setting program is, in itself, the most powerful tool available to our industry today to create motivation.

Goal Setting and Store Success

Any supermarket company, whether it operates one store or a thousand, must above all serve and satisfy its public. Though it has an obligation to its stockholders to make a profit, and to its employees to provide wages, the profit and wages are always the products of filling customer needs satisfactorily.

The company's growth, increased profits, and expanded benefits are all dependent on customer satisfaction. An organization which recognizes its primary role will encourage employees to realize that their own personal success and their future with the company are dependent on whether or not they serve the customer to his or her satisfaction. The goal-setting technique effectively involves employees in the growth and operation of the store, with the result that they are willing to contribute to the common effort to satisfy customers and, thereby, to insure their own and the store's success.

16 | Criteria for Promotions

There is a desperate need in the supermarket industry to establish and apply more objective criteria in selecting people for promotion.

The personnel vice-president of a large chain fixed the cost of training and developing a qualified store manager for his chain at more than $140,000. In this particular chain, the manager turnover rate is more than three times the national average. The high cost of training managers is only one of the expenses incurred. Consideration must also be given to the additional profit that can be earned over a ten-year period by a store run by a really efficient manager. Some experts even claim that the selection of a person for promotion to the job of store manager is a $250,000 decision. Therefore, any tool that could be used to improve the odds of making a good promotion decision should be examined and adopted.

What Is Promotion?

Promotion refers to the selection and placement of an employee into a higher level position within the same company. Though this

261

may seem to be an obvious definition, what is not so obvious is that such a promotion implies the rejection of outside hiring. Thus, a company that promotes only from within its own ranks is committed to using one of its own employees, whether or not it has an employee who can perform the given work or who can learn to perform it better than an outsider.

Many companies still do not have firm, well-planned procedures and policies for hiring outsiders or for promoting from within. Nor have they established systematic promotion criteria. It was not until higher operating costs had driven some companies to re-examine every part of their operation, that they investigated the promotion process. Indeed, they often reconsidered their promotion policies only after they had examined other functions, such as transportation, warehousing, store layout, and accounting procedures. Many supermarket companies have still not yet methodically re-evaluated their promotion procedures.

The Need for a Formal Promotion System

In companies where an informal appraisal and promotion system, or the "no-system" prevails, investigation has shown that many of the people who are selected for promotion are the same people who would have been promoted under the most systematic, rational selection system. Such success would seem to support the theory that "you can't keep a good man down." But this theory quickly falls apart when, all too often, serious, obvious (or not so obvious) mistakes are made. A low performer, for example, may produce the same operating figures in a new job as did his or her predecessor, whereas a strong performer would have doubled the net profit. There are many intangibles and matters beyond the control of store and district managers which may mask promotion mistakes for some time.

The decision to promote an employee is just about the most difficult of all business decisions to make, not because of the skill or intelligence it requires, but because of the personal involvement of decision makers with the people who may be promoted or who may be skipped over. Supervisors obviously have a much closer emotional relationship with their subordinates than they do with outside applicants for employment. Knowing a person as an individual—knowing his personality and family—often makes it difficult, if not impossible, to deal with him objectively, to make a clear, straight business decision. Moreover, most business people overestimate their competence to judge people, and often feel qualified to make decisions about promoting people they know when, in fact, they are not truly competent in this respect.

Problems of Informal Promotion Systems

Supervisors who do not use a carefully planned, formal promotion system generally encounter six major problems:

1. They fail to be completely objective because of their emotional involvement with some of the candidates.
2. They lack the ability or knowledge to make promotions based exclusively on merit.
3. They accept the myth that success on one job qualifies a person for promotion to the next higher job.
4. They accept the myth that a person cannot effectively supervise a subordinate if he himself is not highly skilled in performing the job.
5. They do not really know which supervisors and personnel specialists to invite to participate in the process of making promotion decisions; which employees to consider as candidates for promotion; or which selection tools to use and how to use them.
6. They exaggerate the importance of such non-merit factors as seniority, traditional promotion methods and loyalty or submissiveness.

There is a proverb popular with management which paraphrases Gresham's law ("bad money drives out good money"): "Bad employees drive out good employees." Antony Jay, a British industrial consultant, has written: "Men who have worked diligently and successfully and then see those who have worked less diligently and less successfully promoted above them start to read the management want ads in the paper the following morning. Gresham's law operates more swiftly and inexorably through bad promotions than by any other agency."[1]

Despite a number of problems, the system of promoting from within has some advantages for companies with merit or non-merit promotion systems. Generally, better information is available on which to base selections than can usually be obtained when hiring an outsider. People who are promoted from within the company have already become adjusted to the company's standards, procedures, management style and pace, factors which would be unfamil-

[1]*Management and Machiavelli* (New York: Holt, Rinehart and Winston, 1968), p. 178.

iar to a newcomer. Promotion from within also provides a way of rewarding competent, faithful employees and of attracting and holding better people.

Changing to a Merit Promotion System

A company that plans to change from an informal to a formal, merit-based promotion system must first carefully examine the entire promotion process. What would such a change cost in terms of time and money? Is management truly ready to commit itself to a formal program, not only on paper, but in fact as well? Is it prepared to face up to the disgruntled rumblings and complaints of the cliques and old guard?

Once the company has determined to make the change, it might consider six essential conditions met by those companies with the most successful merit promotion systems.

1. A formal program must be instituted. The merit promotion program must be based on a comprehensive, specially-designed, formal, written program that takes into account the technical selection skills of the people who will administer it. It should include those selection procedures that can be effectively carried out by the managers and personnel people who will screen candidates and make promotion decisions.

2. Employees must be convinced that the company is sincere in its desire to institute an objective merit promotion system; that it is not just giving lip-service to the program.

3. Objective standards must be set. Those who make the promotion decision must choose the employee who best meets an objective, predetermined standard of performance. Irrelevant promotion qualifications must be discarded. Management should recognize that the employee best qualified for promotion is not necessarily the one with the most seniority or a relative or a friend.

4. All qualified candidates must be considered. Each person in the company or unit who appears to have a reasonable chance of becoming a successful candidate must be given the opportunity to compete openly for the promotion.

5. The preference policy must be stated. Management may prefer, but should not require, that each opening above base level be filled by a promotion from within. Only when it is bound by union contracts should management limit promotions solely to employees from within the company. When outside candidates are better quali-

fied than those from within, management should consider them very carefully before promoting the insider.

6. All candidates must be ranked and those who make the promotion decision must genuinely believe that the employee formally selected is the best available candidate from within (or from outside) the company.

Though a number of companies follow each of these steps in setting up a merit promotion program, some occasionally revert to non-merit systems. They argue that they must sometimes bend the rules a little, for example, when they consider it absolutely essential to promote the boss's son or daughter or someone else who fails to meet the prescribed objective standards. When a person is promoted because he or she is a relative, the true reason for the promotion should be given. Few people would question the right of the owner of a business to promote a relative, but many would question such a promotion if it were falsely described as based on merit. However, if the company's firm policy is to promote only on merit, there should be no compromises, exceptions or rationalizations which undermine the program by weakening employee morale and robbing the employee of the chance to be promoted to a better job.

Requirements for Promotions

There is no single set of requirements that will guarantee success in all supervisory jobs. Requirements are affected by (1) the different levels of supervisory work to be performed, (2) the different styles of management, and (3) the different functional areas in which the supervisor will operate. Promotions, like original job selections, are best made by first determining the necessary requirements for success on a particular job, and then by judging how well each candidate fulfills those requirements.

Requirements Vary by Job Levels.   At the lowest supervisory level, such as a department manager who must physically work with a crew throughout most of the day, knowledge of the job, physical vigor and coordination must be emphasized far more than at higher supervisory levels. Indeed, in some companies low-volume store managers perform manual tasks, starting the morning off by putting up bread, and then spending the day assisting in different departments, performing such managerial functions as planning and supervising only when they can find some free time. Problems that arise from the failure to plan or supervise must be dealt with on the spot.

In some companies, the least competent district manager also does a fair share of physical work, frequently spending an hour at one store or another, working at such lower-level chores as lining up packages in frozen food cases or straightening a produce display. Such district managers spend their time at work which is in no way connected with employee supervision or training because they probably prefer to deal with things rather than with people; in other words, they prefer to perform non-supervisory tasks. They are "mismatched"; they do not possess the essential qualities of a good supervisor.

A successful low-level supervisor, on the other hand, always has a strong interest in, though not necessarily a strong preference for dealing with people as well as with things. He or she must also be more mentally alert than most clerks and most unsuccessful low-level supervisors because greater intelligence is required for the job.

An effective middle-level supervisor is adaptable to new situations and is skilled in breaking a problem into its components and in coming up with a sound solution.

A research study has shown that the best higher-level supervisor is outstanding because of four qualities more conspicuous at high than at low levels; he or she (1) is able to set and meet high standards; (2) can accomplish a great deal of work; (3) is dependable; and, above all, (4) is strongly motivated.[2]

Requirements Vary by Management Styles. Job requirements differ in accordance with the particular type of management style adopted by the company. For example, a chain that uses a goal-setting program would require that its grocery managers play a far greater role in planning than they would in a chain in which top management does all the planning. In a democratic management system, where even low-level management people have an important voice in setting goals, more creativity would be required than in an autocratic, paternalistic system where the employee must simply follow orders as they are handed down.

There are other styles of management, each requiring a special type of behavior, and each demanding that a person adapt to the established style for the particular job. The company's management style must be considered when promoting employees to supervisory jobs.

[2]For a landmark study reporting basic research in identifying qualities needed for managerial success, see C. Wilson Randle, "How to Identify Promotable Executives," *Harvard Business Review*, Vol. 34 (May-June, 1956), pp. 122–134.

Requirements Vary by Functional Areas. The different functional areas of work, including store operations, warehousing, manufacturing, accounting and others, require supervisors with different qualities. While warehouse, accounting, and manufacturing managers need supervisory skill, store-level department managers must, to varying degrees, possess a combination of supervisory and sales skills. A manager of a service delicatessen department, for example, requires far more sales skill than a manager of a self-service meat department; both, however, must have supervisory skills. Before any promotion decision can be considered, the special requirements of the different functional areas must be determined. Then the skills of the candidates must be matched with those requirements.

Eight Key Supervisory Requirements

Despite the differences in managerial levels, management styles and functional areas, there are certain common requirements for all supervisors. Successful supervisors tend to possess eight qualities, and tend to have a better balance of these qualities than do less successful supervisors. They are usually (1) effective in their present positions; they possess (2) the drive and determination to get things done; (3) general mental ability; (4) leadership qualities which enable them to give and receive cooperation and loyalty; (5) the administrative ability to plan, organize, delegate, follow-up and control; and (6) initiative; they are (7) motivated; and (8) creative. It is not enough simply to possess some of these qualities; all eight are important. Other qualities, such as good attitude, self-control and good health, though important for supervisory jobs, are often possessed by poor supervisors and therefore cannot be used to effectively distinguish the potentially successful from the unsuccessful supervisor.

Because so many factors are important in making promotion decisions, a selection system must first concentrate on the eight key qualities so that unqualified candidates are screened out and the selection process is not needlessly prolonged. Only candidates who meet minimum standards in all eight requirements should be examined for other specialized needs.

Spotting Potential Talent

In order for a promotion program to be successful, it must be based on a great deal of advance planning. Promotions cannot be made simply on the basis of filling an immediate opening. A successful program must single out the most talented people in the organization in order to eventually promote them to job levels several notches above their present level. These people should then be promoted through a planned series of jobs. A management trainee, for example, should normally follow a predetermined promotion route which leads to a specific position, such as store manager or higher.

It is precisely at this advance planning stage that many companies falter in their promotion programs. Some companies fail to realize that there are times when a promotion for a given position must bypass an equally qualified senior employee for one with the potential for higher-level work. Moving potential talent along at a faster than average rate sometimes becomes necessary when employees at higher levels of management are either approaching retirement, are less than fully adequate, or when rapid expansion is planned.

It is a serious mistake to overfill the lower levels of a company with obviously over-qualified people, unless expansion or turnover is expected to provide a sufficient number of higher-level openings. Poor employee morale and high turnover almost certainly result when over-qualified people are frozen into lower-level jobs. For example, suppose a thirty-store supermarket chain had a policy of hiring only college graduates for all store manager trainee jobs. If it had five such manager trainees on the payroll, opened an average of only one new store a year, and had a very low manager turnover rate, it would soon become obvious to the manager trainees that they were not about to advance for a long time and that they would do well to look for better opportunities elsewhere. Meanwhile, non-college educated clerks or department managers in the same company would have even less chance to advance, and turnover in this group would also be a major problem.

Using Entrance Selection Tools

Some of the personnel tools used in selecting new employees (see Chapter 4) are, to varying degrees, also useful in measuring candidates for promotion. The employment application and other material in the employee's personnel folder should be reviewed when making promotion decisions. One or more interviews are also basic tools in making promotions. A general mental ability test is important and written tests of knowledge of supervisory principles may also be useful. Adult scores on general mental ability tests are usually stable so that results of an examination given at entrance may be consulted. On the other hand, scores on supervisory knowledge tests change as experience is gained and the test should be repeated if a year or more has elapsed since it was last given. Reference check notes made at the time of application for initial employment may also be reviewed when an employee is being considered for promotion, though apart from some occasional information about an employee's past which may affect the promotion, reference checks are not generally significant to the promotion process.

As performance standards for all levels of supervisors continue to rise, and as more emotional pressure is exerted on supervisors, there will be an increasing need for medical examinations. Such examinations may be conducted at or close to the time of the screening for promotion. Medical examinations for middle- and upper-level management jobs are becoming more comprehensive and expensive, many now costing more than $500.

Finally, there is as much validity to instituting a probationary period for promoted employees as for new employees. However, whereas newly-hired employees who fail to pass their probationary periods are usually discharged, promoted employees who fail are either demoted or, too often, allowed to remain in their new jobs as poor performers. A few union contracts even guarantee that recently promoted union members who fail as supervisors be permitted to retreat to their former jobs. Occasionally, a new supervisor who fails because of an inability to deal with people, rather than because of low motivation or low general mental ability, will succeed in another type of staff position which requires less interpersonal contact.

Predicting Performance

There are two general methods of predicting whether or not a person will succeed in a higher-level job: (1) Past accomplishments may be evaluated, and (2) present performance of the key tasks which are demanded in the job for which the person is being considered may be appraised.

Evaluating Past Performance. Written records of past accomplishments and recorded samples of the candidate's own work may be used as direct sources in judging the past performances of candidates for promotion. When the candidate is a department or store manager, the most frequently used and best available written records are usually such operational data as dollar or percentage figures based on the performance of the individual's unit in given areas, including sales, gross profit and controllable expenses. This type of information is available in performance reports produced by the accounting department. These records should always be interpreted in the light of such conditions as the competitive picture that existed at the time they were compiled and the quality of people the candidate inherited. Samples of material developed by the candidate, including manuals, reports, or written suggestions, can also serve as guidelines in evaluating past performance; however, these are normally scarcer than operational-type records.

There are, in addition, two indirect sources of information on the past performances of prospective candidates:

1. Written performance appraisal reports.
2. Group conferences of supervisors and personnel specialists.

1. *Apprasial reports*: The most frequently used, and often the only available indirect material for evaluating a candidate's past performance, are written performance appraisal reports. There are, however, two good reasons why these reports should not be taken at face value when evaluating a candidate. First, many such performance reports are inaccurate and often conceal as much as they reveal. Second, unless they are made on an employee already in a supervisory position, they generally do not cover the qualities most needed for success on higher-level jobs and, thus, do not constitute a fully relevant guide when a supervisory position is to be filled. When a district supervisor predicts next week's sales volume for one of his stores or for his district, he is usually very close to the mark. But when the same supervisor reports that one subordinate in a given store possesses a certain quality, he is less likely to be correct. Moreover, most supervisors tend to protect themselves and their people when they make performance appraisals.

Yet employee evaluations must be made, and unless objective performance measurements are available, a subjective appraisal system is better than none at all. Formal performance appraisal systems can be valuable when they are made by supervisors with full knowledge of the candidate's job performance, and when the ratings adequately cover the factors that are significant for the job under consideration.

2. *Supervisor and specialist conferences*: A second indirect method of checking past behavior is to set up a group conference between two or more of the candidate's supervisors and a personnel specialist. At this meeting, the specialist should systematically compare the supervisors' opinions and evaluate them in light of the qualities which are essential to success on the particular job. Group conferences are of great value when the job specifications have

been agreed upon, when supervisors are personally familiar with the candidate's performance, and when members of the group are candid and honest with one another. If any of these requirements is lacking, such a group conference will prove useless.

Evaluating Performance on the Job.   One of the best ways to find out which candidate will function best on the job is to actually give each one a chance to perform it. For example, a meat cutter who is being considered for promotion to meat manager might be required to lay out a completely new case plan or to make out the week's order for the department; a store manager may be given a one-week assignment to help develop a new training program with the company trainer in order to test his training ability; an assistant manager may be asked to take over when the manager is on vacation in order to judge his ability to perform the store manager's function; and a head cashier who is being considered for the job of cashier trainer in the personnel department may be required to help out for a week by training new cashiers for the opening of a new store.

Many companies are making excellent use of this trial period technique before announcing a permanent promotion. In effect, they screen each candidate right on the job for the specific requirements. This system works much better than handing out temporary or probationary promotions whereby the candidate is put into the new job and demoted if he or she does not succeed. Such demotions can occur quite frequently if temporary promotions are not based on good, solid selection techniques; employees who are thus demoted are humiliated far more seriously than if they had been merely bypassed for promotion.

The Assessment Session

Some of the most recently developed selection tools are especially valuable in identifying employees with middle-level management abilities, such as managers of very large stores or district supervisors. These tools have been successfully tested primarily in other industries.

A number of performance tests are administered, preferably by the personnel department, during a one- or two-day assessment session at company or district headquarters. If trained personnel specialists are not available, some other qualified person at headquarters might conduct the session, but it is extremely important that the leader be competent and experienced in the use of the assessment tools. The following are eight of the most practical and valid screening devices that may be used during the assessment session.

1. *Directed group oral performance test*: A broad discussion topic should be presented to a group of from four to nine candidates, who are preferably at the same job level. The topic should be one with which all candidates are familiar (store methods, work improvement, absenteeism or others), but sufficiently complex so that there is no single correct answer. The candidates should be seated at a round conference table. (If the table is rectangular, no candidate should be seated at the head.) Written instructions should be distributed to the candidates, informing them that they are in a test situation. After the topic is presented to the group, the discussion should last about one and one-half hours and the specialist who serves as discussion leader should remain neutral while trying to draw the participants out and to elicit more information. It is important never to put a person in the same group with his or her boss. Several raters should sit in the background and take notes. Later they should join the discussion leader to rate the candidates on a check list of requirements for the job.

2. *Undirected group oral performance test*: This technique differs from the directed group oral performance test in that there is no discussion leader. During the discussion, a leader emerges from among the candidates. Like the directed discussion, this device creates an intensely social situation for testing interpersonal skills, adaptability, leadership abilities, judgment, creativity and oral and analytical aptitude.

3. *Role playing*: In role playing, a conflict situation such as occurs often in every store (handling an irate customer, a tardy employee and so on) is artificially constructed, and each candidate is rated on how well he solves the problem. Two people participate in the role playing assignment: the candidate who plays the protagonist, and a member of the selection team who acts as the antagonist. It is important that the non-candidate give the same performance with each candidate so that the problem situation is standardized for all. Each candidate should be evaluated by qualified raters who sit in the background and observe the performance. The non-candidate role player should also contribute to the information collected by the raters.

4. *Written test*: A simple written test can be used to measure mental ability and word skill, as well as to obtain information on the candidate's personal background, motivation and prior leadership experience. The candidate may be asked to write a short essay on such topics as the following: his leadership abilities as demonstrated

in athletics, school, military, community, religious, scouting, politics, previous employment, or elsewhere; his personal reaction when faced with such common business situations as opposition and disagreement; the type of work or people he prefers to avoid; the two or three things he has done that have given him the greatest sense of achievement or personal satisfaction; his greatest strengths and weaknesses; or the situations which would cause him the most worry, concern or anxiety. The candidate's essay should not only indicate his estimate of his own worth, but should also supply useful insight into whether or not he possesses the eight key qualities common to good supervisors.

5. *Short talk*: Any topic which is generally familiar to all candidates and yet not so specialized that any single candidate would have a marked advantage over another is suitable for a short speech. For example, the candidate may be given ten minutes to prepare a speech on the advantages of food store retailing as a career, which he should deliver from a lectern and for which he may refer to notes. The candidate should be scored on such factors as organization of material, content, fluency, delivery, and his effectiveness as a company public relations representative.

6. *Teaching test*: Every supervisor must be capable of training his subordinates so that he can ultimately delegate work to them. In order to measure their teaching skills, candidates should be brought into a room one at a time, and assigned the same problem of teaching an elementary physical task to a beginner; for example, to stock Number 303 cans, two at a time with each hand, from a box on a platform to a shelf, label-side forward. The member of the selection team acting as the learner should pretend to learn slowly and to have little aptitude. The scoring should be done by the learner and a rater, who compare the instructions given by the candidate with the company's standard training methods.

7. *Candidate ranking*: Candidates in an assessment session tend to form judgments about each other. Each candidate may therefore be asked to fill out a questionnaire ranking his fellow candidates (excluding himself) on such questions as: Who is the best person to be promoted to a specific job now? Two years from now? Who will reach the highest supervisory executive level at the peak of his career? With whom would he most prefer to attend a three-day out-of-town supermarket conference? And who would be most skillful in persuading high-ranking company officials to change their minds on a problem affecting his department?

8. *Interview with a personnel specialist*: Toward the close of the assessment session, each candidate should have a twenty to thirty minute interview with a personnel specialist who might also have

participated in the session as a rater, and possibly as a role player or learner. The candidate should be asked to describe his reactions to the assessment session, as well as his long-range goals with the company. This interview gives each candidate an opportunity to release the anxieties he may have experienced during the assessment session. The results of the interview should help the selection team to draw the remaining loose ends together.

Using Assessment Information

Because a great mass of information is obtained about each candidate during an assessment session, the personnel specialist must summarize the material and consolidate it with all relevant material obtained from other selection devices. The summarized information on each candidate must also be compared with the job requirements previously agreed upon by the personnel and store operations departments. Then the personnel specialist should prepare an oral and written report containing all the pertinent information, to be presented to the director of store operations and to those assistants who will make the promotion decision. Finally, the personnel department should follow-up the employee selected in order to evaluate and, where appropriate, to improve selection procedures.

In addition to the oral and written reports, the personnel department should prepare a chart on which every candidate is evaluated and ranked for each selection factor. If the top-ranking candidate does not meet the minimum standards that have been set for the job, the personnel department should recommend rejection of that candidate. Other inside and/or outside candidates should then be considered, but only as a last resort should job requirements be lowered.

When the selection decision is not clear-cut, personnel and store operations people should discuss and consider such factors as trade-off qualifications among candidates, immediate promotability versus long-range promotability, and others. Sometimes, even at this late stage, it may be necessary to get more information and even to settle differences in value judgments between the personnel department and store operations. But if the opening is in store operations, that department must ultimately be allowed to establish the job specifications and to decide who will be promoted.

Handling Rejected Candidates

Management can best cope with disappointed candidates by convincing them that the comprehensive selection procedures were devised to find the best person for each opening, and that the future success of the company and of its most able employees is dependent on having a thorough and effective promotion program. Management should also assure rejected candidates that they will be considered for future openings if they are qualified or if their present qualifications change. It should further emphasize to each candidate the value of the managerial training received during the assessment session.

Assessment sessions are being used increasingly by companies committed to making managerial promotions on a merit basis. Much can be gained from reading about the experience of these companies in the business press and from consulting basic sources on screening sessions.

17 | Laws Affecting Employment

The first store that Johnny Keane managed was an independent market owned by a single-store operator in a middle-sized northern Florida city. Although the store was scheduled to close when the owner retired, Keane still got the most out of it. Even though sales depended heavily on local traffic, in 1988 Keane increased store volume by $70,000, to almost $480,000 a year, and boosted gross profit by one-half of one percent.

Keane's success did not go unnoticed, and in December 1988 he was hired by a large chain with annual sales well in excess of two billion dollars. He was assigned to manage one of the chain's units near the state line in Asheville, North Carolina.

Apart from the obvious difference between the independent grocery store in Florida and a supermarket that was part of a chain grossing considerably more, there were still other changes to which even a bright, experienced manager like Johnny Keane had to adjust. Luckily, his supervisor prepared him for the transition. If he had not, Keane might have tried operating as he did in Florida and would have violated both local and federal regulations.[1]

---

[1] The material in this revised chapter reflects labor laws in force as of August 1, 1990.

Though Johnny Keane was working in the same industry, his move to a large chain in a new state required that he make important changes in his hiring policies at the store level. In Florida he had employed twelve-year-old students in his backroom. The students worked after school, sometimes until six at night. Since his annual sales were less than $500,000, he had been exempt from federal minimum wage provisions and was able to pay the youngsters as little as $2.50 an hour. In North Carolina, however, the chain's overall volume brought the federal wage provisions into effect, and North Carolina's stricter state laws governed the hours and conditions of employment of minors. For example, minors under fourteen years of age would not be permitted to work, even in a retail establishment.

Like Johnny Keane, today's store managers are expected to have some knowledge of the laws governing retail employment. They are, after all, employers as well as employees. Unless they know something about federal and state labor laws, chances are they will run afoul of them.

Federal Regulations

All retailers should be familiar with the provisions of the Fair Labor Standards Act of 1938 and its amendments. The basic statute covers millions of workers throughout the country, many of whom are in the retailing industry. The provisions of the Act are interpreted and administered by the Wage and Hour Division of the United States Department of Labor.

The Fair Labor Standards Act establishes minimum wages, maximum hours, overtime pay, equal pay, and child labor standards for covered employees. A section of the Act specifies that covered employees are those who are (1) engaged in interstate commerce; (2) engaged in the production of goods for commerce; or (3) working in "an enterprise engaged in commerce or the production of goods for commerce." Retail employees are normally covered under the third section, provided their employer meets the so-called "enterprise test." The word *enterprise* refers to the entire company, while its individual units (stores, warehouses, and so on) are called "establishments." Persons who are employed by an "enterprise engaged in commerce or in the production of goods for commerce" must be compensated in accordance with the provisions of the Fair Labor Standards Act.

Recent amendments have varied the applicability of the Act. In 1977, the Act was narrowed to exclude from its coverage employees of a retail outlet that made over half its sales within the state in which the outlet was located, provided that the outlet was not part of a larger enterprise (company) with an annual gross volume (exclusive of excise taxes) of more than $250,000. On December 31, 1981, this figure was raised to $362,500. Effective April 1, 1990, the enterprise coverage test was utilized to establish a uniform $500,000 "business volume threshold" for both retail and non-retail firms.

Therefore, a retail chain (or an independent operator) with over $500,000 in gross annual sales is automatically covered under the provisions of the Fair Labor Standards Act. By the same token, the employees of an independent operator or a chain with aggregate gross sales of less than $500,000 are excluded from the Act's coverage. (Also exempt are single establishments with less than two employees.)

Although a store or retail chain is covered by the Act, every employee of that enterprise is not necessarily covered by all of its clauses. Executive and other administrative personnel, for example, are usually exempt from the minimum wage and overtime pay provisions. These exemptions are not arbitrary but, rather, dependent upon a combination of the employee's (1) duties and responsibilities, and his or her (2) wages or salary schedule.

Wage Standards

The Federal Minimum Wage Law of the Fair Labor Standards Act sets a minimum wage ($3.80 an hour beginning April 1, 1990, $4.25 an hour beginning April 1, 1991) for a maximum number of hours (forty hours during any one workweek), after which overtime must be paid at the rate of 1 ½ times the employee's regular rate of pay.

Complete and accurate time records must be kept. Each week is a separate unit and hours cannot be traded off from one week to the next; for example, an employee who has worked 42 hours during one week cannot be compensated by being asked to work 38 hours the following week. In addition, a company may establish a rounding practice to the nearest quarter- or sixth-hour; for example, under a quarter-hour rounding practice, the employer may decide that an employee whose regular workday runs from 8:00 AM to 5:00 PM should not be docked if he signs in at 8:14 AM or that he should not be credited with additional time if he signs out at 5:14 PM. A rounding practice may be used only when it operates fairly and when overtime and undertime average out.

An employee's regular rate of pay is determined by dividing the total pay for the period by the number of hours worked. For example, a worker who earns a straight salary of $240 for a forty-hour week receives a regular rate of pay of $6.00 per hour. An employee who works 44 hours during a particular week must be paid $9.00 (1 ½ times the regular rate of $6.00) for every hour over forty worked. In this case, overtime pay would amount to $36 (four hours at $9.00 an hour) and the employee's gross pay for the week would be $276.

When figuring an employee's rate of pay, certain items should be excluded, such as vacations, sick leave, holidays, Christmas gifts, certain bonuses, reimbursement for expenses, and bona fide overtime premiums. The Act also does not require employers to give extra pay for work on Saturdays, Sundays, or holidays if the total time worked does not exceed forty hours during the week; nor does the Act regulate holiday pay, vacations, severance pay or discharge procedures.

To prevent curtailment of employment opportunities for specific categories of workers, special minimum wage rates are provided for retarded people, for learners and apprentices, and for full-time high school students who work part-time outside school hours in retail establishments. The Act provides that such employment should not be of the type ordinarily given to full-time employees. Moreover, before these special rates can be paid, a certificate must be obtained from the Regional Wage-Hour Office. However, even those employees who must be so certified are subject to the Act's overtime pay provisions. The wage rates paid to students may not be less than 85 percent of the minimum wage, and the students' duties must conform with child labor laws.

Child Labor

The Fair Labor Standards Act sets three minimum ages for the employment of minors. The minimum age is, in part, determined by the type of work to be done. The highest minimum age is eighteen, and applies to minors engaged in occupations classified as "particularly hazardous." Such occupations include, but are not limited to (1) motor vehicle and helper occupations; (2) occupations involved in the operation of power-driven hoisting apparatus; (3) occupations involving slaughtering, meat packing or processing, or rendering; (4) occupations involved in the operation of bakery machines; and (5) occupations involved in the operation of paper-products machines.

In most other cases, the minimum age for employment is sixteen. However, under certain closely regulated conditions, this age requirement is reduced to fourteen. Fourteen-year-olds may be employed in retailing but a number of regulations govern their employment. Minors between the ages of fourteen and sixteen may be employed only outside of school hours; when school is in session, this employment may not total more than three hours in any single day, or more than eighteen hours in any workweek; when school is not in session, they may not work more than eight hours a day or forty hours a week. In addition, such minors may be employed only between the hours of seven in the morning and seven in the evening.

Any violation of these rules constitutes oppressive child labor. Willful violators of the Act are liable to fines of up to $10,000 or imprisonment for six months or both. In addition, there is a civil penalty of $1,000 for each violation. Imprisonment, however, may not be imposed as a punishment upon a defendant's first conviction under the Act. When the employer has on file a certificate that shows that the employee is above the minimum age required for a particular job, oppressive child labor is considered not to exist. Thus, employers who wish to protect themselves against unintentional violations of the child labor provisions should obtain such a certificate whenever there is any question concerning the age of any applicant and his or her eligibility for a certain job.

One of the general principles of federal wage and hour regulations is that state laws prevail whenever they are more strict than federal laws. Since this principle usually has a direct bearing on the hiring of minors, store managers should also be familiar with the relevant state child labor laws.

Discrimination in Employment

The Equal Pay Act of 1963, a section of the Fair Labor Standards Act, outlaws discrimination in rates of pay on the basis of sex. All employees covered by the Fair Labor Standards Act are also protected by the Equal Pay Act standard, and many exemptions from the Fair Labor Standards Act represent exemptions from the Equal Pay Act.

The Equal Pay Act provision prohibits an employer from paying lower wages to an employee of one sex than is paid to an employee of the opposite sex. It applies only when (1) the amount of work is the same, (2) the job requires equal skill and responsibility, (3) working conditions are identical, and (4) the function is performed in the same establishment. If an employer can prove that any of these conditions are not met, or that the difference in wages is based on seniority, merit, or some other objective measurement like quality or quantity, or any other factor not based on sex, the Equal Pay Act standard does not apply.

Most states also have fair employment practices laws which prohibit discrimination on the basis of sex. For example, Ohio law prohibits an employer of four or more persons from, among other things, discriminating between sexes in any way in matters of wages, salaries, or other compensation.

When sex is a relevant factor, employers should be careful in arranging wage scales. When a vacancy occurs, for example, and a female employee replaces a male, the employer may not legally pay the woman a lower wage unless such a differential can be justified on sex neutral criteria. Since the Federal Act considers such fringe benefits as hospitalization "remuneration," an employer may not make these benefits available to employees of only one sex.

Discrimination by employers (or unions) on the basis of race, color, religion, sex, or national origin is outlawed by Title VII of the Civil Rights Act of 1964, as amended. The Pregnancy Discrimination Act of 1978 extends the coverage of Title VII to pregnant women. The language of Title VII is so broad that it can be applied to almost every area of employment.

There are only two exceptions to Title VII. One is for bona fide occupational requirements tied to religion, sex, or national origin. An example of such an exception might be found in a supermarket operating near the Mexican border where a high percentage of the store's customers speaks Spanish. The manager of the store might recruit a cashier of Mexican descent rather than another applicant. The manager can legitimately do this if it can be demonstrated that knowing the customers' language and customs is a bona fide occupational qualification. If there is doubt whether this is a bona fide occupational qualification, it is best to seek approval from the Equal Employment Opportunity Commission (EEOC) *before* filling the job.

The second exception to Title VII is based on the size of the enterprise. The law applies to all enterprises employing 15 or more persons, including supervisors and executives. No special provisions are made for retailers.

A five-member Equal Employment Opportunity Commission was created by the Act to oversee the provisions of Title VII. The Commission (1) receives information about "alleged" violations; (2) investigates complaints; (3) helps complainants file charges; (4) initiates charges of its own when it uncovers unlawful practices; (5) assists complainants in legal proceedings before state or local authorities; and (6) in general, acts as a mediator in cases between employers and employees.

The Commission has the authority to obtain injunctions in federal court. Persons claiming discrimination must first appeal to their state or local Fair Employment Practices agency. In most states there is a work sharing arrangement between the EEOC and the State Civil Rights Commission, so that a charge filed with one agency is also considered to be filed with the other. In addition, only one agency will investigate the complaint. If the complaint is not satisfactorily handled at the agency level (and the Commission is unable to settle it voluntarily), the individual involved or the Commission may initiate federal court action after complying with administrative procedural requirements.

When a charge of prejudice is made against an employer, the person making the charge has the burden of proving it; but this burden is easily shifted. If any evidence of discriminatory practice is presented, the employer is immediately on the defensive. Even when no specific evidence is presented, a pattern of discriminatory practice is sufficient for a charge to be made.

In most cases it is a relatively simple matter to uncover an area of discrimination. The Act is so broadly written that the provisions of Title VII apply with equal force not only to hiring and firing, but also to working conditions in general. For instance, it is unlawful for any employer to limit, segregate, or classify employees in any way that would deprive the individual of employment opportunities or otherwise adversely affect his or her employment status. Thus, seniority rosters maintained separately for males and females, or white and black employees, are violations of the Civil Rights Act. The same holds true for positions classified in any way as "male" or "white." Discrimination in training or apprenticeship programs, including discrimination in selection for on-the-job training programs, is a clear violation of the Civil Rights Act.

Help-wanted advertisements may not indicate a preference based on sex, unless sex is a bona fide occupational qualification for the job involved. In retail operations, most jobs will not satisfy the requirement for a bona fide occupational qualification. When a newspaper classifies advertisements in separate "male" or "female" columns, and alternatively, in "male and female" columns, the combined column should be used. If only separate columns are available, the individual advertisement should make it clear that the job is open to persons of either sex, if this, indeed, is the case.

The Age Discrimination in Employment act of 1967 (ADEA) is still another federal law prohibiting discrimination. All employers of 20 or more persons, in an industry affecting interstate or foreign commerce, are included under this Act.

The original ADEA protected people who were at least forty years old but less than 65. Today, there is no upper age limit; the law protects everyone 40 years old or older. The ADEA bans discriminatory hiring or firing, or unequal compensation, terms, conditions, or privileges of employment because of age. The only instances in which bias is lawful is when the distinction is tied to a genuine occupational qualification (medical factors, for example); when it is based on a reasonable factor other than age; or when it stems from a bona fide seniority system.

Other federal laws include: the Immigration Reform and Control Act of 1986, which broadens Title VII's prohibition against national origin discrimination; the Civil Rights Restoration Act of 1988, which applies to establishments receiving federal funds; and the Americans with Disabilities Act of 1990, which prohibits discrimination against handicapped individuals in establishments offering public services.

Keeping Records

The Fair Labor Standards Act (FLSA) requires all employers to keep complete and accurate records. The Act empowers the Secretary of Labor or his representatives to examine employer records at any time. The Secretary may issue subpoenas or invoke the aid of the courts to obtain these records. Willful failure to keep records, or falsification of records, is a criminal offense. Keeping records assists employers, too, because accurate records provide a basis for defense against employee suits or actions brought by the federal government for alleged violations of the FLSA. In addition, the Immigration Reform and Control Act of 1986 requires employers to obtain proof that a person may lawfully be employed in the United States and to maintain records accordingly.

The employer should maintain records for each employee and preserve those records for at least three years. The records should contain the following information:

1. Name in full (and an identifying symbol or number if these are normally used instead of names for the purpose of payroll records).
2. Home address, including zip code.
3. Date of birth, if the employee is under nineteen years of age.
4. Sex and occupation (sex may be indicated by Mr., Mrs., Ms. or Miss).
5. Time of day, and the day of the week that the employee's normal workweek begins. (If the workweek begins on the same day

284 MANAGING AND TRAINING PEOPLE

of the week for the entire establishment, a single notation for the entire establishment will suffice).

6. Regular hourly rate of pay for any week when overtime is worked. The basis on which wages are paid must also be indicated (such as $5.00 per hour, or $300 per week), as well as the amount and nature—perhaps shown by vouchers—of each payment excluded from regular pay (for example, reimbursement for expenses).

7. Hours worked each day and the total hours worked each week.

8. Total earnings during the workweek including all earnings from overtime.

9. The compensation for overtime worked over and above all straight-time earnings during overtime.

10. Total additions to (or deductions from) wages paid each pay period. More specifically, records must be kept of the dates, amounts, and nature of items that make up total additions (or deductions).

11. Total wages paid each pay period.

12. Date of payment and pay period covered.

13. The I-9 Certificate indicating the employer saw appropriate documents evidencing the employee's ability to lawfully be employed in the United States.

14. Certificate of age and/or work permit if minors are employed.

An employer does not have to maintain records showing the hours worked for each day and each week by employees who are on fixed work schedules. Instead, the employer can enter the normal work hours once and, for future weeks, utilize some type of marking to indicate that the hours were indeed worked. Finally, the employer must post any notice pertaining to the applicability of the FLSA to store employees that the Department of Labor says must be posted. These notices must be posted in places where the employee is most likely to see them.

State Regulations

Federal law, by its very nature, is uniform throughout the country. State law, on the other hand, is a quilt of fifty patches. Each supermarket manager, however, must be familiar with the pertinent state regulations.

In most cases, state minimum wage legislation is not as strict as that of the federal government. Therefore, according to the general rule of thumb, federal law prevails. However, the state codes governing hours and conditions of employment are often more comprehensive and more favorable to the employee than the federal law. When this is the case, the state law prevails.

The basis for these laws is the police powers which every state possesses. Police powers, in this sense, do not refer to the maintenance of public order but, rather, to the right and obligation of state governments to police the health, education and general welfare of its citizens. Restricting the hours, and specifying the conditions of employment of citizens who, as a group, are not equal in strength or endurance to the labor force as a whole is one of the state's police powers. Since minors fall into this category, most states have legislated extensively in their behalf.

It is impossible to give a single abstract that would apply to all situations in all states. Instead, the following charts give, in digest form, the important features of ten representative state codes. The charts provide some indication of how laws vary from state to state on the basis of occupation and point out the need for a thorough study of local statutes.

STATE RESTRICTIONS ON WORKING HOURS AND CONDITIONS

California

Coverage:	Anyone employed in any occupation, trade, or industry.
Exemptions:	All employees in executive, administrative or professional capacity whose work is predominantly intellectual, managerial, or creative; and requires the exercise of discretion and independent judgment; and who earn at least $900.00 per month. Outside sales people.
Minimum Wage:	$4.25/hour effective July 1, 1988. Reduced wage rates permissible with special license, for apprentices and learners during their first 160 hours of employment and for handicapped employees. Minors' rate in special circumstances. Reduced wage rate is not less than 85 percent of the state minimum.
	Split shifts: One hour's pay at minimum wage shall be paid in addition to minimum wage for that work day.
Overtime:	Time and a half for work in excess of 40 hours/week. Special provisions apply to 4 day, 10 hour/day schedules.
Hours:	Special provisions may apply depending on the occupations involved.
Child Labor:	Must be 21 to sell alcohol or to work in an establishment primarily designed for sale of alcoholic beverages.
	Under 18: cannot drive for compensation.
	16-18: cannot work more than 8 hours on a school day.
	14-16 year-olds may work with a permit from school officials, but can only work in specified occupations and cannot work more than 4 hours on a school day.
Hours:	Under 18 years: no more than 8 hours a day or 48 hours a week, with some exceptions. Cannot work between 10:00 p.m. and 5:00 a.m. on a school night, or past 12:30 a.m. on a non-school night. Minors under 18 who have graduated from high school or the equivalent may be employed the same hours as adults.
	16-17 year-olds: Special exceptions for agricultural occupations. May work after 10:00 p.m. but not later than 12:30 a.m. with parental consent as part of approved work experience program. Must be paid at least minimum wage between 10:00 p.m. and 12:30 a.m.
Employment Permit:	Employer must obtain employment permit to employ minors. Special restrictions apply depending on age and occupation. Special exceptions for younger minors in hardship cases.
School Attendance:	Full-time required for those under 18, except high school graduates, having work permit if otherwise required by law to attend school. Part-time school attendance at least 4 hours per week is normally required for minors 16-17 who have not graduated from high school or received certificate of proficiency.

Source: BNA Policy and Practice Series, Labor Policy and Practices—Wages and Hours: State. Published by The Bureau of National Affairs, Inc., Washington, D.C. A codification of state laws that brings together in organized and easily used form the substantive regulations. Published in loose-leaf pages, since 1959, and updated annually.

STATE RESTRICTIONS ON WORKING HOURS AND CONDITIONS (Cont.)

Illinois

Coverage:	Any individual permitted to work.
Exemptions:	An employer of fewer than 4 employees.
	Outside sales people.
	Students at an accredited Illinois college or university employed by the same institution under the FLSA.[1]
Minimum Wages:	$3.80/hour effective 4/1/90; $4.25/hour effective 4/1/91.
	State minimum wage is not to be less than federal minimum.
	Minors' Rates: $3.30/hour effective 4/1/90; $3.75/hour effective 4/1/91.
	Handicapped workers: The director may issue regulations regarding wage rates and permits.
	Learners' rate of pay during learning period may be lower, but must be equal to at least 70 percent of minimum wage rate.
Overtime:	Time and one-half in excess of 40 hours per week.
Hours:	No regulations limiting the hours a person may work.
Days of Rest:	An employee must have 24 consecutive hours in every calendar week in addition to the regular period of rest at the close of each work day. Does not apply to part-time employees who work less than 20 hours per week.
Rest Periods:	If a day is over 7½ hours long, employee must have 20 minutes for meal period no later than 5 hours after start of work period.
Child Labor:	Minors may not work in establishment where alcoholic beverages are sold or served for consumption on the premises. Minimum age is 16 in any gainful employment during school hours.
	14-16: may work outside school hours and during vacations, but not in hazardous or dangerous occupations. Employment certificate needed in special circumstances.
	Under 18: may not operate any motor vehicle as a carrier of property. Special exceptions for some occupations.
Hours:	16 years and under may not exceed 8 hours/day, 48 hours/week, 6 days/week. Cannot work between 7:00 p.m. and 7:00 a.m. on school days, or between 9:00 p.m. and 7:00 a.m. from June 1 until Labor Day. Cannot exceed 5 continuous hours without 30 minute meal period. Age certificates are issued on request by school officials for minors 16-20.
School Attendance:	Full-time attendance required for minors 7 to 16, with some exceptions.
	16-18: part-time attendance required.
Voting:	Two hours off. Application must be made before previous day. Employer may specify hours during which employees may be absent.
Facilities:	Employer to furnish place of employment which is free from recognized hazards that are causing or are likely to cause death or serious physical injury.

[1] Fair Labor Standards Act.

STATE RESTRICTIONS ON WORKING HOURS AND CONDITIONS (Cont.)

Maryland

Coverage:	Any individual employed by a firm which employs one or more employees at any one time.
Exemptions:	Executive, administrative, and professionals. Employees who work no more than 20 hours a week and are less than 16 years old.
	People over 62 who work no more than 25 hours a week.
	Special education students.
	Outside sales people and those compensated by commission.
Minimum Wages:	FLSA wage rates to apply, but special provisions for training rates.
Overtime:	Time and a half for over 40 hours.
Hours:	Retail establishments may conduct regular business on Sunday, but employee may choose Sunday or Sabbath as day of rest. Some counties have restrictions prohibiting Sunday work or limiting the type of work that can be performed.
Child Labor:	Under 18: must have work permit. May not work in hazardous occupations.
	Under 16: may not work during school day or in specified occupations.
	Below 14: no gainful employment.
Hours:	Under 18: no more than 12 hours combined school and work hours per day. Must have 30-minute break time after 5 hours of work.
	Under 16: no more than 8 hours/day, 40 hours/week when school not in session. 4 hours/day on school days; 23 hours/week during full school week.
	Special exceptions for bona fide work study programs.
Night Work:	Under 16: no work between 8:00 p.m. and 7:00 a.m., except between Memorial Day and Labor Day, when they can work until 9:00 p.m.
Employment Permit:	Required for all under 18.
School Attendance:	Required for 6-16 year olds. Certain exceptions exist.
Voting:	Maximum 2 hours time off with pay. Must furnish proof of vote.
Facilities:	Minimum standards, refer to OSHA regulations.[2] Employer to furnish place of employment free from recognized hazards that are causing or likely to cause death or serious physical harm to employees.

Massachusetts

Coverage:	Anyone employed in any occupation, trade or business.
Exemptions:	Employees whose duties are rendered away from employer's premises and who are not required to report daily. Apprentices, learners, and students, with license may be paid not less than 80 percent of minimum rate. Handicapped workers with license may be paid less than minimum rate.
Minimum Wages:	$3.75/hour effective July 1, 1988. Apprentice and learners' rate not less than 80 percent of experienced rates, must have license.

[2] Occupational Safety and Health Act

STATE RESTRICTIONS ON WORKING HOURS AND CONDITIONS (Cont.)

	Special license and special rate for handicapped workers.
Overtime:	Time and a half for over 40 hours. Overtime rate for those below experienced rates is 1½ times regular rate. Sunday labor in retail establishments is 1½ times regular rate.
Day of Rest:	Restrictions apply to Sunday work. Must have 24 consecutive hours including unbroken period between 8:00 a.m. and 5:00 p.m., in each of 7 consecutive days, except in mercantile trades, and others, when employees working Sundays are to be allowed 24 consecutive hours without work in the 6 days following.
Rest Period:	30 minutes break required after a maximum of 6 continuous hours of work.
Child Labor:	Under 18: must have an age and education certificate, except pupils in cooperative education courses. Under 16: cannot be employed during school hours, must have employment permit. Under 14: no permits available in some occupations, except during summers.
Hours:	Under 18: 9 hours/day, 48 hours/week, 6 days/week maximum.
Night Work:	Under 18: prohibited from 10:00 p.m. to 6:00 a.m. 16 year-olds: prohibited from 6:00 p.m. to 6:30 a.m., 7:00 p.m. to 6:30 a.m. July 1 through Labor Day; may work until 9:00 p.m. with employment permit.
Employment Permit:	Educational certificate showing age is required for 16-18, except in cooperative educational course. If they have not completed sixth grade, must attend night school if available. Employment certificate required for 14-16, issued by school officials for cooperative courses involving work programs.
School Attendance:	Full-time school attendance from age 7 through 16, except 14 and 15 year-olds who have completed sixth grade and have special permit. 14-16: part-time attendance for 4 hours a week required of all who are regularly employed. Special exceptions apply.
Voting:	2 hours time off to be allowed, the first 2 after the polls open. Does not have to be paid time off.
Facilities:	Employees must have access to fresh and pure drinking water. If 20 or more employees, must have first-aid kit available. Retail facilities must be well-lighted, well-ventilated, clean, sanitary, heated from October 15 through April 15, adequate seats required.

Michigan

Coverage:	An employer is one who employs 2 or more people at any one time during a calendar year.
Exemptions:	Employers subject to FLSA, higher rate of pay is applicable if state differs from federal rate.
Minimum Wages:	$3.35 an hour, effective 1/1/81, with executives, administrators and professionals exempted. Handicapped rate less than minimum with certificate.

STATE RESTRICTIONS ON WORKING HOURS AND CONDITIONS (Cont.)

Overtime:	One and a half times regular rate for over 40 hours.
Child Labor:	Under 18: a work permit is required unless high school graduate or equivalent. If emancipated minor, certificate of emancipation required.
	Under 14: no permit available.
Hours:	Under 18: 10 hours/day, 48 hours/week, 6 days/week; when combined with school, not more than 48 total hours/week. Must have 30-minute meal break after 5 continuous hours.
Night Hours:	18 and 17 year-olds: 10:30 p.m. to 6:00 a.m. prohibited, if attending school; may work to 11:30 p.m. if not attending school. 14-16 year-olds: prohibited from 9:00 p.m. to 7:00 a.m.
School Attendance:	Required for all from 6 through 16, except eighth grade graduates or the highest possible grade, if more than eight grades are maintained in the public schools.
Voting:	No provision.
Facilities:	Place of employment must be free from recognized hazards that are causing or likely to cause death or serious physical harm to employees.

New Jersey

Coverage:	Any individual employed by an employer.
Exemptions:	Outside sales people, executives, administrative and professional employees.
Minimum Wage:	$3.80/hour effective 5/3/90. $4.25/hour effective 4/1/91, $5.05/hour effective 4/1/92.
	Learners, apprentices, full-time students employed by the college where they are enrolled and handicapped employees are under special regulations that allow lower rates, permit required.
Overtime:	Time and a half over 40 hours, each work week to stand alone.
Hours:	Sunday selling of specified goods is prohibited.
Child Labor:	Under 16: forbidden to engage in any gainful employment except 14-16 year-olds may work outside school hours and during vacations.
	17 year-olds: may use a diploma from a vocational school approved by the Commissioner of Education as an employment certificate to work during hours allowed for 18 year-olds. Extensive regulations by occupation.
Hours:	Under 18: limited to 8 hours/day, 40 hours/week, 6 days/week, when school attendance is not required. Must have 30 minutes for meal break after 5 hours of work.
	Under 16: employment outside school hours not to exceed 3 hours/day.
Night Work:	16-18: may not work between 11:00 p.m. and 6:00 p.m. when school is in session.
	16 year-olds: no work from 7:00 p.m. to 7:00 a.m.
	16 years and under: in some forms of employment, permitted to work until 7:00 p.m.; in others, only until 6:00 p.m.
	14-15: may work until 9:00 p.m. from last day of school to Labor

STATE RESTRICTIONS ON WORKING HOURS AND CONDITIONS (Cont.)

	Day, with parental permission.
Employment Permit:	Required for all under 18.
School Attendance:	Everyone between the ages of 7 and 16 must attend school, with specified exceptions.
Voting:	No mandatory provision.
Facilities:	Must provide facility reasonably safe and healthful. Seating facilities required for employees. Separate toilet and washroom facilities required in mercantile establishments. Must provide proper ventilation and heat. Must have smoking/no smoking regulations.

New York

Coverage:	All individuals permitted to work.
Exemptions:	Executives, administrators, professionals, outside sales people, taxi cab drivers and learners. Special rates are possible for students, learners, and handicapped workers, for not more than 17 consecutive weeks.
Minimum Wages:	$3.80/hour effective 4/1/90, $4.25/hour effective 4/1/91. Learners and handicapped workers may not be paid less than 75 percent of appropriate minimum wage. Youths under 18 may be employed at subminimum rate with special certificate issued by the Commissioner when he deems it necessary to prevent curtailment of youth job opportunities; he may issue certificate to authorize employment at 25 cents below the minimum wage, if there are no more than 2 employees per employer or if no more than 10 percent of the total work force is involved, whichever is greater on any one day.
Retail and Wholesale Trades:	
Overtime:	Time and a half for over 40 hours. An employee directed or permitted to report to work on any day must be paid at least for 4 hours at the appropriate minimum wage. Split Shift: additional hour's pay at full-time hourly rate required on days in which spread exceeds 10 hours.
Day of Rest:	At least 24 consecutive hours of rest required in each calendar week. Sunday labor prohibitions vary by location and type of business.
Rest Periods:	At least 45 minutes required for noon or midway break or after 6 hours of work starting between 1:00 p.m. and 6:00 a.m. Factory employees get at least one hour. Additional meal period required of at least $\frac{1}{3}$ hour between 5:00 p.m. and 7:00 p.m. if shifts starts before noon and continues after 7:00. May get permission for a shorter meal period.
Child Labor:	
Hours:	Under 18: may not work when attendance at school is required. Age 16-17: when school is in session, maximum of 4 hours/day, 28 hours/week, 6 days/week. When not in session, 8 hours/day maximum. Below 16: maximum of 3 hours/day, 23 hours/week, and 6 days/week; 8 hours/day, 40 hours/week, 6 days/week when school is not in session.

STATE RESTRICTIONS ON WORKING HOURS AND CONDITIONS (Cont.)

---

	14 and 15 year-olds enrolled in supervised work-study program may work up to 4 hours/day, 28 hours/week, 6 days/week; or up to 8 hours per day when school is not in session.
Night Work:	Under 16: prohibited from 7:00 p.m. to 7:00 a.m. when school is in session. 16 and 17 year-olds may work until midnight, but not before 6:00 a.m.
Special Mercantile Provisions:	16 and 17 year olds: permitted to work 8 hours/day, 40 hours/week, 6 days/week, except when working one or more shorter work days or holiday in a week, may be employed up to 10 hours, but not more than 48 hours a week. Limits do not apply for (1) December 18-24 or for any 7 consecutive days from December 4-23 inclusive or (2) additional periods each year for the purpose of taking inventory. (Extra hour regulations outlined in detail for these periods.)
	Limits also inapplicable to (1) recognized florists on day before Easter Sunday, Easter Sunday morning, and December 23, and (2) licensed pharmacists. Over 6 days of work allowed.
School Attendance:	Required for 6-16 year olds, except high school graduates 15 and over and those incapable of learning; these may be employed providing they have a special certificate.
Voting:	No loss of pay for up to 2 hours, employer may designate time off at beginning or end of shift.
Facilities:	Must have proper lighting in facility and seats for employees. Must have dressing rooms and washrooms. Must have smoke-free work areas for non-smoking employees.

Ohio

Coverage:	Any individual, but does not include any employer "whose annual gross volume of sales is less than $150,000, exclusive of excise taxes at the retail level which are separately stated."
Exemptions:	Executives, administrators, professionals and outside sales people.
Minimum Wages:	$3.80/hour; $4.25/hour effective 3/31/91.
	Learners: 80 percent of minimum for a maximum of 90 days.
	Apprentices: 85 percent of minimum, with license, for periods not to exceed 90 days.
	Special exception for small establishments whose gross sales volume is more than $362,500 but less than $500,000.
	Handicapped: Director of Industrial Relations may issue special licenses for wages lower than minimum.
Overtime:	Time and a half after 40 hours.
Hours:	
Child Labor:	No minor required to attend school shall be employed during school hours.
	Under 18: must have age and schooling certificate or special certificate issued in certain circumstances. Occupational limitations.
Hours:	After 5 continuous hours of work, must have 30-minute rest

STATE RESTRICTIONS ON WORKING HOURS AND CONDITIONS (Cont.)

	period.
	Under 16: 3 hours/day, 18 hours/week maximum when school is in session (40 hours/week if enrolled in bona fide vocational or work-study program); 8 hours/day, 40 hours/week when school is not in session.
	14-15 year-olds: may work between 6:00 a.m. and 10:00 p.m. on days immediately prior to day when school is not in session, provided hours of employment shall not be more than 6 days a week, 48 hours a week, or 8 hours daily.
Night Work:	Under 16: may not work before 7:00 a.m. or after 9:00 p.m. during summer or vacations of more than 5 days. May not work after 7:00 p.m. any other time.
	16-17 year-olds: may not work before 7:00 a.m., M-F; Sunday through Thursday may not work after 11:00 p.m.; Saturday and Sundays may not work past 1:00 a.m. or before 6:00 a.m. if school is in session.
Employment Permit:	Employment certificates for 18 and under required, if minor attends school. Physician's certificate of physical fitness required and, during school hours, completion of seventh grade required. During summer months, no employment certificate required if over 16.
School Attendance:	Required of 6-18 for the entire session, except those employed on a certificate, high school graduates, and incapacitated people. Part-time attendance required for 16-18 year olds, not less than 4 hours a week, while school is in session, or 144 hours a year, between 7:00 a.m. and 6:00 p.m., school days. Establishment of continuation schools is mandatory and no employer shall refuse to permit minor to attend part-time schools.
Voting:	Reasonable time must be given, without loss of pay.
Facilities:	Employers must furnish place of employment which is safe for employees.

Pennsylvania

Coverage:	Any individual employed by any employer.
Exemptions:	Executives, administrators, and professionals, and outside sales people.
Minimum Wages:	$3.70/hour effective 2/1/89. For learners and students with special certificate, 85 percent of statutory rate.
Overtime:	Time and a half for over 40 hours.
Hours:	
Days of Rest:	"Worldly employment or business on Sunday is prohibited" . . . except for some types of selling activities listed in the Penal Code.
Rest Period:	½ hour break time required after 5 consecutive hours of work. (Interval of less than ½ hour not deemed an interruption.)
Child Labor:	Under 18: an employment certificate is required.
	Under 17: if a high school graduate or is declared to have achieved academic potential by the school administrator, may

STATE RESTRICTIONS ON WORKING HOURS AND CONDITIONS (Cont.)

	be treated as an 18 year-old.
	Under 16: can only be employed in specified occupations.
Hours:	Under 18: 8 hours/day, 44 hours/week, 6 consecutive days. Cannot work over 28 hours during school week if attending school and working outside school hours.
	Under 16: if enrolled in school and working outside school hours, 4 hours maximum on school days, 8 hours on other days; but no more than 18 hours/week.
	Over 14: can work outside school in part of a recognized school work program.
Night Work:	Under 18: no work from 12:00 midnight to 6:00 a.m., if in school. 16-17 year-olds: may work until 1:00 a.m. on Friday and Saturday and days before vacations.
	Under 16 year-olds: may not work between 7:00 p.m. and 7:00 a.m. During June, July, and August, may work from 7:00 a.m. to 10:00 p.m.
Employment Permit:	Required for all under 18, may require physical fitness certificate.
School Attendance:	Required for everyone from 8 through 17, except high school graduates, with specified exceptions.
Voting:	No provision.
Facilities:	Detailed safety precautions. Access to drinking water, toilets and washrooms required. Ventilation and heating suitable for work; policies to regulate smoking required.

Texas

Coverage:	Any individual employed by an employer.
Exemptions:	Executives, administrative, professional or outside sales people.
Minimum Wages:	$3.35/hour effective 9/1/87. Lower rates for handicapped workers with certificate.
Hours:	No provision. May not work 7 consecutive days in a retail establishment. Must allow employee to have 24 consecutive hours time off for rest or worship in each 7 days.
Child Labor:	Minors over 14 may obtain special work orders in cases of hardship, if they have completed seventh grade and have a doctor's certificate of health.
Hours:	Under 15: maximum of 8 hours/day and 48 hours/week.
Night Work:	15 and under: no work from 10:00 p.m. to 5:00 a.m. While in school, 12:00 midnight to 5:00 a.m. on days not preceding school days and during summer.
School Attendance:	Between 7 and 17, required to attend 170 days annually, a full term.
Voting:	Entitled to vote in any election. Time off is paid, employer may prescribe the time allowed.
Facilities:	Facility must be reasonably safe and healthful.

18 | Union Relations

It has been said that in geographic areas where there is substantial union penetration, there are few, if any, differences in the management of a union and non-union operation. Indeed, it is generally true that non-union retail food chains in the same geographic area as their unionized counterparts pay approximately the same wages and provide approximately the same types of major fringe benefits (for example, pensions, vacations, holidays), if for no other reason than that a non-union company must be competitive in the economics of employment in order to remain non-union. However, beyond basic employment economics, there is a vast and often vague region of union relations which, quite obviously, concerns only the management of a unionized company.

Union Relations and the Store Manager

In the area of union relations, the store manager's first and truly paramount duty is to be an effective store-level representative of the company's labor relations policy. It is essential that a manager

295

quickly become familiar with the company's general approach and attitude in union dealings. The manager must know the extent to which he or she should become involved in union matters. A store manager who makes decisions regarding company-union relations without considering company policy may be inadvertently setting a precedent.

The manager must also know what working relationship, if any, should be maintained with union authorities. Most companies prefer that the store manager limit contact to the shop steward or possibly the union's business representative. Finally, the manager must know what his or her working relationship should be with the company's labor relations department. The usual practice in this regard is for the store manager to contact the personnel department when advice or assistance is needed; the personnel department, in turn, might request that the person in charge of labor relations find out the intent of the language of the contract. In a smaller company, the owner would probably check with an attorney. In addition to knowing what role to play within the corporate-union relations framework, the store manager must also have a thorough understanding of the collective bargaining agreements covering the employees in the store.

Union Membership

Food retailing employees customarily belong to one of two unions, which are now combined nationally: The Meat Cutters Union (Amalgamated Meat Cutters and Butcher Workmen of North America, AFL-CIO) generally represents employees involved in the preparation and sale of meat, including counter service personnel; the United Food and Commercial Workers Union generally represents all other store employees.

In several cities, the Meat Cutters Union represents all store employees; this is referred to as "wall-to-wall" jurisdiction. Moreover, in some cities, food employees belong to unions other than these two. However, since all unions involved in the food industry have had the same basic approach toward collective bargaining, there has been surprisingly little negotiating competition between unions. In fact, a striking similarity exists between retail food labor contracts throughout the country.

Collective Bargaining Agreements

The primary function of the labor union is to act as its members' agent in negotiations with their collective employer. The result of these negotiations is a collective bargaining agreement. From the store manager's point of view, a collective bargaining agreement contains three general functional groupings; (1) the company's economic obligations under the contract; (2) operational rights and restrictions; and (3) procedures for settling disputes. While there is some degree of overlap among these three groupings, they nevertheless provide a useful guideline in analyzing a collective bargaining agreement.

1. *Economic obligations*: In order to control and reduce labor costs, a store manager must have a thorough understanding of the company's negotiated economic obligations. The store manager should know, for example, what rate differentials (if any) exist between part-and full-time employees, and between student and non-student employees. It is also necessary to be familiar with premium pay requirements; for instance, for work in excess of eight hours in any one day or forty hours in any one workweek, or for work on Saturdays, Sundays, holidays, or at night. The store manager should be informed of eligibility requirements for pension and welfare coverage, of guaranteed minimum working hours for part- and full-time employees, and of special job classifications which have either lower or higher pay rates and which usually contain restricted or expanded job duties to fit the adjusted rates.

2. *Operational rights and restrictions*: In order to schedule employees efficiently, the store manager should also understand what operating rights and restrictions are binding on management under the terms of the agreement. These "operational provisions" can be either expressly stated in the contract or implied by its wording. The operational areas on which the manager should focus include store operating hours, work schedules, the right of part-time employees to claim priority for new work opportunities, the use of outside sales people to construct and/or maintain displays, union jurisdictional boundaries, and seniority rights.

3. *Settling disputes*: The two provisions which form the foundation of any rational and durable collective bargaining relationship are (1) the prohibition of strikes or other disruptive activities; and (2) the establishment of a procedure for settling differences between the company and the union. Today, almost all labor contracts in the retail food industry include a provision stipulating that neither the union nor the company will resort to strikes, lockouts, or other disruptive pressures as a means of settling problems during the term of the contract. The restraint is always coupled with a companion agreement which provides for the settlement of all disputes through a specified procedure ending in binding arbitration by a neutral

third party. The economic restraint provision is commonly referred to as the "no strike" clause, and its companion, the "grievance procedure."

Grievance Procedures

Although grievance procedures vary widely in form and scope, there are two types commonly found in food industry labor contracts. The first and older form is the loose procedure, which has practically no formal shape. Except perhaps in its informality, it offers few advantages; for example, it provides for very little protection from the unnecessary delays or abuses caused by the filing of old and generally frivolous grievances. The tight grievance procedure, on the other hand, is formal, protects from abuse, and is much more exacting at all levels of management.

Loose Procedure.   The following is an example of the loose grievance procedure, with its rather flexible procedures and time limits for settling disputes.

Section 1. The Employer recognizes the right of the Union to select one Steward at each store to represent the employees on all grievances concerning the interpretation or application of this Agreement.

Section 2. Should there be a dispute concerning the terms of this Agreement or their application which cannot be settled between the parties, the Union may submit the matter to arbitration. Upon written notice of the Union's intent to arbitrate a grievance, the parties shall each designate a representative who shall attempt to agree upon an impartial arbitrator. If the designated representatives are unable to reach agreement, the Union may request the Federal Mediation and Conciliation Service to submit a panel of seven (7) arbitrators, and the arbitrator shall be selected in accordance with the Service's then applicable rules.

Section 3. In the event a grievance goes to arbitration, this Agreement shall be the basis on which the arbitrator's decision is rendered: in reaching a decision the arbitrator shall have no authority to amend, modify, or in any way change its terms.

Section 4. Expenses and fees of the arbitrator shall be borne equally by the parties.

Tight Procedure.   A fairly representative tight grievance procedure, which leaves little to chance with regard to the steps to be followed in settling a dispute, was established by the Cleveland Food

Industry Committee (representing the area's major food chains) and United Food and Commercial Workers Union Local 880. The provisions of this agreement are as follows:

ARTICLE XV
GRIEVANCE PROCEDURE

Section 1. Should any dispute or grievance arise under this Agreement, it shall be settled in accordance with the procedure set forth in this Article, and, except as otherwise specifically provided in this Agreement, this procedure is the sole and exclusive method of disposing of such grievances.

Step 1.

In order to be considered as a grievance under this Article, a dispute or grievance shall be submitted to the Employer in writing within fourteen (14) days after the occurrence of the incident causing such dispute or grievance, or within fourteen (14) days from the date when the employee or Union became aware or reasonably should have become aware of the incident or events in question.

Step 2.

There shall be an effort on the part of the parties to settle and resolve any dispute or grievance and the Employer shall answer all disputes or grievances in writing within fourteen (14) days after receipt of the same.

Step 3.

If the grievance is not satisfactorily settled in Step 2, the Union has two (2) weeks from receipt of the Step 2 answer to submit a written appeal to an appropriate management administrative official. A meeting shall be held between Employee and Union officials and a final written answer shall be issued by the Employer within one (1) week of the meeting. Provided, that the parties may agree to hold additional Step 3 meetings without loss of rights under this Article.

Step 4.

In the event that the parties are unable to settle or resolve a grievance, the Union may refer the grievance to arbitration by requesting the Federal Mediation and Conciliation Service or the American Arbitration Association to submit a panel of arbitrators. Within fourteen (14) days of receipt of the first panel, the Employer and Union may mutually agree to request the Agency to submit additional panels of arbitrators. The arbitrator shall then be selected in accordance with the agency's then applicable rules, unless the Employer and the Union agree to select the arbitrator in some other manner.

Section 2. The Union may refer a dispute or grievance which has not been resolved to arbitration on the forty-fifth (45th) day after the dispute or grievance has been submitted in writing to the Employer in Step 1, or at any time thereafter. The Union must refer a dispute or grievance to arbitration no later than thirty (30) days after the last Step 3 meeting is held.

Section 3. The arbitrator's decision shall be issued within thirty (30) days after the dispute or grievance is submitted to the arbitrator and shall be final and binding upon the Employer, the Union, and the employee or employees involved. The expenses of the arbitrator shall be borne equally by the Employer and the Union.

Section 4. The time limits specified in Section 1 above may be extended by mutual agreement but shall otherwise be enforced in that the dispute or grievance shall be decided against any employee or party failing to observe the time limits.

Section 5. In the event a grievance goes to arbitration, this Agreement, including any Supplements or Addenda, shall be the basis on which the arbitrator's decision is rendered, and in reaching a decision the arbitrator shall have no authority to amend, modify, or in any way change its terms.

Section 6. At any step in this grievance procedure, the Executive Board of the Local Union shall have final authority in respect to any aggrieved employees covered by this Agreement to decline to process further a grievance, complaint, disagreement, or dispute if in the judgment of the Executive Board such grievance or dispute lacks merit or justification under the terms of this Agreement, or has been adjusted or rectified under the terms of this Agreement to the satisfaction of the Union Executive Board.

Section 7. In the investigation and processing of a dispute or grievance, the Union and the Employer shall upon request provide each other all relevant and pertinent records, papers, and data including the names of any and all witnesses whose testimony would have bearing on the grievance, except where a failure to follow established check-out procedure may be involved or where the security of the Union and/or the Employer would be at issue.

The Differences Between the Loose and Tight Procedures. While the types of problems that can be submitted under a loose or tight agreement are substantially the same, the methods of settling the problems differ radically. For example, consider the case of front-end cashiers who claim they were never relieved in time to take full advantage of their breaks, a period guaranteed under the terms of the collective bargaining agreement.

If the agreement provides for a loose grievance procedure, the union representing the cashiers can either file or hold the complaint for as long or as short a time as it wishes; and when it does decide to file it, it may file the complaint at whichever level of management it chooses, regardless of the relative weight of the difficulty.

The union might have a number of reasons for wanting to hold a complaint instead of filing it when it is received. The union could, for example, be accumulating grievances in the hope of winning a major concession from management in an unrelated matter; or it could be using the grievances as leverage in the re-negotiations of the collective bargaining agreement.

The lack of specific language in the loose procedure of a collective bargaining agreement also allows unions to bypass management's table of organization. The cashiers' complaint, for instance, could be easily solved, under most circumstances, at the store level; but the grievance can, at the sole discretion of the union, be brought to the attention of the head of the corporation's labor relations department, thereby ignoring all intermediary supervisory personnel. This permits the Union to "forum shop" by taking a grievance to the most sympathetic manager.

On the other hand, if the collective bargaining agreement contains a tight grievance procedure, claims must be filed and processed within a mandatory time limit in order to be valid. Furthermore, the union must take into account the hierarchical arrangement of management so that small claims may be settled on the lowest possible administrative level.

The Store Manager and Grievance Settlement

Because store managers are often involved in the settlement of grievances, they must learn how the grievance procedure is administered. They should know the proper method of settling grievances at the store level; the types of grievances that should be referred to the store operations supervisor or to the company's central labor relations authority; the preferred technique and style of responding to a grievance, especially if a written answer from the manager is required; and the time limits for filing and answering grievances, with whom they should be filed, by whom they should be answered, and the form the filing and answering should take.

Employee discipline is perhaps the most sensitive area of grievance administration. The store manager must know exactly what the company's position is on such matters as absenteeism, insubordination, and poor work performance, to name only three of the major disciplinary violations. Of course, the manager should attempt to be fair in all disciplinary decisions. But even though all employees should be treated equally and uniformly in comparable disciplinary situations, the manager should not be blind to some very legitimate reasons for differentiation, such as an employee's work record or length of service. The manager must also know how the company deals with the critically important problem of thefts committed by employees, to assure that discipline is consistent within the company. Each time a manager disciplines an employee there is a chance the action will be cited as precedent for future actions. Furthermore, the manager should ascertain at what point in a grievance situation the labor agreement requires or the company prefers union involvement.

The store manager should also be aware of the series of steps that could be taken in a grievance procedure. Sometimes the company and the union cannot settle a grievance and the dispute goes to arbitration. When that happens, the company's burden of providing evidence often falls on the store manager, either as a witness to the event in question or to explain the background in which the incident occurred. At least a basic knowledge of the arbitration process (binding arbitration by an impartial "judge") will be useful to the store manager in making an educated judgment on the strengths and weaknesses of a potential grievance.

If a manager's decision on a grievance is reversed as a result of a subsequent step or in arbitration, letting the manager know this has happened may avoid a repeating the mistake. There are occasions, however, when a company will compromise a grievance where there has been no managerial error because of broader and more important company considerations or, sometimes, even for the sake of expediency. In such cases the store manager should try to make the best of an admittedly bad situation. Grievances represent only one of several points of contact in the continual process of developing a sound company-union relationship. The manager must understand that broader and more important considerations designed to achieve this objective of company-union compatibility occasionally dictate certain decisions that are not readily justified at the store level.

| 19 | Customer and Public Relations |

A store's or company's success or failure in the area of public relations is determined by the quality of its contact with customers. Customers represent an important segment of the general public. Their attitudes reflect a first-hand knowledge of a store or company and they wield a very strong influence on public opinion. Favorable customer relations create the foundation of strong and favorable public relations. It is not enough simply to advertise "courteous service" as a store feature; customers, by their patronage, will testify whether or not a store lives up to such a claim.

Poor customer relations, even by a single employee, can have devastating results. Several years ago, a part-time employee in a small town branch of a supermarket chain insulted a customer who happened to be a community leader and president of the local P.T.A. The customer was not appeased despite the manager's apologies and even though the part-timer was terminated on the day of the incident. The customer related the incident to all her acquaintances, who included almost every woman in town, and succeeded in bringing about a virtual customer boycott of the store. The word-of-mouth boycott was so effective and lasting that the unit was forced to close. To this day, the chain has a poor image in the community.

Customer Relations and the Manager

The establishment of good customer relations in any supermarket requires careful, daily planning and effort. Customer relations demand that every single store employee show genuine concern for the customer, a concern that can only be generated from the top down. The manager who consistently demonstrates a real interest in his customers is very likely to have employees who do the same. The supervisor, store and department managers must set the pattern of customer courtesy because employees will look to them to lead the way.

Most store managers in almost every supermarket chain are classified by their companies as either "good customer people" or "good operations people." These, unfortunately, are realistic appraisals because few managers excel at both production and customer relations. A person who is equally skillful in both areas is almost invariably identified as a top manager in the company.

Frequently, a store manager who is considered a strong customer person is assigned an assistant manager who is judged strong in operations so that the store would enjoy the necessary balance in both vital areas. Under the circumstances, such combinations are undoubtedly useful, but they do little to correct the basic problem of developing managers with talent in both areas. The problem of developing such managers has been given little attention in the manager training programs of most companies.

Factors Affecting Customer Relations

Once the factors that influence customer relations are identified, steps may be taken to improve customer satisfaction and loyalty. Among these factors are employee friendliness and courtesy and the company's operating policies, which include its position on cashing checks, returning merchandise, providing rainchecks for advertised items temporarily out of stock, and handling such checkstand problems as ringup and change-making errors, poor bagging and discourtesy. Product quality, variety and price, the level of store service, and the company's public relations policies also significantly influence customer relations. Many other factors could be listed because each time a customer comes in contact with a store employee, customer relations are involved.

Employee friendliness and courtesy are perhaps the most important factors affecting customer relations. One major regional chain noted for its employee friendliness and courtesy far out-distances its competition even though its prices are consistently higher.

Hiring, Training and Customer Relations

Good customer relations should be taken into account at the out-set, during the employee selection process. Orientation and training procedures should emphasize the importance of all types of customer contacts, including the value of greeting customers pleasantly, assisting them and handling their complaints.

Companies in which trained, competent people do the hiring have a better chance of weeding out the sullen, gloomy person or the troublemaker. But in most companies it is impractical for the personnel department to hire all employees because of the wide geographic distribution of individual stores. Yet even where geography is not a problem, part-timers are usually hired by store managers and a great majority of problems occurring in employee-customer relations may be traced to part-time employees. The store manager must therefore be trained in such basic hiring techniques as effective interviewing and employee selection.

Any competent personnel department can construct a one- or two-day training program to instruct the store manager in the fundamentals of recruiting, interviewing and selecting part- and full-time employees. Because most present full-time supermarket employees begin their careers as part-timers, such a training program would raise the level of employee quality, as well as improve customer relations.

Hiring is only the first step in building better customer relations. The next step is to orient and train the new employee in store or company policies and in the proper procedures of customer relations. Most supermarket training programs, however, emphasize the mechanics of the job, and hardly discuss customer contacts.

Indeed, many employees are never even encouraged to be friendly to customers. In one Midwestern chain, Mary, a part-time clerk, was described by a customer as unfriendly. When the store manager presented the problem to Mary, she told him that she had actually given the matter of friendliness toward customers some thought and that she had decided against it. She was concerned that customers, particularly men, might consider her bold or forward. "Besides," she concluded, "no one ever told me how to treat customers."

On the other hand, customers quickly identify a friendly employee. Every store manager has regular customers who insist on being checked out by a particular cashier, even when they must wait longer in line. These cashiers inspire strong customer loyalty because they show a genuine interest in people, treat them pleasantly, considerately and with respect.

If supermarket employees could be convinced, through orientation and training, that their attitudes and actions in their contacts with customers are vital to store volume and store success, there would be a better chance of them becoming motivated to be pleasant and concerned about customer needs. The loss or gain of even one average customer who spends over $3,500 a year in a store is a matter of great concern.

The better store managers, however, do not rely solely on the initial customer relations training given to new employees. They know that this vital area must be discussed and reviewed repeatedly. They also know that the more emphasis they put on the subject, the more likely they are to obtain and maintain a high level of customer relations. Top managers, therefore, schedule periodic meetings of all employees who come in contact with customers. At these meetings they review store-customer relations policies, work out solutions to problems that arise, and solicit ideas from employees to improve customer relations. They also report and emphasize all favorable customer comments regarding an employee's outstanding courtesy and pleasantness.

Public Relations

Not only are public relations in the community strongly influenced by that segment of the public which constitutes a store's or company's customers, but effective public relations programs can also add even more customers to a store or company. The primary objective of any public relations program is to earn and maintain the good will of the community. Each action or policy must be examined for its long-term effect on community relations, and not merely for its immediate effect.

By showing concern for the welfare of the community, a manager can earn its good will. Every supermarket company has a stake in the communities in which its stores are located. If the communities prosper, the stores can prosper; if the communities suffer, the chain is also hurt. Because every store manager benefits from the community in which he operates, he has an obligation to contribute to its welfare. The community deserves more than token financial support for such programs as the United Fund, Cerebral Palsy or Multiple

Sclerosis drives. More than anything else, the community needs the leadership of capable, honest business people.

The extent to which key personnel participate in community affairs often depends on the attitude of top management. The feeling of moral obligation to the community varies from company to company. A company that actively encourages participation by managers and other key personnel in activities related to the community's welfare, not for the good of the store or the company but, rather, for the good of the individual and the community, will usually earn the respect of the community as well as of its own employees.

The size of a company or the location of its headquarters is irrelevant to establishing a policy of active participation in community affairs. Independent store owners and operators collectively exert as much influence as a chain and have as great a moral obligation to the community. Larger chains, because of top management's lack of intimate knowledge of community problems as a result of absentee ownership, have at least an equal, if not greater responsibility to promote employee participation in community activities.

Public Relations Policies

Policies relating to employee participation in community affairs should be clear and specific, and should recognize that (1) service to the community will, on occasion, require that employees be absent from their jobs or otherwise give of company time to community affairs; and (2) the time and effort expended on community affairs should not infringe on a manager's or company's first obligation to make a success of the business; such a policy would be harmful to the community as well as to the company. These two conditions of community involvement are not contradictory. They recognize that community affairs will require time away from the job, but not to the extent that the job is neglected. On the other hand, a company that takes the position that the manager must give only of his or her own time to community affairs will, in effect, contribute nothing to the community.

Many years ago it was not uncommon for management to consider the seeking of public favors the prime objective of its public relations policy. It contributed gifts, used publicity techniques, and established personal contacts with community officials, in the belief that what is good for the company is good for the community. But the days have passed when it was considered sufficient to promote the company's image solely through press agents or institutional advertising. A company cannot simply insist that it is interested in the community; it must support its words with action.

Today there is a growing recognition by all people in business that a company has a social responsibility to the community it serves, a responsibility that can be met only through real service. Enlightened management has also recognized that leaving it up to the other person to solve the problems of the community will eventually invite the assistance of the state or federal government, to the detriment of both the company and the community.

Modern public relations require that management examine how each of its policies will promote or detract from the welfare of the community. A negative policy should be changed or abandoned. A primary objective of the public relations function is to advise management of the anticipated effect on the community of company policies, decisions and actions. Public relations are based on the philosophy that what is good for the community is good for the company. Management must recognize that employees should devote their talents, as well as their means, to community betterment. Time away from the job that does not adversely affect the business is a small price to pay for good company-community relations.

Management's growing concern for public acceptance and approval is becoming more evident as the supermarket industry becomes more competitive. Moreover, as the labor market becomes tight and competent employees become more scarce, it is increasingly recognized that capable young people are difficult to attract and more difficult to hold. Many of these young people desire, and are entitled to have the opportunity to make a significant contribution to the community and to society in general. Companies that do not attempt to satisfy such worthwhile desires by providing opportunities for their employees to participate in a meaningful fashion in community affairs will find themselves at a future disadvantage when competing for labor.

Community Activity

What are some supermarket companies doing today to promote public acceptance and approval through involvement in community affairs? The executive vice-president of one large regional chain has observed that he spends at least 60 percent of his time in activities not directly related to business. He has served or serves as officer or director of his local service club, his church, his political party, Chamber of Commerce, United Fund, hospital board, community civic club, and of many other organizations. In the evening he can usually be found at his desk, catching up on his business work.

An independent owner of a small Texas supermarket, though not especially prosperous, places his business in the hands of subordinates and, at considerable personal sacrifice, on two occasions served a full year as a district governor of his Lions Organization. The president of a small chain organized a panel of one hundred influential women to help him to design a supermarket which would become "their" store and which would benefit the community. Among the panel's recommendations, which was later incorporated into the building, was a large community meeting hall supervised, controlled and operated by panel members, and used by all types of civic and service groups.

Once every three months, a large regional chain is host to a selected group of community leaders. It provides a free dinner, a warehouse and office tour, and an informal discussion of the supermarket business. These gatherings include forty to fifty different persons each time; one meeting will be called specifically for school officials, counselors and teachers; another for high school or college students; still another for civic leaders or service club officers; and a fourth for scout leaders and officials.

Dick Richard, former president of Richard's Lido Market in Newport Beach, California, has, by his actions, shown how a devoted executive can build public acceptance and approval through active service to the community. Mr. Richard has described community relations as "having the people concerned about you and your business." He succeeded at inspiring and maintaining such concern by devoting a major share of his time to providing leadership in solving community problems. This is his philosophy regarding community affairs: "I don't care what you do, but be a big part in the little things, and be a little part in the big things. If you haven't got money, give them your time. If you don't have the wherewithal, work for them, and go out and raise for them. . . . If you don't think that this will increase your business, without trying, at least 5 percent, then you have a great experience coming to you."[1]

Thus, according to Mr. Richard, the material reward for the many hours spent each week in community relations is increased profits. This, however, does not account for what is perhaps an even greater reward: the sense of contributing to the welfare of the community and the real pleasure derived from making such a contribution.

---

[1] "The Personal Problems of Management," *Proceedings of the 1966 Midwestern Executive Conference* (Chicago: Super Market Institute, 1966), p. 31.

These few illustrations merely scratch the surface of what super-market management and personnel are doing for the betterment of their communities. What is most important is the awareness that stores and companies have a social and moral obligation to give of their means and talents to help solve the problems of the communities they serve and from which they receive their daily bread.

Appendix

THE 1990 TURNOVER STUDY

(Supplementary Material for Chapter 1)

TABLE 1

Statistical Profile of the Participating Companies

Number of Participating Companies	30
Number of Supermarkets/Super Stores	3,955
Combined Annual Sales (Billions)	$35.595
Average Annual Sales per Supermarket/Super Store (Millions)	$9
Average Weekly Sales per Supermarket/Super Store	$173,077
Number of Employees	345,969
Full-Time	120,355
Part-Time	225,614
Average Number of Employees per Store	87
Full-Time	30 = 35%
Part-Time	57 = 65%

TABLE 2

Companies Participating in the Employee Turnover Study

A. LOCATION OF PARTICIPATING COMPANIES

Thirty chains, representing 3,955 supermarkets operating in all areas of the United States and doing a combined annual volume of $35.595 billion, participated in the study.

Location of Headquarters	Number of Companies	Number of Supermarkets	Annual Sales (in millions)	Primary Operating Areas
East	17	1,806	$25,152	All states east of the Mississippi River, excluding five Midwest States
Midwest	4	1,637	2,616	Wis., Mich., Ohio, Ind., Ill.
West	9	512	7,827	All states west of the Mississippi River
Total	30	3,955	$35,595	—

B. TYPES OF PARTICIPATING COMPANIES

Local and regional chains constituted 83 percent of the companies included in the study, while national and multi-regional chains accounted for 17 percent of the companies.

Location of Headquarters	Local and Regional Chains[1]	National and Multi-Regional Chains[2]	Total
East	15	1	16
Midwest	3	1	4
West	7	3	10
Total	25	5	30

[1] Chains operating stores in part or all of the states in the region in which they are headquartered.
[2] Chains operating stores in part or all of the states in the region in which they are headquartered, as well as stores in one or more additional region.

C. SIZES OF PARTICIPATING COMPANIES

Nineteen participating chains have sales of less than $1 billion, but the eleven participants with sales of more than $1 billion account for almost 80 percent of the group's combined sales total of $35.595 billion.

Sales Group (millions)	Number of Chains	Percentage of Total Sales
Under $100	4	0.63%
$100 to $500	7	4.41
$500 to $1,000	8	15.19
Over $1,000	11	79.77
Total	30	100.0%

D. EMPLOYEES COVERED IN THE STUDY

The participating chains employ almost 346,000 persons, with part-timers having a numerical edge over full-timers. Chains based in the East have the greatest proportion of full-time employees 936.0 percent of store personnel). Midwest companies operate with the greatest proportion of part-timers (72.6 percent of store personnel).

Location of Headquarters	Total Number of Employees	Full-Time Employees	Percentage of Total	Part-Time Employees	Percentage of Total
East	255,385	92,016	36.0%	163,369	64.0%
Midwest	40,521	11,100	27.4	29,421	72.6
West	50,063	17,239	34.4	32,824	65.6
Total	345,969	120,355	—	225,614	—

TABLE 3
Annual Turnover per 100-Full-Time and Part-Time Employees
Based on Causes of Turnover
(Twenty Companies)

The major portion of full-time and part-time separations are voluntary, and account for over 70 percent of all terminations; involuntary separations account for the balance. The full-time turnover ratio is highest for companies based in the West, while companies in the Midwest have the highest part-time turnover ratio.

Causes of Turnover	East	Midwest	West	Average
Separations per 100 Full-Time Employees				
Quits	5.5	6.1	5.4	5.7
Discharges	1.6	0.9	1.6	1.4
Retirements, Illnesses, Deaths	0.3	0.6	1.3	0.7
Layoffs, Reductions in Workforce, Store Closings, Temporary Hires	0.1	—[1]	0.5	0.2
Total	7.5	7.6	8.8	8.0
Separations per 100 Part-Time Employees				
Quits	49.4	68.0	37.7	51.7
Discharges	14.3	8.9	9.3	10.8
Retirements, Illnesses, Deaths	1.0	0.6	1.6	1.1
Layoffs, Reductions in Workforce, Store Closings, Temporary Hires	0.1	0.1	1.4	0.5
Total	64.8	77.6	50.0	64.1

[1] Less than .05 percent.

TABLE 4
Full-Time Employee Turnover by Tenure
(Fifteen Companies)

More than half of the separated full-time employees leave their job within the first year. In an identical study conducted seven years ago, fewer than one in four full-timers left during the first year of employment.

Tenure	Percentage of Full-Time Male Turnover	Percentage of Full-Time Female Turnover	Average Percentage of Full-Time Employee Turnover*
0-1 Month	24.66%	8.37%	19.30%
1-3 Months	17.38	9.68	14.85
3-6 Months	11.44	10.18	11.03
6-12 Months	12.14	14.32	12.85
12-24 Months	9.82	23.30	14.26
24-36 Months	5.34	7.47	6.04
36+ Months	19.22	26.68	21.67
Total	100.0%	100.0%	100.0%

*Weighted Average: Based on the proportion of male to female full-time employees in the reporting companies.

TABLE 5
Part-Time Employee Turnover by Tenure
(Fifteen Companies)

More than one in four separated part-time employees leave their job within the first thirty days of employment. Almost two in three leave during the first ninety days, and over 85 percent leave within the first year.

Tenure	Percentage of Part-Time Male Turnover	Percentage of Part-Time Female Turnover	Average Percentage of Part-Time Employee Turnover*
0-1 Month	29.02	25.46	27.07%
1-3 Months	28.67	39.83	34.81
3-6 Months	15.69	12.82	14.11
6-12 Months	12.43	10.36	11.29
12-24 Months	8.41	6.06	7.11
24-36 Months	2.46	2.04	2.23
36+ Months	3.32	3.43	3.38
Total	100.0%	100.0%	100.0%

*Weighted Average: Based on the proportion of male to female part-time employees in the reporting companies.

TABLE 6

Full- and Part-Time Employee Turnover by Tenure
(Thirty Companies)

In this larger sample, which includes data from companies that did not report male and female turnover separately, almost two in three separated full-time employees and nine in ten separated part-time employees leave their job within the first year.

Tenure	Percentage of Full-Time Turnover	Percentage of Part-Time Turnover
0-1 Month	24.04	29.00
1-3 Months	14.71	28.00
3-6 Months	12.59	12.51
6-12 Months	12.21	18.44
12-24 Months	9.80	6.70
24-36 Months	5.97	2.31
36+ Months	20.68	3.04
Total	100.0%	100.0%

TABLE 7
Reasons for Employee Separations
(Nineteen Companies)

Roughly three in four full- and part-time separations are voluntary (resignations); one in five separated full- and part-time employees are separated for cause (discharged).

Reasons	Full-Time Employees		Part-Time Employees		Full- and Part-Time Employees	
	Number	Percentage	Number	Percentage	Number	Percentage of Total
Resignations (For other employment; dissatisfaction with hours, wages, etc.)	6,690	72.58%	114,781	77.39%	121,471	77.10%
Discharges (Unsatisfactory work; violation of policies, etc.)	1,888	20.48	30,672	20.68	32,560	20.67
Unavoidable Separations (Retirement; death; illness, etc.)	553	6.00	2,307	1.55	2,860	1.82
Operational Discharges (Layoff; store closing; temporary hiring, etc.)	87	0.94	561	0.38	648	0.41
Total	9,218	100.0%	148,321	100.0%	157,539	100.0%

TABLE 8
Estimated Annual Turnover Costs
(Thirty Companies)

Each company used the same formula to estimate its turnover costs. The formula included costs for recruiting (search, interview, screen); hiring and induction (administration, orientation, uniforms, training, travel, wages, monitoring); and separation (administration, separation pay, severance allowance, exit interview, taxes).

In the average $9 million supermarket/super store, where net profit after taxes is approximately 1.0 percent ($90,000), the cost of turnover ($42,795) is equivalent to roughly 48 percent of the store's net profit.

Average Cost per Incident		Average Cost per Supermarket/Super Store		Total Cost per Supermarket/Super Store
Full-Time	Part-Time	Full-Time	Part-Time	
$1,021	$557	$7,147	$35,648	$42,795

FORECASTING MEAT DEPARTMENT TONNAGE AND LABOR-HOUR REQUIREMENTS

(Supplementary Material for Chapter 10)

This system of forecasting tonnage and labor-hour requirements, developed and used by one chain, is included here to illustrate how store and meat department managers can provide the best possible customer service at the lowest possible labor cost.

Work sampling studies were made in selected stores. These samplings were used to determine labor-hour requirements, depending on tonnage processed and product mix. The work samplings identified two types of activities in the meat department: variable functions and fixed functions. Variable functions (for example, breaking, cutting, boning, grinding, traying, wrapping, weighing, displaying, rewrapping, preparing special cuts, and others) are those in which labor-hour requirements vary directly according to the tonnage sold. Fixed functions (such as cleaning, policing case, receiving, preparing reports, supervising, traveling, breaks and personal time, and others) are those that require approximately the same number of labor-hours in a store regardless of fluctuations in tonnage.

Work sampling studies for all variable functions established the number of labor-hours required to process 100 pounds (45 kg) of product for each meat commodity group (beef, veal, lamb, pork, poultry, sea foods, and so on). Typically, the time required to perform each of the fixed functions was established as the average number of labor-hours actually expended in that function in the stores in which work sampling studies were made.

In forecasting tonnage and labor-hour requirements each week, the meat department manager fills out only columns X and Y of

TABLE 9
Labor-Hour Requirements for Fixed Functions

Fixed Functions	Labor-Hours Required per Week in Each Store
1. Cleaning	19.5
2. Handling Supplies	2.1
3. Taking Inventory	2.4
4. Ordering	.9
5. Policing Case	9.0
6. Changing Prices	3.0
7. Receiving	4.2
8. Preparing Reports	4.8
9. Handling Salvage	4.0
10. Supervising	5.7
11. Traveling (walking)	22.0
12. Others	2.4
Total Fixed Functions	80.0

Table 10. The number of pounds of each commodity group to be sold during the coming week must be forecast and entered in column X. The number of pounds forecast must then be multiplied by the labor-hours required per 100 pounds (45 kg) for each commodity group; four decimal places should be marked off and the labor-hours should be entered to two decimal points under "Required Labor-Hours: Forecast" (column Y).

The tonnage and labor-hour forecasts should be completed in duplicate and the original mailed to the meat office no later than Saturday of each week for the following week. The meat office then computes figures in all columns other than X and Y on the forecast form, and returns a completed copy to the meat department manager, the store manager and the supervisor no later than Wednesday night following the week in question.

In forecasting meat tonnage for each commodity group, certain factors should be taken into account. For any item to be advertised in the coming week, reference should be made to several past weekly promotion bulletins in which the same items were advertised. The season of the year, the advertised price, and any factors (for example, competitive ads) which have been shown to influence the sale of

TABLE 10
Meat Department Tonnage and Labor-Hour Forecast

Store Number _____   Week Ending _____

Commodity Group	Pounds Sold			Required Labor-Hours		
	Forecast (X)	Actual	± Variance	Per 100 Lbs. (45 kg)	Forecast (Y)	Actual
A. Variable Functions						
Beef				1.32		
Veal				1.06		
Lamb				1.16		
Pork Loins				1.29		
All Other Pork				.87		
Variety Meats				1.29		
Smoked Hams				.60		
All Other Smoked Meats				.93		
Table-Ready Meats and Sausages				.30		
Sliced Bacon				.21		
Canned Meats				.67		
Poultry (ice packed)				.80		
Sea Foods				1.06		
Frozen Meats				.30		
B. Total						
C. Fixed Functions					80.0*	80.0*
D. Barbecue Allowance (maximum of 4.2 hours)						
E. Customer Relations Allowance (maximum of 6.5 hours)						
F. Subtotal of Variable and Fixed Functions (sum of B, C, D and E)						
G. Add 7.5 Percent of F for Personal Time and Breaks						
H. Total Weekly Labor-Hours Required Based on Tonnage Forecast (sum of F and G)						
I. Total Weekly Labor-Hours Scheduled						
J. Total Weekly Labor-Hours Required Based on Actual Tonnage (I adjusted to H)						
K. Weekly Labor-Hours Paid—Actual						
L. ± Variance (difference between J and K)						

*See Table 9.

those items, should be considered. How much tonnage was moved and how these sales affected the movement of other commodity groups should also be noted.

One of the major responsibilities of the meat manager is to plan weekly in-store promotions which will maximize the sales and gross profit of the department. These special in-store promotions will, of course, affect the movement of the items promoted and of other items, and this must be considered in projecting tonnage figures. Store-wide special promotions, such as anniversary sales, store manager sales, and others, can also influence movement of various commodity groups. The past weekly movement in pounds of each commodity group of all non-advertised items should also be reviewed and, on the basis of sound judgment and reasoning, a projection should be made of the number of pounds of product that will probably be sold during the coming week.

Once the pounds are forecast and the labor-hours required are determined for each commodity group, the labor-hour forecasts in column Y are added to find the total variable labor-hours required (B). To this figure are added the 80.0 labor-hours required for fixed functions (C); an allowance of up to 4.2 labor-hours for a barbecue operation, if the store has one (D); and an extra allowance of up to 6.5 hours for customer relations (E), if the supervisor feels that this is warranted. These figures (B, C, D and E) are added to obtain a subtotal of variable and fixed labor-hours required (F). Then, 7.5 percent of this figure (G) is added to F to obtain the total labor-hours required for the coming week (H).

Once total labor-hour requirements have been established, daily schedules for each employee can be developed, keeping in mind the activities that must be performed each day and the scheduling principles covering people and products. (These principles, not provided here, are printed in a manual and distributed to department managers.) To adjust labor-hours scheduled from week to week in accordance with the forecast of labor-hours required, one or more part-timers are needed to provide scheduling flexibility. Part-timers may be employed and trained in some of the required non-technical areas of work, such as sanitation, grinding, cubing, cutting fryers, pricing and displaying table-ready meats; or, with the approval of the store manager and where union agreements do not prohibit it, employees from other departments in the store may be used to perform non-technical work in the meat department on a part-time basis, in accordance with the forecast requirements.

If it becomes evident during the course of any week that department sales will not meet expectations, every effort should be made to reduce the part-time employee schedule for the balance of the week to insure that no more labor-hours are used than are necessary to cover the functions to be performed. On the other hand, if it becomes evident that department sales will considerably exceed expectations, part-time hours should be increased to make sure that all variable functions are covered.

What follows is a system applied to three stores for forecasting and scheduling the required weekly labor-hours. The system is based on the one shown in Table 10.

TABLE 11
Forecasting and Scheduling System

Commodity Group	Hours Required per 100 Pounds (45 kg)	Labor-Hours Required Based on Forecast of Tonnage to Be Processed During Week		
		Store A	Store B	Store C
Total Weekly Meat Volume		$34,562	$33,330	$31,867
A. Variable Functions				
Beef	1.32 hours	103.0 hours	89.4 hours	45.6 hours
Veal	1.06	1.4	4.8	—
Lamb	1.16	1.6	1.2	—
Pork Loins	1.29	32.9	16.0	30.1
All Other Pork	.87	3.7	.8	13.1
Variety Meats	1.29	2.0	1.6	4.3
Smoked Hams	.60	5.6	20.4	5.6
All Other Smoked Meats	.93	4.4	4.4	6.4
Table-Ready Meats and Sausages	.30	7.0	3.0	5.4
Sliced Bacon	.21	2.8	4.0	4.3
Canned Meats	.67	.4	—	—
Poultry (ice packed)	.80	26.8	23.0	30.4
Sea Foods	1.06	1.4	.2	1.0
Frozen Meats	.30	2.2	1.0	1.4
B. Total		195.2	169.8	147.6
C. Fixed Functions		80.0	80.0	80.0
D. Barbecue Allowance (maximum of 4.2 hours)		4.2	.8	4.2
E. Customer Relations Allowance (maximum of 6.5 hours)		0.0	6.5	1.6
F. Subtotal of Variable and Fixed Functions (sum of B, C, D and E)		279.4	257.1	233.4
G. Add 7.5 percent of F for Breaks and Personal Time		21.0	19.3	17.5
H. Total Weekly Labor-Hours Required Based on Tonnage Forecast (sum of F and G)		300.4	276.4	250.9

Selected
Bibliography

Argyris, Chris, *Personality and Organization*. New York: Harper & Row, 1957.

Blake, Robert R. and Mouton, Jane S., *The New Managerial Grid*. Houston: Gulf Publishing Company, 1978.

Dowling, William, ed., *Effective Management and the Behavioral Sciences*. New York: AMACON, 1978.

Drucker, Peter F., *Managing for Results*. New York: Harper & Row, 1964.

Drucker, Peter F., *Managing in Turbulent Times*. New York: Harper & Row, 1980.

Drucker, Peter F., *The New Realities*. New York: Harper & Row, 1989.

Drucker, Peter F., *The Practice of Management*. New York: Harper & Row, 1954.

Harwell, Edward M. and Kinslow, William E., *New Horizons in Checkout Management*. New York: Lebhar-Friedman Books, 1988.

Harwell, Edward M., *The Complete Manager*. New York: Lebhar-Friedman Books, 1986.

Herzberg, Frederick, "One More Time: How Do You Motivate Employees?" *Harvard Business Review:* January-February, 1968.

Herzberg F., Mausner, B. and Snyderman, B., *The Motivation to Work.* New York: John Wiley & Sons, Inc., 1959.

Jay, Antony, *Management and Machiavelli.* New York: Holt, Rinehart and Winston, 1968.

Kay, Emanuel, *The Crisis in Middle Management.* New York: AMACON, 1974.

Keil, E.C., *Performance Appraisal and the Manager.* New York: Lebhar-Friedman Books, 1977.

Kepner, Charles H. and Tregoe, Benjamin B., *The Rational Manager,* New York: McGraw-Hill, 1965.

Likert, Rensis, *New Patterns of Management.* New York: McGraw-Hill, 1961.

Likert, Rensis, *The Human Organization: Its Management and Value.* New York: McGraw-Hill, 1967.

Livingston, J. Sterling, "Pygmalion in Management." *Harvard Business Review*, July-August, 1969.

Lunding, Frank, *The Sharing of a Business*, Scarsdale, New York: The Updegraff Press, Ltd., 1954.

Marrow, Alfred J., *Behind the Executive Mask.* New York: American Management Association, 1964.

Maslow, Abraham, *Motivation and Personality.* New York: Harper & Row, 1954.

McGregor, Douglas, *The Human Side of Enterprise.* New York: McGraw Hill, 1960.

McGregor, Douglas, "An Uneasy Look at Performance Appraisal." *Harvard Business Review*, Vol. 35 (May-June, 1957), p. 89.

Myers, M. Scott, *Every Employee a Manager.* New York: McGraw-Hill, 1970.

Odiorne, George, *Management by Objectives.* New York: Pitman, 1965.

Ouchi, William, *Theory Z.* Reading, Ma.: Addison-Wesley, 1981.

Peters, Thomas J. and Waterman, Robert H., *In Search of Excellence.* New York: Harper & Row, 1982.

Randle, C. Wilson, "How to Identify Promotable Executives." *Harvard Business Review*, Vol. 34 (May-June 1956), pp. 122–134.

Reddin, W.J., *Effective Management by Objectives.* New York: McGraw-Hill, 1971.

Robbins, James G. and Jones, Barbara S., *Effective Communication for Today's Manager.* New York: Chain Store Publishing Corp., 1979.

Scobel, Donald N., *Creative Worklife.* Houston: Gulf Publishing Company, 1981.

Shtogren, John A., ed., *Models for Management: The Structure of Competence*. The Woodlands, Tx.: Teleometrics, International, 1981.
Sloan, Alfred, *My Years with General Motors*. New York: Doubleday & Company, Inc. 1963.
Steinmetz, Lawrence L., *The Art and Skill of Delegation*. Reading, Ma.: Addison-Wesley, 1976.
Yoder, Dale, *Personnel Management and Industrial Relations*. New Jersey: Prentice-Hall, Inc., 1962.

Glossary
of Terms

adjusted gross profit (dollars): gross profit minus controllable expenses.

Age Discrimination in Employment Act of 1967: a Federal law which protects persons aged 40 or older from discriminatory hiring, firing, or unequal compensation, terms, conditions or privileges because of age. The Act covers all employers of 20 persons or more in an industry affecting interstate or foreign commerce.

AAA: American Arbitration Association, a nonprofit organization that can be named in a contract as the source for settling future labor-management disputes. The AAA functions as a private court system and the arbitrator's decision is final and binding.

AMA: American Management Association, a nonprofit educational organization whose purpose is to develop, improve and communicate management techniques.

Anti-Discrimination Law: a Federal law which prohibits discrimination in hiring and in all phases of employer-employee relationships because of race, color, religion, sex or national origin. The law applies to all employers of 15 persons or more in an industry affecting commerce.

aptitude test: a test designed to determine an individual's potential to successfully perform an activity.

back-up personnel: employees from other departments or on call, who may be summoned to assist regular employees during peak volume hours or in emergencies.

base rate: an employee's regular hourly, daily or weekly wage rate before overtime begins.

basic elemental time: the time required to perform a basic element or segment of a manual task.

behavior modeling: a training program in which trainees practice proper managerial behavior, imitating a model demonstration, as shown in a video tape or film.

binding arbitration: the settlement of a dispute by a person or persons whom the contesting parties have chosen to hear their respective claims and have authorized to reach a decision, and whose decision the contestants agree in advance to accept as binding.

bonding: an insurance contract which an employer takes out with a bonding agency. The employer is guaranteed payment of a certain sum if a financial loss is incurred because of the act of an employee or because of some event over which the employer has no control.

buddy system: as part of the induction process, a new employee may be assigned a "buddy" to help him become oriented to the company, the store, his job and his fellow employees.

central training: a structured program in which employees are trained at a central location by a trained instructor who administers standardized instruction.

C.I.E.S.: International Association of Chain Stores (*Comite International des Enterprises a Succursales*), an organization whose membership is comprised of food chains and manufacturers from 23 countries, including the U.S., whose purpose is to exchange information and ideas on an international level.

coaching session: a meeting between a superior and his or her immediate subordinate, scheduled approximately every six months. The superior discusses the subordinate's progress, praising where appropriate and offering helpful advice in order to improve future performance.

collective bargaining agreement: the result of labor negotiations between union and company. The agreement defines (1) the company's and union's rights and obligations under the contract; (2)

operational rights and restrictions; and (3) procedures for settling disputes.

commodity group: a general class of merchandise, or family group, comprised of related items in a department.

company goals: as part of a goal-setting program, the combined department goals become the store goals; the combined store goals become the supervisor goals; and the combined supervisor goals become the company goals.

controllable factors: practices that influence or affect performance in specific areas of responsibility, which are controllable by store personnel, such as ordering accuracy.

daily activities form: a form on which a department manager lists, in proper sequence, the major activities to be performed each day by each employee in the department.

department goals: the specific department goals and steps for the coming target period. They are designed by each department manager participating in the goal-setting program.

department to total sales (ratio): a percent figure which is computed by dividing the department sales by the total store sales.

discharge procedure: a system detailed in the labor agreement which sets forth the basis for discharge or discipline, provides an appeal procedure and possibly gives grounds for reinstatement.

discontinued items: products which are no longer available to a store either from the manufacturer or the warehouse.

distress items: items which demand forced sale because of damage or deterioration.

Distributive Education: local high school and post-secondary school programs which combine classroom instruction in marketing and distribution with on-the-job experience.

district manager: an executive who supervises six to twelve stores; sometimes called a zone manager.

employee turnover: employees who are voluntarily or involuntarily separated from the work force and must be replaced.

engineered labor standards: standards of performance developed for specific jobs by means of motion and time studies.

enterprise: legal term used to describe the entire company.

Equal Employment Opportunity Commission: a five-member committee set up to oversee provisions of Title VII of the Federal Civil Rights Act of 1964.

Equal Pay Act of 1963: a section of the Fair Labor Standards Act which outlaws discrimination in rates of pay on the basis of sex.

establishment: the individual operational units of a company (or *enterprise*), including stores, warehouses, etc.

excessive turnover: turnover that is avoidable, such as voluntary separations which occur as a result of dissatisfaction with the job, wages, hours, working conditions or opportunities; leaving for other employment, etc.

excise taxes: Federal sales taxes imposed on certain retail items.

exit interview: an interview with a departing employee. Its purposes are to accurately determine reasons for turnover and to obtain information regarding deficiencies within the company so that corrective action may be taken to avoid excessive turnover in the future.

Fair Employment Practices Agency: local and state agencies to which, according to the Federal Civil Rights Act of 1964, persons claiming discrimination must appeal.

Fair Labor Standards Act of 1938: Federal act which establishes minimum wage, maximum hours, overtime pay, equal pay and child labor standards for covered employees, unless a specific exemption applies.

Federal Civil Rights Act of 1964: Title VII of the Act outlaws discrimination by employers and unions on the basis of race, color, religion, sex or national origin.

Federal Mediation and Conciliation Service: an independent Federal agency which has jurisdiction in labor disputes that affect commerce but do not involve unfair labor practices or representation questions. The agency seeks to bring about voluntary settlements by persuading the opposing parties to continue negotiations and by suggesting solutions.

Federal Minimum Wage Law: a section of the Fair Labor Standards Act. It sets a minimum wage and a maximum number of hours after which overtime must be paid at the rate of $1\frac{1}{2}$ times the employee's regular rate of pay.

FIFO: first in, first out, a method of rotating inventory.

fiscal year: the twelve-month period designated as the tax year for a given company.

fixed activity (function): an activity which requires the same number of labor-hours regardless of increases or decreases in volume, such as ordering, price changing, cleaning and others.

flannel board card (FBC): a training aid consisting of a plywood board covered with flannel, to which sandpaper-backed preprinted cards will adhere. It is used as a substitute for a blackboard.

flip chart: a training aid consisting of a number of charts or other material designed to be shown in sequence.

floater: a transient laborer or person who frequently moves or changes his or her place of work.

flow diagram: a plan drawing of a building or area on which a flow process chart is placed.

flow process chart: a means of presenting graphically, by the use of symbols, the sequence of all operations that occur during an activity, process or procedure.

FMI: Food Marketing Institute, an educational and research organization composed of independent and chain supermarket companies, whose purpose is to establish a forum for the interchange of ideas and information on supermarket operations.

forced choice rating technique: a rating technique whereby the rater is asked to choose, for each of a series of statements or questions, the best word to describe the employee being rated.

forequarter: the front half of a side of beef or veal.

formal performance appraisal: a system whereby the superior writes down his evaluation of the subordinate's performance.

fringe benefits: payments made to an employee other than wages or salaries. They often include life insurance, hospitalization, retirement and/or a variety of other plans.

grievance procedure: part of a collective bargaining agreement. It provides for the settlement of labor disputes through a specified procedure, usually ending in binding arbitration by a neutral third party.

grievance procedure, loose: the settlement of all disputes through a specified procedure, which is rather informal and flexible, particularly with regard to the time limits for bringing and processing grievances.

grievance procedure, tight: the settlement of disputes in a formal manner, specifying a time limit for settlement and providing protection from abuse.

gross pay: wages before such deductions as Social Security, income tax, etc.

gross profit dollars: the difference between the cost of merchandise received by a store and the amount rung up on the cash register for that merchandise.

gross profit percentage: the total department sales dollars rung up, divided into the difference between the sales and the total cost of the merchandise.

impulse buying: customer purchases unanticipated in advance of shopping.

incentive program: a bonus system whereby certain employees (usually managers) are remunerated in direct proportion to the performances of their departments or stores.

in-depth interview: a thoroughly detailed probe into an individual's background, experience, aptitudes, attitudes and accomplishments. It is sometimes used to screen job applicants, but more frequently to evaluate candidates for promotion to managerial positions.

induction: the process of introducing and orienting a new employee to his company, store and job.

informal performance appraisal: casual, word-of-mouth evaluation of an employee's performance.

in-stock position: the quantity of a commodity or item in stock, expressed in dollars or cases.

in-store merchandising: promotional efforts (displays, signing, extra footage, etc.) originating within the store.

intelligence test: a test designed to determine an individual's intelligence quotient (I.Q.).

inter-department merchandising: the displaying of an item from one department in another department; for example, cabbage with corned beef, displayed in the meat department.

internal pilferage: thefts committed within a store or company by its employees.

inventory control: control of current stock (shelf, backroom, warehouse, on order, etc.) so that merchandise received conforms to sales demands and out-of-stocks or over-stocks are avoided.

island display: a free-standing merchandise display built in an aisle of the store.

item movement: the number of cases or units sold per week or per fixed period.

job analysis: the determination, through observation, of the tasks which comprise a job, as well as the minimum knowledge, skills and abilities required to perform it successfully.

job description: a clear and systematic written summary of the contents and requirements of a specific job.

job induction: the introduction and orientation of the new employee to his job and to his role in the department.

journeyman: an experienced worker, as distinguished from an apprentice who is learning his or her trade.

key personnel: those employees who hold managerial, supervisory and administrative positions with a company.

labor dollars: the dollars expended on direct labor costs (employees' wages and salaries).

labor-hour requirements: the number of labor-hours needed depending on the functions to be performed, the volume to be handled, and other factors.

laundry expense: the cost of cleaning uniforms, jackets, towels, rags, aprons, etc.

LCI: Learner Controlled Instruction, a training program wherein the responsibility for seeking out and mastering specific skills or knowledge is shifted to the trainee, who, within limits, determines the time needed to complete the program.

learning cost: the cost to the company of the new employee's lower rate of productivity (compared to the productivity of an experienced worker) during the learning period, as well as the cost of product damage and errors made by the new employee.

lockout: a term sometimes applied to an employer's action in temporarily shutting down a plant and temporarily laying off employees during a labor dispute.

long-term disability benefits: payments made over an extended period of time to an employee who becomes ill or who suffers a disabling accident off the job.

maintenance cost: the cost of maintaining a given piece of equipment or other physical asset.

markdown: the amount by which the regular selling price is reduced.

markdown percent: determined by dividing the markdown by the original selling price.

markup: the amount added on to the cost of an item. Cost plus markup equals the selling price.

markup percent: determined by dividing the markup by the cost of the item.

merit increase: wage or salary raise based on quality of performance rather than tenure.

merit promotion: promotion based on superior performance.

nepotism: favoritism shown to a relative.

net loss: the amount of loss resulting when total expenses exceed total income.

net profit: the dollar profit remaining after all expenses are subtracted from total income.

noncontrollable factors: practices that influence or affect performance in specific areas of responsibility, which may not be con-

trolled or altered by store personnel, such as company-wide promotions.

no-strike clause: a provision in a labor agreement by which the
union agrees that there will be no strikes, picketing, or other
interference with business operations during the time of the labor
agreement.

on-the-job training: the structured training of an employee in the
store by the department or store manager or by a trainer. The
employee learns through planned instruction and by performing
the job for which he or she was hired.

opaque projector: a training device which enlarges and projects
printed material on a screen.

operating payroll: wages paid to store personnel, usually computed
on a weekly or period basis. Fringe benefits may or may not be
included.

operational discharge: the separation of an employee for such operational reasons as store closings and employee layoffs.

oppressive child labor: legal term used to describe any violation of
the child labor laws as set down in the Fair Labor Standards Act.

osmosis (training): a procedure whereby an employee is exposed to
his job, and learns to perform it on an informal, unplanned basis.

overhead projector: a training device which enlarges and projects
transparencies (up to 8 ½" x 11") onto a screen and on which an
instructor can write.

performance indicators: measurements used to evaluate performance. For example, performance indicators in sales include dollar
sales per week and the ratio of department sales to total store
sales.

performance review: a semi-annual or annual review of an employee's performance during which the superior and subordinate discuss the subordinate's performance, identify his strengths and
weaknesses, and agree on ways in which the subordinate can
improve his future performance.

performance standard: a specific level of performance expected of
an employee in each area of his responsibility.

performance test: a standardized test administered to experienced
applicants for certain skilled jobs in order to determine whether
they can perform specific segments of the job.

perishable item: an item whose freshness is short lived, for example,
produce, dairy products, baked goods, or meat. (Frozen foods and
ice cream are also considered perishables because of their quick
deterioration without proper refrigeration.)

personnel forecast: a program whereby a company predicts and anticipates its future personnel requirements.

personnel inventory: a survey of present employee resources and an evaluation of employee job performance.

pilferage: the amount of shortage estimated to result from customer, employee or vendor theft within the store as opposed to break-ins or burglaries.

pirating: the recruiting of employees from competing or other companies.

point-of-sale material: signs and other promotional material, usually supplied by the manufacturer for use where the item is displayed.

premium pay: a wage rate higher than the employee's regular rate, usually given for overtime hours, holiday, off-time, unusual or hazardous work.

primary job assignment: the job which represents the major responsibility of an employee. The cashier's primary job assignment is to check-out customers.

private label: a brand name owned and used by a wholesaler or retailer for exclusive distribution.

probationary process: a trial period during which an employee's performance on the job is evaluated in order to determine whether or not he will become a successful and qualified employee.

probationary promotion: a provisional promotion whereby the candidate is placed in a new job and tested during a probationary period. If he is unsuccessful during this period, he is returned to his former position.

product life: the number of days before a product will lose its flavor, taste or color appeal.

product mix: the variety of items within a given commodity group and their sales relative to total movement.

product rotation: placing new merchandise beneath or behind merchandise already on hand so that the oldest merchandise is sold first.

programmed instruction: a standardized teaching technique by which the trainee proceeds at his own rate depending on his understanding of the material. The material is presented in "frames" or small blocks.

promotional item: an item which is promoted to increase store traffic and/or to increase item movement.

promotion from within: the policy of selecting an employee for promotion from within the ranks of the company.

recruitment program: a program designed to fill each opening at the proper time with the most competent individual available.

sales per labor-hour: an index of employee productivity, computed by dividing the number of payroll hours into store or department sales.

salvage: the processing of containers, cardboard boxes, etc., that accumulate in each department.

seasonal item: an item that has increased appeal at certain times of the year, for example, turkeys during Thanksgiving.

secondary job assignment: all job assignments which are not primary. For instance, the secondary job assignment of a cashier might be to price and stock candy or health and beauty aids.

self-imposed goals: goals designed by the employee for his own work rather than goals imposed on him by his superior.

severance pay: special payment, usually in a lump sum, made to employees upon discharge or permanent layoff and intended to help tide the employee over a period of unemployment immediately following termination.

shelf extender: a wood or metal shelf attached to a display edge, which protrudes into the aisle, thereby extending the display shelf.

shelf talker: a point-of-purchase merchandising device usually attached to the moulding on a gondola shelf, and designed to attract the customer to that particular location.

shop steward: an individual elected by fellow employees in a local branch of a labor union. The steward's job is to see that labor union rules are enforced and to represent employees in primary-level dealings with the employer.

shrinkage: the difference between book gross profit (i.e., the gross profit dollars that would be received if there were no losses due to pilferage, cashier errors, etc.) and the actual gross profit dollars realized.

SLIM: Store Labor and Inventory Management, an inventory control system designed to increase labor productivity and reduce capital investment in inventory in the grocery department.

SMI: Super Market Institute, a trade association, merged into the Food Marketing Institute in 1977.

Standard Practices (Manual): a written description of departmental policies and practices that have been adopted as standard operating procedure by the company.

stockout: an item that is out of stock in the display area.

store induction: the process of introducing and orienting the new employee to his store.

subpoena: a writ commanding an individual to appear in court under penalty for failure to appear.

tare weight: the weight of packaging materials used in traying, wrapping and pricing meat, produce, dairy or bakery items.

target period: the period of time (usually three or six months) designated for the accomplishment of objectives established in a goal-setting program.

tenure: status granted after a trial period to an employee protecting the person from summary dismissal.

tie-in merchandising: merchandising related items in the same location within a department.

tight labor market: a situation in which there are few prospective employees in number and/or quality, available for work in a community.

time study: measuring with a stop watch the time required to perform a given task, based on detailed segments or elements of the task.

training aids: such devices as flannel board cards, slides and transparencies, which are helpful in communicating knowledge and information during a training session.

variable activity (function): an activity for which the labor-hour requirements increase or decrease in direct proportion to volume or sales.

visual aids: teaching devices such as slides, motion pictures, transparencies and others.

Wage and Hour Division: a division of the U.S. Department of Labor whose job is to administer and interpret the provisions of the Fair Labor Standards Act of 1938.

Wage and Hour Laws: the Fair Labor Standards Act; a Federal law establishing a floor under wages, a premium wage rate for work above a specified number of hours per week and restrictions on the employment of child labor. It is administered by the Wage and Hour Division of the Department of Labor.

wage expense: the cost to the company of wages and salaries paid to employees.

wage percent: a ratio of wages to sales, computed by dividing payroll dollars by sales volume.

wall-to-wall jurisdiction: a situation in which all employees in a particular establishment are represented by a single union.

Worker's Compensation: payments to an employee who is injured while performing on the job. These payments are required by law and contributed to by the employer.

work sampling study: a technique for determining the labor-hours being used and the frequency of occurrence of various functions performed in a department or store. An observer records the activity being performed by each employee in the department at pre-selected, specified intervals.

work simplification: a structured technique whereby a job is broken down into its components. By the application of the principles of motion economy, attempts are made to eliminate, combine, change the sequence, or simplify elements in order to determine the best way to perform the job.

Index